glimpse

glimpse

Publication of
The Society for Phenomenology and Media
Vol. 19, 2018

The Society for Phenomenology and Media

Glimpse is the annual publication of the Society for Phenomenology and Media.

This volume of *Glimpse* is dedicated to "mute and glorious" philosophers everywhere.

Contents

Introduction

For the first time in the 20-year history of the Society for Phenomenology and Media's annual international conferences, last year's conference featured a theme that was not directly related to media. The conference organizers of our lively and very successful 2017 meeting in Brussels, Belgium, selected the theme of the Anthropocene, a current and widely discussed topic in the social sciences as well as in philosophy. Although many of the papers presented at the conference did not take up this theme, a significant number of them did so, and examples of both are represented in the current (2018) volumes of *Glimpse* and *Proceedings*. SPM has always encouraged philosophical diversity and a wide variety of perspectives; our conferences are open to all papers insofar as they discuss media.

Back to Brussels: as our main keynote speaker, SPM was lucky enough to enlist one of the leading thinkers today working in the area of intersection between politics and technology, Langdon Winner, a perfect fit for a conference themed around the notion of the Anthropocene. His keynote paper fronts the selection of papers in this volume of *Glimpse* that comprise the first grouping of essays dealing directly and primarily with the theme of the Anthropocene. While Winner takes an analytical approach to the philosophy of technology that appeals to the political, sociological, and ethical dimensions of technics that is grounded in the natural sciences, several other authors in this first section of essays adopt a Heideggerian metaphysical stance that employs a vernacular of neologisms in a critical under-standing of the philosophy of technology, calling on the theoretical work of Bernard Stiegler as well as Peter Sloterdijk. Although these approaches are different in their analyses of causes and possible cures, they concur with the idea that however we describe or narrowly define it, the Anthropocene represents an impending environ-mental calamity not only for humanity, but also for all other living things on the planet.

In his timely and engaging article, "Biosphere Meets Public Sphere in the Post-Truth Era," Winner begins his exposé of the topic of the Anthropocene with a look at the current situation in politics and popular forms of media, which have contributed to the spreading of doubt not just about some particular news item or scientific claim, but about what should count as a fact and what should be recognized as truth. Enveloped within this umbrella of doubt is the reality of climate change, which has been spreading into public discourse for almost as long as it has been recognized as an issue of concern. This atmosphere of doubting the claims of science has fostered postponement of and even hostility toward any widespread initiatives aimed at reducing activities that contribute to the resulting problems, some of which are, or may soon be, reaching catastrophic proportions.

Winner develops this critique in his examination of the terminology of the Anthropocene, which he regards as inadequate and misleading in guiding our thinking about the Anthropocene. Sometimes with tongue-in-cheek and sometimes with alarmed seriousness, he punctures the balloon of self-inflated "science(s) of technology" that situate the discussion of the global situation within the regime of what he sees as a biased terminology. Winner opposes the use of the term, "Anthropocene," tying it to the Trumpian "post-truth" era of "fake news," propaganda-laden social media platforms, and other forms of Orwellian rhetoric that confront us at this juncture in our history, non-stop and seemingly from all corners. Winner wonders whether, rather than being helpful in understanding and addressing the problems we face, the linguistic creativity we intellectuals, scientists, scholars, political activists, and other concerned commentators employ in posing problems for academic analysis is nothing more than a production of beguiling fictions. He argues that although there may be plausible reasons for humans naming an entire geological epoch after themselves, to Winner, "it smacks of an obvious, species-centered narcissism."

Next up is Mark Coeckelbergh's "Scientific Subjects, Romantic Witnesses? Magic Technologies, Alienation, and Self-Destruction in the Anthropocene," which is more in line with the Heideggerian approach mentioned above. Adopting what in the end turns out to be a somewhat hopeful outlook, Coeckelbergh alerts us to a paradox of agency faced by humans in the age of the Anthropocene. We are the cause of the negative consequences of climate change, yet we seem to be at a loss in coming up with solutions. We have become impotent, alienated by-standers in the face of the threat of human self-destruction. He takes an imaginative leap into the suggestion that in addition to the contemporary cultures of science and technology that have played a significant role in the emergence of the problem, we must now also recognize the potential of the cultural movement of romanticism whose aesthetics generate their own technological manifestations. This would be a kind of "romantic science." The element of romance enables new imaginaries and makes space for our creation of "enchanted and artificial spaces for living elsewhere." With this romantic and, as Coeckelbergh suggests, magical idea of technology, we can re-enchant the ordinary, problem-laden world, or even create a new world that will satisfy our desire for romance and magic.

However, Coeckelbergh concludes that our "Earth alienation" and magical escape into new (romantic) worlds would be nothing more than an artistic solution, a way of conceiving of the world, or of nature, and our connection to it. He ends by saying that we need to "create technologies that give us more agency and a different, less alienated epistemic relation to our environment. We can avoid a romantic escape into magical thinking and a fascination with the spectacle of the Anthropocene and its attendant problems by engaging directly with nature, not through theory, but through hands-on contact with natural things and also by reinterpreting science and technology as thoroughly bound up with culture and political reality.

In "The Anthropocene as Event," Jan Jasper Mathé continues the discussion of anthropogenic events with his claim that we make the mistake of overlooking the fact that the Anthropocene is itself a kind of event. Just as Coeckelbergh notes that we feel powerless to solve the very problems we create, Mathé, calling on the work of Slavoj Žižek and Bernard Stiegler, argues that our attempts to deal with the disruption and destruction that have surfaced in the age of the Anthropocene are only obscured by framing them within the boundaries of science and technology. Mathé sees techno-scientific culture as a source for the belief that human history is conjoined with the history of the planet itself. As an event, the Anthropocene is an object that transforms reality by shattering the notion that the Anthropocene is just another fantasy. Mathé sees a way forward by conceiving the very interplay of appearances, which may be taken as perspectival distortions of reality, as genuine aspects of reality in itself. Tapping into the

Stieglerian idea of technicity – that humans are in themselves incomplete and contingently determined beings in need of supplementation through various forms of technology – Mathé urges that we need to see technology as "a constructive medium for human experience and practice.... [and] to integrate technological development into who and what we are as human beings." This will ideally lead us to create new perspectives from which to generate actions that make sense of and deal with the urgency of the Anthropocene. We really have no alternative but to obey the imperative of acting in response to it as a real event in both geological and human history.

In the elaborately detailed essay, "Re-Orienting the Noösphere: Imagining a New Role for Digital Media in the Era of the Anthropocene," Pieter Lemmens re-introduces the concept of the noösphere, first introduced by Jesuit philosopher, Pierre Teilhard de Chardin, as a framework for conceiving of human evolution. Lemmens continues the exposition of Stieglerian thinking and also calls on the work of Peter Sloterdijk, whose ideas he uses to frame his essay, however, Lemmens' main argument is clearly based on Stiegler's philosophy and cultural politics. He avoids wading into the more controversial issues of genetic engineering or technological tampering with human reproduction in order to produce "better" (culturally tamed, "de-bestialized") humans that Sloterdijk provocatively promotes, which led the renowned German philosopher and public intellectual,

Jürgen Habermas, to charge Sloterdijk with more than a glancing flirtation with fascism. This is not the place to air this debate but only to note that the "homeo-technological turn" brought about by the "Neganthropocene" envisioned by Stiegler and championed by Lemmens as a "synergetic co-operation, co-production, co-construction" that results in a conjugated *biotechnosphere* through which "the digital noösphere would be intelligently transformed from a *de*structive into a *con*structive force" is not in itself a fascist ambition. However, there is a need to be wary of such connections. Lemmens references Sloterdijk to call for a "co-natural, non-despotic and Earth-caring technological paradigm."

In "A New Telluric Force: Humans in the Age of the Anthropocene," Melinda Campbell and Patricia King Dávalos develop an approach that acknowledges both the empirical observations of the natural sciences and the phenomenological data of lived experience as integral to understanding, addressing, and solving the problems that attend the issues raised by the Anthropocene. They see the situation that confronts the planet and the life it supports in the crisis of the Anthropocene as signaling a need to move from subjective phenomenological investigations into human-environment relations to a re-conceptualized and naturalized phenomenology, which merges the ability of the natural sciences to produce objective accounts of the natural world with the methods of phenomenology that give proper recognition to the lived experience of the creatures who

inhabit, enjoy, and exploit that world. The "telluric force" in question is that of humans themselves, who, in the age of the Anthropocene, figure not simply as both perpetrators and victims of the new geological and climatological conditions, but who themselves are a geologic entity or force. All of which leads, the authors claim, to new political, social, and ethical confrontations and opportunities for cooperation and conflict resolution.

We now move into a second grouping of the essays in this volume that focus on specific effects of technological innovations and advanced technics on the quality and indeed the very form of human life. We start with Richard S. Lewis's "Hello Anthropocene, Goodbye Humanity: Reframing Transhumanism through Postphenomenology." Lewis weighs in on the "human enhancement" debate generated by the development of new technologies that exploit untested possibilities in genetic engineering and technological bodily alterations and augmentations that promise (or threaten) to dramatically change our conception of what it is to be human. This harks back to the controversial "eugenics question" that Sloterdijk has injected into philosophical public discourse mentioned above. Lewis, however, does not call on Sloterdijk, but instead considers two opposing sides on the issue, the transhumanists (e.g., Nick Bostrom and Ray Kurzweil) and the bioconservatives (e.g., Francis Fukuyama, Jürgen Habermas, and Michael Sandel). He sees the field of postphenomenology, developed by Don Ihde, as an effective way to engage the human-enhancement debate through identifying flaws in transhumanist thinking and introducing an empirically grounded, realistic approach to the notion of human enhancement.

In an outstanding summary and penetrating analysis of the new media collectively known as the "social network," Valeria Ferraretto, Silvia Ferrari, and Verbena Giambastiani situate their discussion of personal identity as it relates to the transformational power of social media. Invoking Foucault's concept of the *dispositif* (cf., "apparatus"), the authors explain that the experience of living one's life online, cultivating a "digital life," puts the apparatus of the social medium into operation, and with this form of experience comes both the maintenance and enhancement of various forms of social, institutional, and personal power. The authors address three important issues: how social media are changing us; the extent to which social media have changed society; and the question of whether social media improve and enhance human life. They countenance the interesting possibility that our digital life may in fact be the start of a new "historical orientation" in which the virtual world is simply an extension of the real world, with no ontological line of separation.

To address this set of questions, Ferraretto, Ferrari, and Giambastiani enlist, among others, Walter Benjamin and Michaela Ott (influenced by Gilles Deleuze) to think through the complex and multi-faceted relationship between the self as ordinarily conceived (as an inhabitant of the actual world) and the online self. The

answer lies, according to the authors, in acknowledging a new kind of community that distinguishes individuals from *dividuals*. The idea here is that we must no longer think of "human beings undivided as individual entities. Individuals have become dividual," which is a state of being that is "affected by and interrelated with countless others, of sharing multiple bio- and socio-technological structures." Again, following Benjamin, the authors conclude that new forms of perception are in fact enabled by the new forms of reproduction (as in social media) because these media multiply our "being-as-self," and as a consequence, all social relationships are thereby transformed. In the end, Ferraretto, Ferrari, and Giambastiani consider a new mode of life in which the "divided individual" is the real and true subject in the postmodern era.

Nicola Liberati continues the investigation of our digitally and technologically enhanced future in "Facing the Digital Partner: A Phenomenological Analysis of Digital Otherness." Liberati is inspired by authentic, Husserlian descriptive phenomenology in his discussion of the possibility of meaningful, even intimate, relationships with digital entities. He explores first how digital entities are perceived as merely fictional because they do not function as part of the everyday world in the same way as, for example, actual human or living beings. However, with the emergence of new iterations of digital technologies (Liberati references the Gatebox virtual-assistant "girl" that takes on human-like characteristics), the digital other breaks through the boundaries of the virtual world to meet the user where he lives, so to speak. Invoking the ideas of Alfred Schütz, Liberati asserts that the quality of otherness is grounded in both intertwined, interconnected activities as well as in resistance. Up until now, digital entities have not been able to meet both of these criteria; however, the newest forms of digital technologies can achieve resistance because they can be programmed to be operational even when switched off. This adds an element of autonomy that approaches the resistance of other human beings. Liberati maintains that, so equipped, these digital programs "can be perceived as 'digital others' with which, or with whom, it is possible to develop intimate relationships."

Continuing the theme of the technologically augmented or disrupted human body as well as introducing the importance of art in thinking through the Anthropocene, Marta G. Trógolo, Alejandra de las Mercedes Fernández, and Rosario Zapponi present an account of subjectivity as a zero-point of orientation in "Living the Body as a New Anthropocene Experience?" In this original and thoughtful essay, they inquire into possibilities for new ways of conceiving the body's role within nature. The authors explore issues related to human self-reference in situations of human invention (such as making art) as well as situations of corporeal interventions like cosmetic surgery or even technological bodily enhancements, claiming that such activities result in a kind of repulsion, or even expulsion (as in bodily dehiscence), thereby negating human morphogenetic nature. They argue that conceiving of the "'body object' as a knotting of meanings given the impossibility of reticulate substance, humanity, and subject" can allow for an opportunity to witness an "immanent Anthropocene experience" rather than a transcendent one. Such a witnessing would mark a "historical passage to techno-science as well as an interpretation of an Anthropocene conversion as power-totalizing."

The role of art as revelatory of human nature continues to be addressed in the next group of articles. In "Anthropocene and Art," Alberto Carillo and May Zindel make an important claim about the value of art in dealing with the issues of the Anthropocene. Pointing to the "three great ecological problems" of pollution, desertification, and the destruction of biodiversity, they claim there is no such thing as a dynamically independent, autonomous nature or planetary environment that is separate from culture and human activity, which itself should be seen as geologic in nature. (This recalls a main theme developed earlier in this volume by Campbell and King Dávalos in "A New Telluric Force.") Carillo and Zindel argue that artists play a special role in making us aware of this aspect of human existence – that we are a geologic force – because the magnitude of our impact on the planet goes beyond what can be seen or known directly in human experience, and the particular kind of conceptual representation achieved in works of art is an important way of "perceiving" and understanding this geological impact.

The next essay in this section develops the theme of art as both a continuation and a disruption of human life as well as providing a "looking glass" (both in the sense of a mirror *and* a window) into reality. Lisa Daus Neville's "Memory of the Future: Cecilia Vicuña's Participatory Poetics and Murray Bookchin's Unfolding Dialectical Freedom" brings together a number of themes and ideas that suggest art's integral role in expressing and creating a communal understanding of life. In this beautifully written essay, Neville introduces us to Chilean poet, artist, and filmmaker, Cecilia Vicuña, whose highly original work weaves together themes at the heart of art-making, metaphysical questioning, spiritual realization, environmental awareness, and social reform (healing). Neville's move here from an exposition and insightful interpretation of Vicuña's work to what she sees as the complementary thought of social ecologist Murray Bookchin is not merely instructional, but also broadens the discussion in helpful ways. She characterizes Bookchin's view as an "ecology of freedom in which human being becomes aware of itself as nature's own self-expression," a stance that lines up with underlying principles as well as the surface expressions of Vicuña's work. She advances the idea, already introduced in Carillo and Zindel's "Anthropocene and Art," as well as in Trógolo, Fernández, and Zapponi's "Living the Body as a New Anthropocene Experience?" that we must turn to art or other activities that integrally involve human intentionality and expressive production in order to "heal our calcified discrete identities and return us to our evolutionary origins in an ecology of interdependence."

David Romero Martín, in "Art and Experiences of Embodied, Disruptive Reality," also underlines the position taken by Carillo and Zindel: art, in its various expressions, is empowered to disrupt and enhance ordinary experiences of reality. Moreover, its analysis indicates a parallelism of the aesthetic experience and psychological disruptions and disorders. Martín probes the effects of immersive technologies (e.g., those which create virtual- or augmented-reality scenarios or situations) that create shifts in the subjective experiential perspectives of user-experimenters to show that the effects of such technologies on the sense of embodiment and of reality itself mimics a level of the sort of detachment and sense of loss of familiarity with self and world that characterize dissociative orders such as depersonalization and derealization. The phenomenological implications are taken to indicate that there is a meaningful interrelation between art, technology, and dissociative disorders.

In "Mediating Knowledge: How Theater Transmits Partial Perspectives," Bjorn Beijnon also sees art, this time considering the medium of theater, as a powerful medium that both disrupts and heals through the formation of community in the transcendence of individual perspectives. Beijnon develops the idea that "the empirical world is a shared space for multiple bodies that agree on the causality of certain events and objects in that space." This results from the fact that humans make sense of the world from their own individual, embodied perspectives, which leads to the creation of multiple individual body-worlds, each of which has its own partial perspective on the empirical world. And theater, as an art form, has a powerful capacity to transmit different partial perspectives to the audience through the techniques of re-enactment and disruption, thereby connecting differently situated knowledges and producing what he calls "ecological knowledge": a kind of transcendent perspective that comes from an awareness of the connected network of situated knowledges and partial perspectives.

The volume closes with two articles that take radically different approaches to the study of media. In "Tools for New Lifestyles: Indigenous Stone Crushing and Public Perception of Television Entertainment Reporting in Jos City," Sarah Lwahas brings us a concrete analysis of television news reporting on the environment, showing how the descriptive medium of TV news falls short in providing adequate or incisive reporting on environmental issues. The example she surveys is the practice of indigenous stone crushing, which, while beneficial to a class of workers, mostly women, who rely for their livelihood on this arduous work, it is at the same time quite destructive of the local environment. Lwahas points out that in addition to an increasing depletion of the impressive rock formations characteristic of the Plateau state of Nigeria, this practice represents an endangering of both indigenous culture and the aesthetics of the surrounding environment of Jos City. She concludes that this environmentally risky practice needs to be thoroughly studied, publicly discussed, and much more frequently reported on by the television stations that themselves make use of the high-altitude rocky outcroppings for their broadcast masts and satellite-signal receivers.

Paul Majkut provides the coda for this year's volume of *Glimpse* with a continuation of his discussion of media in "Time Machines and the Appropriation of Time: Mediated, Unmediated, Immediated" in a discussion of clocks, calendars, and the appropriation of time. In this he considers clocks and calendars as media, tracing their development and use in everyday life as well as in the domains of class struggle and power relationships. His extensive exposition and fascinating digressions take us through historical time to reveal the advent and demise of various forms of temporal media (as media of communication) and the shifting dynamics associated with the "ownership of time," showing how "technological mediation forms and defaces experience, representationally removing it from the direct experience of *immediated* reality." Majkut's stated purpose, however, is to *return* to us to immediated reality, conceived as "inherent, simultaneous, and spontaneous knowledge of the world."

—Melinda Campbell
Editor

Founder's Statement

"The unpreparedness of the educated classes, the lack of practical links between them and the mass of the people, their laziness, and, let it be said, their cowardice at the decisive moment of the struggle will give rise to tragic mishaps."

— *Frantz Fanon*, The Wretched of the Earth

Over 50 years ago, one of the twentieth century's most insightful realists gave fair warning of the failure of the intelligentsia of his own generation of thinkers to act. His warning is as pertinent now as then. Frantz Fanon's insights into the ethical and political shortcomings of the educated are a call to arms directly addressed to members and participants of academic societies throughout the world.

The Society for Phenomenology and Media is no exception. Since its inception in 1998, SPM has worn the intellectual blinders common to all ideologically partisan groups of thinkers, whether Anglo-American analytic and linguistic or continental philosophers. Diversity of thought is not one of the virtues of contemporary academic thought. And, while wary travelers in the sea of controversy must avoid the Scylla and Charybdis of Anglo-American and continental positions, the world sinks deeper and deeper into political-economic despair. Our academic frames reveal that we are interested in explaining the world to each other, not changing it for the betterment of all. As Marx commented in his eleventh thesis in *Theses on Feuerbach*, "Philosophers have hitherto only interpreted the world in various ways; the point is to change it."

Frantz Fanon makes the same point.

Because SPM has erred on the side of continental philosophy and not reached out to other traditions, I will not chastise Anglo-American philosophers for "cowardice at the decisive moment of the struggle" that gives "rise to tragic mishaps." That is left to gatherings of those in that tradition.

As a first step, our time is more appropriately spent in a critique and censure of the varieties of phenomenology that have, despite claims of embodiment and lived experience, ignored the real world:

Edmund Husserl's blind subjective-transcendental idealism that spoke of *The Crisis of European Sciences and Transcendental Phenomenology* while not seeing the political crisis that was everywhere apparent in Germany in 1936; the loathsome exuberance of Martin Heidegger's Nazi "phenomenology" and his acolytes; Alfred Schütz's libertarian "realist" phenomenology with its deep roots in Austrofascism and its racist consequences when transferred to the United States, especially those associated with the New School for Social Research; the reactionary Catholic phenomenology of Pope John Paul II that draws inspiration from the crypto-Catholic thought of Merleau-Ponty; the elitist proclamations of Anna-Teresa Tymieniecka that are nourished by Roman Ingarden's seminal and overly-precious "new criticism."

Phenomenology has for long politely flirted with fascism and Eurocentric "educated" supremacists. Many today decry the anti-science of the demagogue Donald Trump and the right who deny global warming, give anti-evolution "creationists" room to impose their theocratic idiocy, believe in "clean coal," etc., but over many decades I have heard worse attacks on the natural sciences from phenomenologists, beginning with Husserl's discounting of the natural attitude, which includes not only ordinary men and women but natural science itself.

We begin by asking who we are and what our purpose is.

Let us be frank.

Many of us are here because our institutions, universities and research centers require annual conference participation and publication. Publish or perish. This does not mean that the work we do and the papers we present and publish are simply intellectual performances on an academic stage. Over the years, SPM has published insightful and fresh studies of media, its history, theory, and practice. Though this has not always been the case, and many papers have been routine schoolbook exercises and academic rehashes of thinkers in vogue at the moment, SPM has also been a place where ideas on media, new and old, have been discussed. This is particularly true of the many essays that have grappled with fast-changing digital media, social (or, as some prefer, *anti-*social) media, virtual reality, augmented "reality," artificial "intelligence," and any number of attendant epistemological, ontological, and aesthetic questions in an enormous number of media – manuscript, print, stage, dance, telephone, TV, radio, Internet, and so on and on.

Some have attended SPM conferences as short interludes from academic work, that is, small vacations to wonderful, new locations throughout the world, meetings where ideas on media are discussed in a privileged setting. Personally, I prize these annual meetings and direct contact and conversation with new and old international colleagues, always learning a great deal more than I would have had I stayed isolated in my university, sheltered in its library among the books and journals. But, then, I do not believe that thinking about fundamentals is a predilection restricted to the literate.

Fanon tells us that the educated

have lost practical contact with the great bulk of humanity. He says the educated are in peril of losing *practical links* to the masses. *Practical* is a pivotal choice of words. Intellectuals may have contact with the masses, but it is not practical. Fanon uses the term in the sense of *praxis*, and here he means political activity, that is, *political activism*. By and large, the contact intellectuals have with the masses is theoretical, framed in an academic argot that is a highly coded language of a cult. Think of our own SPM conference last year. I have in mind the keynote given by Michel Puech in Brussels that praised Harry G. Frankfurt's book, *On Bullshit,* while at the same time not pausing to notice that he and others at the conference were drowning in bullshit. Nonetheless, it was one of SPM's best conferences in 20 years of existence. If phenomenologists and others are to be truly *embodied* and not merely perceptually embodied, they must be *politically embodied,* that is, politically active.

Throughout the world today, we see fascism ascendant. Apartheid and religious fanaticism is widespread everywhere, white supremacy is openly discussed. In Africa and Asia, corrupt tyrannies are the rule and neo-colonialism prevails. In Europe and North America, coalition governments include the extreme right, openly fascist parties.

While the rich dance, the gap between haves and have-nots has never been greater, and we daily witness the *dance macabre* of late capitalism in the era of the Anthropocene or, as I prefer, the Capitalocene. It is said that a president of an impoverished former colony sent an urgent email to the World Bank, saying, "Send food. 50 million people starving," to which the Bank replied, "Tighten your belts," to which the leader replied, "Send 50 million belts."

Along with Fanon, the California poet, Lawrence Ferlinghetti, is also worth remembering today. In *A World Awash with Fascism & Fear,* written a half-century ago, he describes the world political scene of his own time that was remarkably the same as the one we find ourselves in today, an era of neo-colonial expansion, dispossessed refugees and economic emigrants, and libertarian-fascist nationalism. We live in a time when neo-Nazis and white supremacists openly march in torch parades in the United States, apartheid and segregation are state policy in Israel, and European intellectuals breathe a sigh of relief when fascist parties in Germany, Austria, Holland, and others have *only* captured 30 percent of the popular vote! In France, "moderates" congratulated themselves, saying that the fascist party of Marine le Pen "only" had about a third of the electoral vote.

I am here to tell you that one-third is a lot of thirds.

Elsewhere, we see that Russia is a social-fascist kleptocracy of dynastics and oligarchs and China proclaims itself as a superpower world leader in grand schemes to colonize Africa and link Europe to its ravenous union of the worst aspects of socialism and capitalism.

The listing of problems could go on and on, but, I suggest, the task ahead of us is to decide what we must do to reconnect ourselves to the mass of humanity.

In the past, I have suggested that we begin with a *phenomenology of listening*. The call for intellectual listening still seems sound. In "Neo-Colonial and 'Post-Colonial' Splitting Hairs and Talking Back," an analysis of the children's book, *Nappy Hair*, I argued that the problem was not, as Gayatri Spivak maintains, that colonial subalterns could not talk back except within the imperial narrative, but that *colonial masters did not listen* – citing the call-and-response oral literature as obvious "talking back" and a refutation of Spivak's theory. Of course, I found nothing "post" about today's economic imperialism. Carolivia Herron, the African-American author of *Nappy Hair*, offered me the opportunity to discuss neo-colonialism and the long-forgotten theory of the internal colony.

Intellectuals prefer to think on comfortable, knotty questions of Western epistemology, ontology, and aesthetics of media, not its worldly reality in economic, social and political reality.

At the SPM Conference in Puebla in 2002, I invited Vicente Marcial Cerqueda to keynote our meeting. I asked him to translate the Zapotec concept of "to know" into Spanish (*saber*) and English. This required a lot of linguistic and cultural contextualizing, but I thought this would be a good first exercise for Europeans and Norteamericanos in a phenomenology of listening. As was to be expected, his discussion was mind-boggling when the Western concept was discussed in terms of "the action or effect of being a jaguar." Europeans and Norte-americanos, who have for so long expected other peoples to work within their educated framework, were unable to do the same in the worldview of an indigenous people.

Ordinary people who are not involved in our enterprise often see us as blabbering idiots detached from reality in our insistence that we have delved its deeper truths.

Ours is to reconnect with the masses and avoid tragedy.

—Paul Majkut
San Diego

Keynote Address

Biosphere Meets Public Sphere in the Post-Truth Era

LANGDON WINNER

RENSSELAER POLYTECHNIC INSTITUTE
TROY, NEW YORK, USA

In our time, especially in the U.S.A., there is a remarkable deterioration in the quality of public discourse and its capacity to illuminate important choices that face society. Corrosion of this kind is evident in the character of political debate, levels of citizen engagement, standards of journalism, as well as in the style and content of conversations on social media. A consequential expression of this malady was the flow of attention and discussion in the 2016 election campaign, including surging tides of what came to be called "fake news," stories propagated on Facebook, Twitter, Instagram and the like. Fake news" – news stories that have no factual basis but are presented as facts"[1] – include on widely circulated on social media during the 2016 election campaign: "The Pope Endorsed Donald Trump." The story was false, totally fabricated; yet it sped around the Net, especially on Facebook and Twitter, like wildfire through dried sagebrush.

Adding to the rhetorical smoke and fire of the 2016 election and was the notable failure in much of American news media to apply standard methods of verification and correction as such dubious claims and politically freighted narratives filled the campaign. More often than not, prominent print, video and Internet "news" would simply echo the claims, memes and images of the presidential campaign with little attention to the validity of the assertions, for example the repeated assertions by Donald J. Trump and his surrogates that the sinking fortunes of working class and middle class Americans are primarily caused by a flood of Mexicans and other immigrants crossing the country's southern border. For many observers in the mainstream journalism and social media it was enough to report Trump's words, leaving the strong impression that his statements were certainly true.

A master of techniques of generating bogus "news" stories within the Trump organization was Steve Bannon, former investment banker, producer of Hollywood films and executive director of the prominent Internet source for right wing media and propaganda, Breitbart News. Promoter of extreme, white nationalist political views associated

---

[1]Amy Merrick, "Did fake news swing the election for Trump?" *Chicago Booth Review*, Feb. 20, 2017, review.chicagobooth.edu/economics/2017/article/did-fake-news-swing-election-trump.

with the "alt-right," Bannon became "chief executive officer" in Trump's presidential campaign and stayed on as "chief strategist" in The White House when Trump took office in January, 2017. In such settings, Bannon and his associates helped Trump hone his rhetorical flourishes, ones laced with anti-immigrant, anti-Muslim, xenophobic, and far right wing "populist" views of the nation's plight, ones summarized in Trump's promise "To make America great again."[2] Although eventually fired as a member of Trump's inner circle, Bannon's basic approach to political communications continued to shape the administration's way of presenting its message even after the master craftsman was removed.

Exactly how attempts to corrupt and undermine public discourse influenced the specific outcome of the 2016 election is open to ongoing study and debate, as is the question of the possibility of Russia's malign influence upon the process. I won't explore those questions here. Of course, the presence of deception, lying, and propaganda in public affairs is an old story. In many ways this craft has always been a crucial part of political life, although twentieth-century techniques of propaganda certainly refined its methods, setting the stage for twenty-first century methods and platforms that can ultimately replace anything remotely resembling reality within the echo chambers of illusory claims that circulate within the twenty-four hour

"news" cycle. What appears to be new and extraordinarily troubling in the present moment is that mischief of this kind has become even more deliberate and cleverly, even cynically executed than ever before.

At its worst, the decline of political communication results in modes of "post-truth" thinking and talking. Chosen as 2016's word of the year by the *Oxford Dictionary*, "post-truth" refers to "relating to or denoting circumstances in which objective facts are less influential in shaping public opinion than appeals to emotion and personal belief."[3] A key feature of a "post-truth" world is that conventional pathways leading back from lies, misrepresentations, toxic fantasies, and blatant propaganda into a space of clear, reliable information and sound judgment have been obliterated so that correction and re-centering is virtually impossible. Indeed political objections and media efforts to refute false claims become just another part of the stream of verbiage that reinforces the lies in much of public consciousness. "There they go again…" Fox News viewers might well conclude, "Those damned liberals trying to discredit the story about the Pope's enthusiastic endorsement."

Trump, Bannon, and others on their team cleverly employed techniques of exaggeration and repetition not merely to communicate lies and a thick fog of confusion, but even more to knock the moorings out from under any reliable sense of reality. We can ask, What's the

[2] Scott Shane, "Combative, Populist Steve Bannon Found His Man in Donald Trump," *New York Times*, Nov. 27, 2016, www.nytimes.com/2016/11/27/us/politics/steve-bannon-white-house.html?_r=0.

[3] "Word of the Year 2016 is…" *English Oxford Living Dictionaries.* en.oxforddictionaries.com/word-of-the-year/word-of-the-year-2016.

evidence? What are your sources? What are the rational foundations for the issues, problems and solutions you are projecting? But such questions became irrelevant to the election process, replaced by questions that boil down to: Are you one of "us"? Or are you one of "them"? As the liberal economist, Robert Reich, noted his list of deceptive patterns common in American print and electronic journalism: "The media start describing Trump's lie as a claim that reflects a partisan divide in America, and is 'found to be true by many.' The public is confused and disoriented about what the facts are. Trump wins."[4]

In this mode, Kellyanne Conway, senior advisor to Donald Trump, denounced those who offered evidence clearly showing that Trump's presidential inaugural was *not* the most-watched such ceremony in American history. "You're saying it's a falsehood. And they're giving – Sean Spicer, our press secretary … gave alternative facts."[5] (Alternative facts?) At roughly the conclusion of his first year as President, editors at *The Washington Post* tabulated the number of lies or misleading claims Trump had spoken during that period. The total came to more than 2,000.[6]

In sum, to an astonishing degree, today's public sphere is littered with alternative facts, fake news, and post-truth political discourse. An event horizon through which American politics has passed is one predicted thirty years ago by communications theorist Neil Postman in his classic work, *Amusing Ourselves to Death.*[7] Postman looked at the increasingly pervasive world of television entertainment and the powerful methods used to capture and hold TV audiences. He observed that two apparently separate and distinct realms of modern society – politics and entertainment – would eventually merge in ways that would leave the public sphere, its language and political figures and recurring rituals – especially elections – indistinguishable from gaudy television programs. Nowadays it's all show business.

The phenomenal rise of Donald J. Trump is clearly the most vivid and consequential realization of Postman's prophecy to date. A mob-connected real estate speculator, scam artist (e.g., "Trump University") and master of techniques of recurring bankruptcy as a way to amass a billionaire's fortune, Trump moved on to become star of the "reality" TV show "The Apprentice," in which he played a hard-driving businessman sending loyal underlings out to accomplish

[4] Robert Reich, "How Trump Lies About His Many Lies," *Newsweek*, Feb. 2, 2017, www.newsweek.com/robert-reich-how-trump-lies-about-his-many-lies-562520.

[5] Eric Bradner, "Conway: Trump White House offered 'alternative facts' on crowd size," CNN, Jan. 23, 2017, www.cnn.com/2017/01/22/politics/kellyanne-conway-alternative-facts/index.html.

[6] Glenn Kessler and Meg Kelly, "President Trump has made more than 2,000 false or misleading claims over 355 days," *The Washington Post*, Jan. 10, 2018, www.washingtonpost.com/news/fact-checker/wp/2018/01/10/president-trump-has-made-more-than-2000-false-or-misleading-claims-over-355-days/?utm_term=.808c31534297.

[7] Neil Postman, *Amusing Ourselves to Death: Public Discourse in the Age of Show Business* (New York: Penguin Books, 1985).

a difficult weekly "task," promoting those who succeeded and dismissing failures with an emphatic "You're fired!" The next step in this trajectory was a flamboyant presidential campaign in which he mowed down a field of seventeen prominent Republican candidates, seized the nomination and became the world's most powerful elected official, a position for which – by most serious assessments of his knowledge, background, ability, and temperament – he is distinctly ill-prepared and ill-suited. The appeal of his candidacy and now his presidential persona – xenophobia, Islamophobia, misogyny, militaristic nationalism, authoritarian posturing, and not-so-covert racism – make for riveting TV entertainment.

It may appear that the onset of post-truth politics is a recent development, something that we've wandered into in a haphazard way during the past several years. Upon closer inspection, however, it is evident that the distressing symptoms we see are the product of an ingenious, well planned, well-financed, well executed campaign to shape the discourse of public life and political institutions, implanting a newly fortified corporatism justified by an ideology that promotes the dominance of business interests realized in a fanciful so-called "free market." Forcefully argued in a memo written in 1971 by attorney Lewis Powell for the U.S. Chamber of Commerce[8] and circulated to persons of wealth and power, the game plan involved: organizing a new collection of conservative think tanks to research and publicize corporate friendly view; establishing networks of radio and television channels (especially what eventually emerged as Fox News) to propagate conservative political views; providing lavish financial support to nurture the rise of a new generation of right wing politicians; and reshaping higher education by funding university professorships and business-friendly departments, to propagate ways of writing, speaking and teaching about the glories of free enterprise and evils of collectivism, a mindset that glorifies winners and heaps scorn on the less fortunate, people depicted as losers and social parasites.[9]

As this movement matured and spread it relied upon backing from a core of billionaire supporters led by ultra "conservative" businessmen Charles and David Koch, who set out to eviscerate the American labor movement, turn back the clock on civil rights (especially voting rights), and to discredit the women's movement, the environmental movement, and any other social insurgency that might threaten corporate power. The story here has many twists and turns. But the result has been an institutional and mindset shift of phenomenal proportions over more than four decades, one that has brought us to the stomach-turning presence of Donald Trump, the social conservatives in the majority party, and his oligarchic, kleptocratic, white supremacist, increasingly autocratic regime. In short, the widely noticed, rapidly spreading derangement in the

---

[8] Lewis F. Powell, Jr., "Confidential Memorandum: Attack on American Enterprise System," brianholmes.files.wordpress.com/2012/06/5b-powell_memorandum.pdf

[9] Jane Mayer, *Dark Money: The Hidden History of the Billionaires Behind the Rise of the Radical Right* (New York: Doubleday, 2016).

America's public sphere is not a "bug" but a "feature."

POST-TRUTH IN THE DISCOURSE OF SCIENCE

A significant accomplishment within the maturation post-truth political communication has been has been an all out campaign to neutralize the authority of scientific research and analysis in key fields of public policy, a set of developments described by historian of science Naomi Oreskes and Eric M. Conway in their book *Merchants of Doubt* as well as the full length documentary film it inspired.[10] Carefully crafted attempts to discredit scientific knowledge about crucial policy questions have a decades-long history from the attacks upon the strong evidence about the dangers of cigarette smoking to the increasingly solid scientific consensus about the magnitude, causes and consequences of climate change. What the merchants of doubt have done is to fashion well-funded, well-rehearsed displays of rhetoric and imagery that instill the impression that relevant scientific findings are not proven, still in doubt, not a solid basis for strong social and political action.

A crucial juncture in Oreskes' movie, *Merchants of Doubt*, comes when she persuades one of the magicians in the art of sowing confusion to share his secrets on exactly how it is done. The trick, he explains, is to recruit a person who appears to have scientific credentials of some kind or other to look in to the TV camera and announce that global warming "has not been proven" and that the question is "still up for debate." Within today's television news-and-talk visuals, there is often a split screen with one scientist explaining the rigorous consensus of 97percent of climate scientists from dozens of research fields, while on the other half of the screen viewers see a climate-change doubter from an organization with a impressive name (often one funded by the large petroleum companies), who argues that he has reservations about the research and that the science is still highly uncertain. Because the screen is split into two equal halves, the lasting impression viewers receive is that there are actually two sides to the story, both plausible, both well-grounded in the facts, but that, alas, they remain in profound disagreement.

Impressions of this kind have a strong presence in post-truth politics as it affects the role of science in Trump-era public policies. Within the Republican Party and The White House, they buttress the conclusion that climate change caused by human activity is not only unproven but actually a flagrant hoax perpetrated by the Chinese. Early in the Trump administration, references to climate change were essentially banned in the Environmental Protection Agency and other offices of the executive branch. Somewhat later, staff members of the E.P.A. were advised to avoid the term, "science-based" standards for environmental policies, and to use the words, "economically and technologically achievable standards" as

---

[10] Naomi Oreskes and Erik M. Conway, *Merchants of Doubt: How a Handful of Scientists Obscured the Truth on Issues of Tobacco Smoke to Global Warming* (London: Bloomsbury Press, 2010).

the preferred alternative.[11] Here one hears echoes of the story of Winston Smith, tormented employee of The Ministry of Truth in George Orwell's novel, *1984*, who processed orders of this sort each day, casting terms condemned by Big Brother into "the memory hole" for immediate incineration.

WELCOME TO THE ANTHROPOCENE

As thoughtful observers become aware of the presence of "fake news," merchants of doubt, targeted propaganda in social media, and the other varieties of post-truth rhetoric that now flood the public realm, a question might well arise. Are we ourselves immune from these tendencies? Do our own concepts and arguments guide us towards reasonable, well-grounded, fruitful paths of action? Are the categories, questions and themes proposed by intellectuals, scientists, scholars, and political activists actually helpful in addressing the central problems that face world societies today? Or does our linguistic creativity sometimes produce what are little more than beguiling fictions?

To my way of thinking, a relevant example here concerns ongoing campaigns to rebrand the geological epoch in which we live. Within the past decade or so there have been a number of colorful proposals. True, the conventional term, "Holocene," is admittedly drab and a little long in the tooth. Perhaps an upgrade of some

kind is warranted. Derived from the Greek, *holos*, Holocene simply means the "whole" or "entire period," beginning at about 11,700 years ago, a period of interglacial warming. One way to describe the present moment is to say, "We're living in the late Holocene." Yes, that's fairly dull. Two appealing alternatives are "Homocene" and "Anthropocene," both of which evoke the aggregate planetary effects of human activity over the centuries. Another contender, "Capitalocene," advanced by sociologist Jason W. Moore, points to the formative influence of capital in modern times. Also on the candidate list are "Atomicocene," noting the arrival of nuclear weapons and nuclear technologies, and "Cthulucene," proposed by Donna Haraway, which pays homage to "Chthonic" entities, ancient spirits of the underworld. A more dreary label is that of "Plutocene," offered by archaeologist Andrew Gilkson, whose book with that title sketches prospects for a post-Holocene world character-ized by a dangerously warming planet accompanied by high levels of radiation from humanity's reckless application of nuclear energy and possible nuclear war.

Among the various contenders, the name "Anthropocene" is now by far and the most popular at present, on display in countless books, journal articles, videos, podcasts, and academic conference titles.[12] Indeed, the label has some notable virtues. For many observers it seems to lend a distinctive air of gravity to attempts to

[11] Emily Atkin, "The EPA's Science Office Removed "Science" From Its Mission Statement," *New Republic*, March 7, 2017, newrepublic.com/article/141174/epas-science-office-removed-science-mission-statement.

[12] J. Zalasiewicz, A. Harwood, and M. Ellis, "The Anthropocene: A New Epoch of Geological Time," *Philosophical Transactions of the Royal Society*, 369, no 1938 (2011).

come to come to terms with a variety of climatological, environmental, and social calamities increasingly apparent around the globe. Rather than call it simply, "Earth's Crisis," the fashion spreads to name the predicament "Anthropocene," a term thought to be more grandiose and seemingly profound. It's possible that earlier renderings of climate crash and its causes, Al Gore's "An Inconvenient Truth" for example, began to seem a little too dull and uninspired to merit the kind of emotional and intellectual spark needed to focus people's attention. In much the same vein, crowds now rush to conferences to debate "Big Data, The Cloud and Horizons of A.I.," while nobody would bother to sign up to discuss "Internet 2.0 and Online Communities." That's so yesterday!

While there seem to be credible, even noble, reasons for adopting "Anthropocene" as a name for the new model era, an awareness of the pitfalls of offering flashy new nomenclature should give us pause. At the top of my own list of concerns about the category is that it smacks of an obvious, species-centered narcissism. Human beings naming a whole geological epoch for them-selves? How marvelous! How fabulously egotistical! Indeed, how exquisitely Anthropocentric!

Feelings of skepticism of this kind have recently prompted me to enter the fray, suggesting a reasonable alternative label, something more specific, focused, rigorous, and concrete. As outlined in talks for philosophy conferences and in an academic journal, I argued that a superior name for this unfolding period of world history would be the "Langdonpocene." It has a nice ring to it, don't you think? It's succinct, intelligible and bound to appeal to a certain slice of the world's populace, namely my friends and family. Of course, the suggestion was pure satire, a send-up similar to others I've offered in other settings over the years. But what's obviously "fake news" about the sudden onset of the Langdonpocene poses an interesting question: Is there really any need to provide a new name for this geologic era *at all*? What is the purpose? What good does the change on the theater marquee serve other than to attract newly enthralled audiences?

Some who dislike my modest proposal have expressed alarm that I'd stoop so low as to worry about a "mere name." My response to that criticism is: "Yes, exactly!" At the same time (and with tongue firmly implanted on cheek) I remain firm in my insistence that "Langdonpocene" is far superior to "Anthropocene" for some rock solid geological reasons. Hear me out!

In important respects, based upon some highly credible data, it's likely that I deserve as much credit for overall biospheric impact as just about any person who has ever lived on Earth, past or present. After all, I've spent more than seven decades here, living contentedly as an average, middle-class American consumer and an active, well-travelled member of the professional class. In those roles I've probably burned as much fossil fuel as anybody during my lifetime, a total of roughly 2.3 billion Btu so far, an impressive accomplishment.[13] I've

---

[13] American Geosciences Institute, "How Much

consumed as many tons of natural resources, driven and flown as many miles and defaced as much of the natural landscape as any of the "anthropos" who've lived on Earth during the past twelve millennia. As one of the leading beneficiaries of the era of fossil fuels, I would gladly pit my largely heedless, unintended geological defacements and excessive burning against any and all contenders.[14] You see, I've been on the "cene" for quite a long while. In fact, it's likely that my most lasting contribution to the world's future will not be my scholarly writings, but the countless tons of greenhouse gases I've emitted into the atmosphere over the years.

Another reason that richly qualifies "Langdonpocene" over the leading but pretentious alternative, I would argue, is that "Anthropocene" includes literally billions of people who have little if any claim to this grandiose geologic title at all. Among them are human beings, "anthropos" if you will, who over many centuries and to the present day have lived modestly with minimal impact on the local or global environs or the Earth's climate systems. Much of the populace of Asia, Africa, South America, island communities, northern Canada and the like, people in the so-called "developing countries" have little if any right to be identified as serious players in this new game of names. No, they should be regarded as mere fakers, pikers, frauds, and utter nobodies if ever they pretend to

have a stake in labeling this momentous epoch! Unlike my own substantial claim, their names would not even appear on a list of plausible nominees for the prize, for their levels of wanton destruction are pathetically miniscule at best. Sorry, folks, you just don't deserve to have a new "cene" named after you.

As outlined in an elegant, well-documented argument, the views of Andreas Malm and Alf Hornborg have offered similar reasons for criticizing the presumptuous term "Anthropocene." "We find it deeply paradoxical and disturbing that the growing acknowledgement of the impact of societal forces on the biosphere should be couched in terms of a narrative so completely dominated by natural science." They note that the prevailing focus upon the human species as a unified whole tends to overlook the actual social and economic institutions and activities that are clearly the cause of the massive effects in the biosphere evident today. "Capitalists in a small corner of the Western world invested in steam, laying the cornerstone for the fossil economy: at no moment did the species vote for it either with feet or ballots, or march in mechanical unison, or exercise any sort of shared authority over its own destiny and that of the Earth System." For example, if one takes into account quantitative measures of actual resource and energy consumption, the gravity of misjudgment about a unified "humanity" in "Anthropocene" discourse immediately becomes clear. "A significant chunk of humanity is not party to the fossil fuel economy at all: hundreds of millions rely on charcoal, firewood or organic waste such as

Energy Does a Person Use in a Year?" www.americangeosciences.org/critical-issues /faq/how-much-energy-does-person-use-year. [14] Ibid.

dung for all domestic purposes....Their contribution is close to zero."[15]

The fundamental error here, Malm and Hornborg observe, is the very one that Karl Marx emphasized in his argument that production is "encased in eternal natural laws independent of history, at which opportunity *bourgeois* relations are then quietly smuggled in as the inviolable natural laws on which society is founded."[16] In this case, the species homo sapiens as a whole is credited (or blamed) for the voracious policies and actions of relatively few members of the group. That is the implication the term "Anthropocene" carries with it.

Today's penchant for linking the activities of modern techno-capitalism and their world-altering consequences to the activities of humanity as a whole has a distant mirror in writings about technology, industry, economics, philosophy, and social change common in the mid-twentieth century. Featured in the titles of a great many books, essays and news stories of the period was a ponderous subject called "Man," a collective name for humanity within the broad sweep of history, especially as regards the accomplishments of modern industrial society. Among book titles, for example, one finds *Man and Nature, Man and the State, Man and Water, Man and Technology, Man and His Nature, Man and His Universe, Man and His Values*, and so forth. My search of the "World Cat" interlibrary catalog at my university turned up more than a hundred books published during that period with "Man" as the central character. What a guy!

Eventually this practice of naming ceased as it dawned on people that, lo and behold, there were also women, not just men, who had made and were making substantial contributions to developments within the domains of life and work under discussion. Hence, a standard anthology in Science and Technology Studies of the 1970s and 1980s, *Technology and Man's Future*, eventually changed its title to *Technology and the Future* in its later editions.[17]

Of course, much of the credit for this awakening is due to the increasing presence of women scholars and feminist perspectives in scholarship and publishing as the years moved on. "What were we thinking?" was a comment frequently heard in university corridors as this correction took place.

Beyond its blatant sexism, another problem with the "Man and…" construction was that it implicitly, sometimes even explicitly, portrayed humanity from the point of view of the European and North American populace, suggesting that such folks were at the apex of all human creativity. The "Man" who had mastered the land and seas, conquered The New World, and brought new kinds of knowledge and technology to prominence was transparently composed of people living in London, Paris, New York, and other hubs of Western industrial influence. Of course,

[15] Andreas Malm, and Alf, Hornborg, 2016 "The geology of mankind? A critique of the Anthropocene narrative," *The Anthropocene Review* I(1): 62-69, 2016.
[16] Karl Marx, *Grundrisse* (London: Penguin Books, 1993, 87).

[17]Albert H. Teich, ed., *Technology and Man's Future* (New York: St. Martin's Press, 1972) and Albert H. Teich, ed., *Technology and the Future*, 6th edition (New York: St. Martin's Press, 1993).

a common underlying intention here was generously, inauspiciously to include the billions of other humans who live on Earth or who have ever lived here as parts, albeit lesser parts, of the populace in question. Writers in the "Man and" tradition seemed to find it magnanimous to include all those other people beyond Europe and North America within the mysterious pronoun "we," employed throughout their books. But any informed, focused attention on the lives and contributions of other large and diverse cultures around the globe was seldom part of the univocal history sketched at the time. A strong implication in the "Man and…" literature was that scattered others around the globe should be pleased to learn that the powerful males in Western Civilization had now given them a nice little tip of the hat, recognizing their otherwise insignificant presence in the story of "Mankind."

Looking at the rise and fall of the "Man and…" literature and its pungent underlying point of view, the rise of the "Anthropocene" appears as a nostalgic revival of a collection of woeful habits. A good many geologists, philosophers, social scientists, journalists, and other prominent thinkers have – yet again! – taken it upon themselves to speak for the diverse populace of human beings who have existed over many generations, using ingenious labels and a set of judgments about who it is that truly matters. In this case, blanket judgments about who is responsible for the widespread, often calamitous reengineering of the Earth's biosphere are placed in the lap of "anthropos," a category that includes literally billions

of people, living and dead, who have had an almost negligible effect upon the world-gouging endeavors the new geologic label recognizes and (alternately) celebrates or bemoans. As a serviceable estimate, far and away the greatest extent of the damage to Earth's biosphere through the burning of fossil fuels, resource extraction and ill-conceived works of engineering comes from 1 billion people on Earth within the total populace of 7.3 billion. In that light a more accurate label for this geological epoch would be "The Fourteen-PerCentPocene." While not as fascinating as "The Langdonpocene," it is several steps closer to reality than that other popular brand.

There is no longer any doubt about the enormous scale and significance of the impacts upon the Earth and its creatures that the activities and projects of some human groups have brought about. In fact, a truly welcome feature of today's vogue for the label "Anthropocene" is the light it sheds upon deteriorating condition of the biosphere and its life-sustaining features. This includes growing awareness of a phenomenon known as the "Sixth Extinction." Scientists have identified five previous mass extinctions of plant and animal life, including the mass die-off at the end of the Cretaceous, sixty-five million years ago, the one that killed off the dinosaurs, evidently caused by the effects of one or more massive asteroids or comets striking the Earth. While estimates of the extent of today's death rate vary according to method and categories of analysis, most of them are starkly ominous. In its *Living Planet Report 2016* the World Wildlife Fund estimates that On average there has been a 58 percent drop in numbers of vertebrates – fish, mammals, birds and reptiles – around the globe between 1970 and 2012.[18] This does not bode well for human settlements that depend upon biodiversity for their livelihood. According to researchers from the United Nations Environment Program and University College London, "For 58.1 percent of the world's land surface, which is home to 71.4 percent of the global population, the level of biodiversity loss is substantial enough to question the ability of ecosystems to support human societies. The loss is due to changes in land use and puts levels of biodiversity beyond the "safe limit" recently proposed by the planetary boundaries – an international frame-work that defines a safe operating space for humanity."[19]

Given the unhappy plight that evidently awaits countless nonhuman species in the years ahead, a section in print and online newspapers called "Anthropocene News" could well become a suitable replacement for the portion now called "Obituaries." Sticking with the convention of proposing names with Greek roots, however, a classy alternative label might be "Thanatopocene," the epoch of death. This would closely match a central theme in many of today's most popular movies and television series, that of apocalyptic and post-apocalyptic crises along with a profusion of zombie narratives. On my own university campus, a wildly popular student organization at present is the Humans vs. Zombies Club, one that "prepares players for the impending zombie apocalypse." In their own fun loving ways, young people seem to be preparing for, perhaps even yearning for, Anthropocenic futures that include encounters with the walking dead. Playing one of the deceased creatures as opposed to a living human is actually a cherished role in these games.

Descriptions of the "Sixth Extinction" emphasize not only the pervasive effects of carbon emissions upon global warming, but also ambitious enterprises that involve transforming and exploiting vast stretches of the natural landscape, projects often identified as signature accomplishments of the "Anthro-pocene" era. Tom Butler's astonishing photo essay, *Overdevelopment, Overpopulation, Overshoot,* offers vivid portraits of many of the places affected.[20] Included on the list would certainly be the huge expanses in the Amazon rain forest now being cleared for lumbering, cattle-raising and other kinds of profit-making enterprise. As an afterthought, one ingenious attempt to preserve some forested areas and the species of flora and fauna in them is the creation of "islands" of forest habitat within zones subject to commercial development, large patches of land in which the trees and plants are left intact. Proponents argue that policies of this kind will preserve the vitality

[18] World Wildlife Fund, "Living Planet Report," 2016. awsassets.panda.org/downloads/lpr_living_planet_report_2016.pdf
[19] University College of London, "Biodiversity falls below safe levels globally," 2016. www.unep-wcmc.org/news /biodiversity-falls-below-safe-levels-globally.

[20] Tom Butler, ed., *Overdevelopment Over-population Overshoot* (San Francisco: Goff Books, 2012.

of the forest and its creatures, while allowing economic enterprise to flourish.

Recognizing the magnitude of the damage done to many of the planet's ecosystems, some biologists and eco-philosophers have begun recommending immediate, large-scale measures to shelter pieces of land and ocean from any further so-called development and to set aside vast portions for recovery. Thus, E. O. Wilson has proposed what he calls "Half Earth," a plan to devote the space of half the planet as permanent shelters for the millions of nonhuman species that exist here.

"The way it could done," he observes, "is to take the remaining wildernesses of the world, on both sea and land, and set those aside as inviolate, while we go on with our chaotic and unpredictable, destructive future….The big task is to settle down before we wreck the planet."[21] Thus, the Half Earth proposal amounts to a call to cease the massively destructive tendencies that have been characteristic of Anthropocene so far, the creation of an Anti-Anthropocene, if you will.

A hallmark of the discourse of renaming a geological epoch and imagining its astonishing features is that it brashly reaffirms what the writings of many ecophilosophers and environmental activists have long called into question – the distinctly anthropocentric standpoint for human reflection about the world in which we live. Thus, the arguments in the philosophy of "deep ecology" offered by Arne Naess and others criticize the traditional, often unstated, prejudice that humans ought to be the crucial point of reference in our reflections. Given the vast plurality of living creatures and habitats on Earth, wouldn't that be a more reasonable standpoint at which to begin, a better way to move forward? Philosophies that fundamentally recognize the situations of other creatures and their needs would likely be far more revealing than one that merely restates, amplifies and tacitly celebrates the hubris of the past several centuries in the West.

In light of what Arne Naess and other ecophilosophers have strongly affirmed, the unvarnished, breast-thumping pride in the reassertion of humans as all that really matters on Planet Earth is the truly astonishing feature of the emerging vogue for Anthropocenism in our time. At this moment in history it's worth asking why this is needed. Why is this necessary? What is the purpose, the practical application of the discourse of the Anthropocene?

True, there are some thinkers who offer the concept essentially without any particular agenda beyond simply bearing witness to what comparisons of different geologic epochs reveal and why the current one might be recognized as distinctive. From that standpoint why not simply refer to the current stage of Earth's lengthy history as "the late Holocene," while noting its peculiar features, even the ones that point to some fairly rapid consequential changes? But modesty of that kind does not seem to be adequate to a good many observers of the situation. For better or worse,

---

[21] Simon Worrall, "Book Talk: E.O. Wilson's Bold Vision for Saving the World," *National Geographic News*, Nov. 1, 2014, news.nationalgeographic.com/news/2014/11/141102-edward-wilson-meaning-existence-darwin-extraterrestrials-ngbooktalk/.

many hope to leverage the rhetoric of the Anthropocene to support policies in tune with a particular ideology or political program.

One contender is a proposal called the "Good Anthropocene." A prominent advocate is Erle Ellis, professor of Geography and Environmental Systems at the University of Maryland. He writes, "Creating the future will mean going beyond fears of transgressing natural limits and nostalgic hopes of returning to some pastoral or pristine era. Most of all, we must not see the Anthropocene as a crisis, but as the beginning of a new geological epoch with human-directed opportunity."[22]

Ellis, along with a good number of others who've embraced similar points of view, favors geoengineering as a promising response to what he sees as a grand challenge. "Geoscientists are ever more actively involved in geoengineering to counter global warming by injecting sulfate aerosols into the stratosphere, industrial carbon sequestration, and other massive technological alterations of Earth systems." His vision is that of ever-expanding management of the workings of the planet with increasing recognition of "human responsibility."[23]

In my reading of the debate, whether the conviction is completely explicit or quietly buried, much of the enthusiasm for the term, "Anthropocene," involves techno-triumphalism, or, more precisely, eco-techno-triumphalism. Some of those who embrace the label enthusiastically praise expanding powers brought by modern science and technology to bring all of nature under systems of dominance, ones very often advertised as ultimately for the good of humanity as a whole. That's always a good way to frame such policies. Just tell people it's for the good of everybody. As techno-enthusiast Stewart Brand once proclaimed, "We are as gods and might as well get used to it."[24]

INSIDE AN ANTHROPOCENIUM: BIOSPHERE 2

An appropriate metaphor and working model for what we are witnessing at present is the grand experiment of the middle 1980s to create Biosphere 2 in the desert of Arizona near the town of Oracle.[25] As a point of reference, Biosphere 1 was understood as the name for the entire collection of ecological systems on Earth as it stands, the environs within which human beings and other living beings have evolved. In contrast, Biosphere 2 was an elaborate work of engineering, a massive structure of metal and glass, a greenhouse on steroids, built near Oracle, Arizona during the late 1980s by the firm Space Biosphere Ventures, under the guidance of visionary inventor/engineer John W. Allen. Its purpose was to create a completely enclosed ecosystem with no inputs from the outside world other than sunlight. Erected at an estimated cost of $200 million, the massive laboratory included several ecological zones called "biomes" — a rainforest, mangrove wetlands, a small

---

[22] Erle C. Ellis, "Earth Science in the Anthropocene: New Epoch, New Paradigm, New Responsibilities," *EOS Forum*, 90:49, 2012, 473.
[23] Ibid.

[24] Steward Brand, *Whole Earth Catalog* (1968, 1).
[25] Jane Poynter, *The Human Experiment: Two Years and Twenty Minutes Inside Biosphere 2* (New York: Basic Books, 2006).

ocean with coral reef, a grassland, and fog desert along with a 2,500-meter agricultural system, as well as places for human habitation. The scientists, architects, and engineers who worked on the project took every detail into account, including ingenious mechanisms for generating ocean waves.

A central goal of the Biosphere 2 experimental facility was to demonstrate the feasibility of self-contained, sustainable living systems for space stations to be built in future decades. To some extent this was inspired by post-Apollo program fascination with extraterrestrial settlements both within Earth's orbit and beyond, ones envisioned and promoted by Gerard O'Neil among others. Advocates for structures of this kind argued that they'd be needed for deep-space exploration, also as a nifty backup in the unfortunate eventuality that the Earth might become uninhabitable. Those who volunteered to live in Biosphere 2 during its two trial runs were called "bionauts," mirroring the reputation of the "astronauts" who went to moon and other space missions. Even their natty blue uniforms looked entirely appropriate for would-be successors to Neil Armstrong and John Glenn.

In fact, there were some notable scientific findings produced by research within parts of Biosphere 2, including insights into effects of ocean acidification on sea life. In the end, however, both of the "missions" of Biosphere 2 – the first from September 1991 to September 1992, the second from March 1994 to September of the same year – were utter disasters, afflicted by a number of ecological and social breakdowns.

The first mission "suffered from CO_2 levels that 'fluctuated wildly' and most of the vertebrate species and all of the pollinating insects died."[26] Insect populations, including cockroaches and other unwanted species grew at an astonishing speed. Other problems included "overstocked fish dying and clogging filtration systems, unanticipated condensation making the 'desert' too wet, population explosions of greenhouse ants and cockroaches, and morning glories overgrowing the 'rainforest,' blocking out other plants."[27]

According to journalist Christopher Turner, during the first mission, "all the bionauts could think about was food, and their memoirs of the two-year project are full of references to their recurring dreams of McDonald's hamburgers, lobster, sushi, Snickers-bar cheesecake, lox and bagels, croissants, and whiskey. They bartered most of their possessions, but food was too precious to trade. They became sluggish and irritable through lack of it, and were driven by hunger to acts of sabotage."[28] According to another published account, "Before the first closure mission was half over, the group had split into two factions and people who had been intimate friends had become implacable enemies, barely on speaking terms."[29]

[26] "Biosphere 2: History 2.2 First Mission" *Environment and Ecology*. environment-ecology.com/ecological-design/255-biosphere-2.html.
[27] Ibid.
[28] Christopher Turner, "Ingestion: Planet in a Bottle," *Cabinet*, Issue 41, Spring 2011, www.cabinetmagazine.org/issues/41/turner.php.
[29] "Biosphere 2: History 2.2 First Mission" *Environment and Ecology*, environment-ecology.com/ecological-design/255-biosphere-2.html.

Although the specific problems that surfaced during the second "mission" were of a somewhat different complexion, that "mission" was also abruptly cancelled when the bionauts split into rival factions, fiercely competing for available resources. Whatever the promise of its natural science-and-engineering horizons may have been, the human relationships within the Oracle facility were largely calamitous and beyond repair, an outcome that does not bode well for the social and political consequences of climate crash now rapidly unfolding around the globe.

Although it may seem that the techno-triumphalist fantasies on display in the Biosphere 2 project are worlds apart from the maladies in the public sphere exemplified by the rise of Donald J. Trump, one suggestive link stands out. In its conception, management, finance, and eventual collapse, a key player in Biosphere 2 was none other than Steve Bannon, Trump's right-hand man in the journey from TV reality showman to the office of President of the United States. From a 1993 C-SPAN television special, Bannon appears seated inside the massive structure, wearing his trademark kaki jacket, waxing eloquent about the project's monumental vision.[30]

A lot of the scientists who are studying global change and studying the effects of greenhouse gases, many of them feel that the Earth's atmosphere in 100 years is what Biosphere 2's atmosphere is today. We have extraordinarily high CO2, we have very high nitrous oxide, and we have high methane. We also have lower oxygen content. So the power of this place is allowing those scientists who are really involved in the study of global change, and who, in the outside world, or Biosphere 1, are limited to working only with just computer simulation, this actually allows them to study and monitor the impact of enhanced CO2 and other greenhouse gases on humans, plants, and animals.

In the end, Bannon's most notable contribution to the utopian scheme was to pull the plug, removing its primary source of funding at the behest of his boss, billionaire oil baron Ed Bass, who had decided that the experiment had become a costly waste of money. From there, Bannon moved on to become a mover and shaker in investment banking, a producer of tacky horror movies and political documentaries, and an impresario of far-right-wing Internet "news" sites. Abandoning his professed ecological ideals of the Biosphere 2 misadventure, he ultimately became a militant climate-change denier, denouncing the whole environmental crisis as "fake news," a key feature in an increasingly reactionary political profile.

In light of the trajectory of Bannon's bizarre career within two important realms of public affairs, an interesting question looms ahead: Will the post-truth political maneuvers in Donald J. Trump's White House 2 fare any better than the triumphalist pseudo-science of Biosphere 2? At this writing it seems unlikely.

---

[30] Quoted in Samathan Cole, "The Strange History of Steve Bannon and the Biosphere 2 Experiment," *Motherboard*, Nov., 2016.

Scientific Suspects, Romantic Witnesses? Magic Technologies, Alienation, and Self-Destruction in the Anthropocene

MARK COECKELBERGH

UNIVERSITY OF VIENNA
VIENNA, AUSTRIA

ABSTRACT: *As in the Anthropocene the fates of humans and the planet become increasingly entangled, we have a paradoxical problem of agency in the face of the changes: we at the same time create the problem and are impotent when it comes to solving it. It seems that we are reduced to bystanders, or worse, distant witnesses. To understand this problem, in particular to identify what makes possible this deadlock in terms of agency and knowledge, this paper uses the concepts of "Earth alienation" (Arendt) and romantic technologies (Coeckelbergh and others). It then explores some paths which may help to deal with this problem: direct engagement with material and natural things, artistic work, changing our understanding of science and technology and of their relation to culture and politics, and critically studying the language and images we use in our analysis and discussion of the problem. It is concluded that the problem under investigation points us to deeper problems and complexities of modernity, to which there is no magic solution.*

KEYWORDS: Anthropocene, technology, alienation, romanticism, magic, engagement

INTRODUCTION: THE PROBLEM REGARDING AGENCY AND KNOWLEDGE IN THE ANTHROPOCENE

The term "Anthropocene" has been introduced to signal that the effects of humans on the global environment have escalated (Crutzen) to such an extent that they overwhelm us and shape the geological future. Global warming, in particular, has raised concerns that human activities have become so pervasive that "they rival the great forces of Nature" (Steffen et al.). Humans have become a geological force. And in the Anthropocene, as the fates of humans and the planet become increasingly entangled, there is the danger of the self-destruction of humankind. The geological force we created seems to be turning against us by destroying the Earth, the very condition for human life.

If this is the situation and the danger, what can we do about it? There is a serious problem regarding human agency in the face of these changes. As Bruno Latour has put it, we are part of the history, part of the drama, but at the same time we are "utterly impotent" when it comes to fixing the problem (Latour 2). We are also not good in dealing with all the data that are communicated to us by scientists; it is not clear what we know. If anyone or anything has agency, it seems, it is the Earth itself.

And we, with our media and our technologies, *witness* what happens, becoming bystanders in a geological drama that we created. We are witnesses and suspects at the same time. This is a problem for ethics and politics: How can we act responsibly if we are at the same time (a) contributing to a history of self-destruction; and (b) feeling impotent? What do we know, and what can we do?

While there is a vast debate about the Anthropocene and the role of technology in the problem and in the solution, in this paper I limit myself to the problem of agency and knowledge, and within this space of discussion I focus here on the technological-cultural conditions that have created this situation in the first place and have *made possible* this somewhat tragic position of the witness and bystander.

For this purpose, I inquire into the problem of "Earth alienation" and its relation to technology, and link this problem to magic and romanticism in our modern use of technology. Then I reflect on what could be alternative ways of relating to our environment and the Earth. On the whole, the paper links the problem of agency and knowledge in the Anthropocene with the problem of (technology in) modernity.

EARTH ALIENATION AND TECHNOLOGY

If today we witness environmental destruction and face the threat of human self-destruction, this can be understood as a form of alienation. Walter Benjamin writes:

> Mankind, which in Homer's time was an object of contemplation for the Olympian gods, now is one for itself. Its self-alienation has reached such a degree that it can experience its own destruction as an aesthetic pleasure of the first order. (Benjamin 235)

For Benjamin, this was what happened in Fascism and its war. But it also seems relevant to the situation described above: we use technologies to change the Earth, and at the same time we contemplate our own self-destruction.

This detached, aesthetic attitude is possible only since we were able to physically distance ourselves from the Earth. Here Hannah Arendt offers an interesting concept: "Earth alienation," which also links the problem to technology. In *The Human Condition,* Arendt starts her prologue with the story of Sputnik, the first artificial satellite that circled the Earth in 1957. She connects this event to the human dream to escape from the Earth (1-2). This is an age-old dream. But what is new in the modern age, according to Arendt is that this dream now goes together with a turning away from "an Earth who was the Mother of all living creatures under the sky" (2). This is a turning away from the human condition itself, from our habitat:

> The Earth is the very quintessence of the human condition, and earthly nature, for all we know, may be unique in the universe in providing human beings with a habitat in which they can move and breathe without effort and without artifice. (Arendt 2)

This turning away is made

possible by science and technology. Later in the book, Arendt argues that science created Earth alienation, by means of modern mathematics which enabled taking a standpoint outside nature (265), an Archimedean point. This, according to Arendt, made possible our mastery over nature and "the enormously increased human power of destruction" (268). She also points to Cartesian doubt, which led to loss of faith and perhaps to the idea that Nature is an illusion.

But keeping in mind the event in Arendt's Prologue, one could also add that, in addition, *technologies* made possible this leaving the Earth and this very *contemplation* or *witnessing* of the Earth and our destructive powers. First there was the telescope and then the space technologies such as satellites and spaceships, which literally enabled humans to leave the Earth and *look at the Earth for the first time*, thus constructing it as "Earth" and "planet," and *taking distance from it*. The very problem of the "Anthropocene" is made possible by this view from space, this technology that enabled us to perceive ourselves as earthbound and Earth-destroying at the same time, this technology that constructed "the Earth" and "the planet" in the first place. It is through modern science with its numbers and measurements, and through modern technologies, that we came to understand ourselves as living on a threatened planet and as living in the Anthropocene.

Giving this kind of phenomenological and hermeneutic role to technologies is not only compatible with work in contemporary philosophy of technology (e.g., Ihde's post-phenomenology, see for instance, *Postphenomenology and Technoscience,* and of course with Arendt's mentor, Heidegger, who analyzed modern technology as a way of thinking rather than simply as an instrument (*The Question Concerning Technology*). But it is also entirely in line with Arendt's own view in *The Human Condition,* which acknowledges the role of technologies in shaping new (world)views:

> It was not reason but a man-made instrument, the telescope, which actually changed the physical world view; it was not contemplation, observation, and speculation which led to the new knowledge, but the active stepping in of *homo faber*, of making and fabricating. (Arendt 274)

For Arendt, science and technology are not spheres that are separate from the lifeworld and from society; they have cultural and political significance. To conclude, inspired by Arendt's concept of Earth alienation, we can say that technology makes possible our detachment from the Earth in the first place, and hence makes possible the problem indicated in the beginning of this paper. Through modern technologies and media, we at the same time cause the problem and aesthetically contemplate it.

However, not only modern science and technology play a crucial role in the emergence of this problem. There is also another cultural (and as I have argued, technological) movement at work, which is also part of modernity and which involves *a particular kind of* aesthetics: romanticism.

ROMANTICISM, MAGIC, AND TECHNOLOGY

Modern science and/or Enlightenment thinking are often blamed for creating alienation. But romanticism is also problematic in this respect, as "witness" it is also "suspect." As has been shown before (Coeckelbergh, *Environmental Skill*), romanticism creates and presupposes a distance between a romantic observer and a Nature which is used for romantic projections. It can also lead to self-absorption, which is the opposite of engagement with the natural environment.

However, romanticism is not only a cultural movement or a psychological attitude; our *technologies* are also romantic (Coeckelbergh, *New Romantic Cyborgs*) and hence contribute to the alienation problem and the problem identified in the beginning of this paper. In the nineteenth century, for instance, there was science fiction that portrayed leaving the Earth as a way of achieving re-enchantment, but there were also material technologies such as automata and all kinds of media such as photography that enabled people to escape reality. There was a romantic science and there were what Tresch has called "romantic machines" (*The Romantic Machine*). We are used to separating culture from technology, but in scientific and technological practices they come together. Here romantic thinking and engineering met, for instance in the romantic adventure of ballooning or in the sublime steam engine. Technologies were not only a threat to romantics; they were also highly fascinating and could be used as re-enchantment engines.

Moreover, as has been argued in Coeckelbergh (*New Romantic Cyborgs*), romantic machines are not a thing of the past alone; contemporary technologies and their use have also a romantic aspect. For example, computer games, augmented reality and virtual reality technologies enable users to enter different worlds. Internet technologies have created a cyberspace which once again enables people to leave the Earth. And fantasies about uploading promise to realize the Platonic and Cartesian dream of leaving the body and leaving the Earth. For our relation to the natural environment, this means that there is once again the danger of alienation, understood as disengagement and distance from the natural environment. And once again technologies are not pheno-menologically and hermeneutically neutral: they change our view of the world. For instance, using all these new technologies, perhaps we start to perceive the Earth not as the condition for human life and existence but a merely accidental house, which we can leave for another one somewhere else in space (see for instance the ideas of some Californian CEOs such as Elon Musk). Maybe the Earth is seen as too boring; in response it is suggested that we can create our own enchanted and artificial spaces for living elsewhere. This romanticism is shared by many artists who are enthusiastic about going to space.

Moreover, the Earth can be seen as something which we can re-build and re-engineer. With regard to the Anthropocene problem, for instance, there are many proposals to geo-engineer the Earth. The Earth itself comes to be seen as a spaceship or a building which we can modify by means of technology. The Earth itself becomes a kind of artifact.

The latter is perhaps not so much a romantic idea as a magical one. Technology can be seen as magic in at least the following senses: First, magic can be seen as the power to change things in the world, to make the world obey one's will. One could say that this kind of magic has created the Anthropocene problem: technology has given us power to do with the Earth what we want. The same kind of thinking is at work in proposals to geo-engineer the Earth as a solution to the Anthropocene problem.

Second, magic can be seen as trickery, fooling, creating illusion. Social robotics, for instance, can be understood as a magician's practice: the roboticist tries to create the illusion that the robot is a human being or a pet. More generally, the design of ICTs [Information and Communication Technologies], from the invention of the first graphical interfaces to today's smartphones, can be seen as a kind of illusionism. There is the illusion that the technology is a human being, for instance when the technology talks to us. But there are also other illusions; for instance, users are given the illusion that ICT is immaterial, that there are no material infrastructures needed and that there is no human labor going into it, and that there are no social and political issues. With regard to the Anthropocene, technology is creating the illusion that we can have full knowledge about what is happening

to the Earth, that it is not a political issue, and that we can solve the issue by means of tricks.

Third, magic can be seen as enchantment. This concerns the romantic technologies already mentioned, which are used to (re-) enchant the dull world or to create another one, in cyberspace or outside the Earth. Consider for instance today's magic of augmented reality, which enables us to overlay philistine reality with wonder and enchantment, or the Internet of things, which promises to create an enchanted garden of smart, quasi-living and talking things.

To conclude, romanticism and magic enable both the attitude of mastery of nature and the detached attitude of the observer. They thus contribute to making possible at the same time the self-destruction of humankind and the enjoyment of that self-destruction as an aesthetic pleasure. The drama of the Anthropocene is fascinating to watch, since it takes us out of the ordinary, turns us into characters in a larger story, and calls for romantic-hero engineers who may save the world. With the Anthropocene, we no longer need Hollywood. Engineering and political Fascism combine to create a great spectacle that satisfies our longing for romance and magic.

EXPLORING ALTERNATIVE PATHS

If this is not the direction we want, then what could be the alternative? Is there a way out of the problem, the Anthropocene dead-lock of agency and impotence? How can we get less magical thinking, less romantic thinking, less alienation?

How can we escape the illusion that the problem is not social and political at all? How can we gain a different relation to the natural environment and get less romantic technologies? What *can* we do? What kind of knowledge and procedures do we need, *instead* of what Benjamin calls "a processing of data in the Fascist sense" (212)?

These are big questions and problems, which are not easy to deal with let alone answer; within the limited space of this paper, let me just indicate *some* paths here that may guide us towards dealing with them.

First, as has been suggested in Coeckelbergh (*New Romantic Cyborgs*; *Environmental Skill*), we can avoid alienation by engaging with things and with nature, which gives us a different kind of knowledge: rather than theoretical knowledge (contemplative knowledge, vision, or *theoria*), it gives us know-how. It also enables us to take back some of the agency we lost in the Anthropocene. We can do gardening, for instance, and enjoy both the agency (but there are also limits to that agency; we never have full control) and the direct, much closer engagement with nature.

Second, if "the Earth" or "the planet" is in danger, can *art save the world*? It can certainly offer a different kind of knowledge and approach to the problem than theory and conceptual work. The challenge is then to contribute to understanding and solving the problem without contributing to the deadlock identified (and indeed without contributing to Fascist aesthetics).

Third, science and technology

themselves can be reinterpreted, as being bound up with culture (e.g., romanticism) and, in the spirit of Latour, as political. Instead of separating science and technology from culture, it should be clear that as practices they are always embedded in a larger form of life, in a way of doing things ("how we do things here"). Instead of hiding the politics, scientists could be more open and straightforward about the political role of science and scientists. And, as Latour argues towards the end of his article, the body of the Earth is a body politic. Is perhaps nature itself political? What does this mean? Furthermore, can we create technologies that create less distance? Can we create technologies that give us more agency and a different, less alienated epistemic relation to our natural environment?

Fourth, one way to achieve the latter is to be critical about the language we use to talk about the problem. Images such as "The Planet" and terms such as "Nature" and "Anthropocene" may themselves prevent a better understanding of the problem, for instance by alienating us from our more concrete and direct relations to the natural and social world, by suggesting that we are not already "Nature" and entangled with "Nature," by putting the human being in the center of the ethical and political attention, or even by denying the social and political dimension of the problem. Further investigation of the language and images used in this discussion are recommended in order to render it more critical.

These are mere suggestions; more

research is needed to develop these points. For instance, I have made several remarks about the political; these need further unpacking.

CONCLUSION

In this paper I started with the problem, the "deadlock" of agency in the Anthropocene (which was in turn connected to a problem regarding knowledge). I have investigated and discussed this problem in several ways. With the help of Arendt I have framed the problem in terms of "Earth alienation," I have discussed it in the light of romanticism and magic in modernity, and I have explored some alternative paths which may help us to avoid or at least deal with the problem. In general the present discussion shows how complex the problems with technology in modernity are, and indeed how problematic and paradoxical modernity itself is. Whether or not we use the term "Anthropocene," it is clear that we – as modern romantics – have a problem. And there is no magical solution.

WORKS CITED

Arendt, Hannah. *The Human Condition.* 2nd ed., Routledge, 1958.

Benjamin, Walter. "The Work of Art in the Age of Mechanical Repro-duction." *Illuminations*, Pimlico, 1999, pp. 211-244.

Coeckelbergh, Mark. *New Romantic Cyborgs: Romanticism, Information Technology, and the End of the Machine.* Cambridge, MA/London: The MIT Press, 2017.

---. *Environmental Skill: Motivation, Knowledge, and the Possibility of a Non-Romantic Environmental Ethics.* New York: Routledge. 2015.

Crutzen, Paul J. "Geology of Mankind: The Anthropocene." *Nature*, vol. 415, 2002, p. 23.

Ihde, Don. *Postphenomenology and Technoscience: The Peking Lectures.* State University of New York Press, 2009.

Heidegger, M. *The question Concerning Technology and Other Essays.* Translated by William Lovitt, Harper & Row, 1977.

Latour, Bruno. "Agency at the time of the Anthropocene." *New Literary History*, vol. 45, 2014, pp. 1-18.

Steffen, Wil, Crutzen, Paul J., and John R. McNeill. "The Anthro-pocene: Are Humans Now Overwhelming the Great Forces of Nature?" *Ambio*, vol. 36, no. 8, Sciences Module, 2007, p. 614.

Tresch, John. *The Romantic Machine.* University of Chicago Press, 2012.

The Anthropocene as Event

JAN JASPER MATHÉ

VRIJE UNIVERSITEIT BRUSSEL
BRUSSELS, BELGIUM

ABSTRACT: *The Anthropocene could become the defining name of our period, yet scholars continue to disagree over the very concept. One important challenge that remains to be addressed is the apparent inability to locate our experience of anthropogenic events into meaningful action. We see what is happening around us and we know that we need to do something. But in the end, there is no actual response. Even in our most promising scientific solutions, the evental nature of the Anthropocene is often overlooked. The very fact that we think about anthropogenic events from within the symbolic framework of science and technology obscures them. Drawing from the philosophy of technology and a critical engagement with Slavoj Žižek and Bernard Stiegler, I argue that technoscientific culture provides a fantasy of reality in our current age of human history, which is now inextricably bound up with the history of the Earth. Therefore, the Anthropocene is an event in every sense of the word, namely an object that is fundamentally transforming reality. It not only challenges the framework that regulates our access to reality – which would introduce it as just another fantasy – it shatters that reality completely. Understanding the Anthropocene as event may offer a solution to a general sense of disorientation that leaves human beings unable to react in ways other than merely acting out.*

KEYWORDS: critical theory, philosophy of technology, Žižek, Stiegler, event

INTRODUCTION

A lot has been said about the Anthropocene since its formal conception almost two decades ago. As Bruno Latour has already pointed out, essentially, "we all seem to converge on the same traumatic claim that human agency has become the main geological force shaping the face of the Earth" (4). The increasing impact of human activities on the structure and functioning of biospheres, ecosystems, and atmospheric and stratospheric composition have united the two cultures of academia across the natural sciences to philosophy, anthropology, law, and human geology. Of course, the topic has also attracted a lot of attention outside academic circles. There have been alarmist concerns about runaway climate change by activists and opinion leaders in media outlets all over the globe.

Surprisingly, however, while we can see what is happening and know what is going on, we seem unable to shape our experience of anthropogenic events into meaningful action. Failing to act now, the "anthropogenic erosion" of the planet's biodiversity will have grave "ecological, economic and social consequences" (Ceballos et al. E6095). But despite many global initiatives like the Paris Agreement or the UN Climate Change Conference, we struggle or, worse, even refuse to translate these warnings into policy and public commitment. Nearly every one of us knows that we need to do something, but we carry on as usual.

Why, then, is it so difficult to make a change? Are we still in denial? Are we afraid? Or we might all be deranged, which is the rather provocative premise of Amitav Ghosh's latest book, *The Great Derangement*. Perhaps we are unable to imagine, let alone understand, the intricate links between the natural environment and a rather abstract anthropos. Who or what is this anthropos and how does it relate to the Earth as a protagonist of history that will probably persist in our absence? These issues are important, and we must keep them in mind. But let me draw our attention to the following question first: Has the nature of the Anthropocene as an event been lost from sight?

THE ANTHROPOCENE AS FACT

Again, referring to Latour and Michel Serres, "human action is visible … in the construction of knowledge as well as in the production of the phenomena those sciences are called to register" (Latour 5). In most of the scientific reports anthropogenic phenomena are described as both the driver of epochal change and as its final cause. This is why our impact on the natural world appears to be a fact of destiny. To partition our geological time unit in terms of the Anthropocene, a number of formal criteria must be met, and they proceed from a specific event.

The GSSP or "golden spike" event (Lewis and Maslin) that kindled the Anthropocene will affect how we think about the future of our species on Earth. In other words, the narrative of the Anthropocene depends on a specific marker, whether we choose for instance the great acceleration triggered by the Industrial Revolution or the transoceanic movement of species in the early seventeenth century. Human history is marked by such events, in an ongoing pattern of growth followed by collapse (Steffen et al.). The world was never a consistent place. But the evental nature of the Anthropocene turns out to be something rather particular. It arises from the fact that we, ourselves, have become the event.

THE MEANING OF EVENTS

In its pure and simple form, an event is something that by happening suspends the regular course of things. It is a moment of transformation. Because it happens, an event overcomes the gap that separates an effect from its cause. This gap becomes elevated into the final moment of what is called the absolutely new. The emergence of the present presupposes a past that is "always moving on," that is "swelling unceasingly with a present that is absolutely new" (Bergson 219). For Henri Bergson, as for Whitehead, the absolutely new appears in subjective experience as if it were always-already there, because every image of the present is related to the past.

We have some kind of process philosophy going on here, which sees a previous moment in time as being maintained in its current state to retroactively bring into being the possible conditions of the present. Things are what they are because they relate to what they were in the past. In the flow of human history, what once seemed impossible becomes completely understandable and is even taken for granted *after* it happens. Accordingly, Antonio Negri claims that there is always a paradoxical imperative hidden in our actions. To act is "to do so knowing that the *aporia* is always present in the action," so that "the subject must act while acknowledging the non-conclusiveness of the universe in which it acts" (Negri 45).

This temporal paradox is interesting because it shows us something about reality itself, in the sense that there is always an immediate frame that regulates our access to the field of reality. To be engaged in the world at all is to assume an invisible order that structures and sustains our experience of reality. Hence, in the spirit of Heidegger, our relationship to reality is set against a temporal horizon of meaning within which all entities appear. Reality, as Brian Massumi (41) reminds us, is what is impossible not to experience *when* we experience it. In response to Heidegger, Peter Sloterdijk goes on to say that our structures of meaning are not merely confined to the scope of time. Equally defining for how humans understand themselves in the world is the space they share, as a "place that humans create in order to have somewhere they can appear as those who they are" (Sloterdijk 28). Now, one may wonder, is the Anthropocene as event only a shift in the frame that regulates our access to reality, or does it pose a radical destruction of the frame as such?

DISRUPTION AND ADAPTATION

When Heidegger wrote about the question concerning technology, he already contemplated a technological frame which, as a transparent background to reality, represents "technology as an instrument," holding us in "the will to master it" (34). According to him, we are fundamentally constituted and conditioned by technics. This has remained, in some way or another, the central outset for contemporary philosophy of technology. For Heidegger at least, the essence of technology unfolds in our relating to reality as a collection of objects of scientific revelation and exploitation. In other words, the essence of technology is first and foremost the technologizing of the essence itself (Žižek, *The Parallax View* 275). I will return to this in a moment.

First, let us assume the worst. Suppose the "shock of the Anthropocene" (Bonneuil and Fressoz; Lemmens and Hui) rushes towards a total disaster for planet Earth and all of its inhabitants. This would be a rapture of theological proportions, both literally and figuratively, for it would bring about the "disappearance of humanity" and, therefore, the radical destruction of "the material support of every symbolic frame" (Žižek, *Event* 28). However, the unhappy conclusion here is not so much our mass extinction, but rather the technoscientific superstructure that renders it all possible. In a world governed by vast infrastructures based on complex technological systems, our technological frame of reality seems very much capable of supporting such a total and devastating disruption.

The crucial point is that we *need* technological disruptions. In keeping with our theory of the temporal paradox, we need a disruption to unfold so that it can become negated, preserved and elevated into new structures of meaning. Disruption remains preserved in adoption as its constituent instance. A technological frame emerges once it starts to cause itself in society, in the midst of an ongoing passage from technological disruption to adoption. However, this "mutual shaping" of society and technology raises a couple of problems.

In his work, philosopher Bernard Stiegler shows that every techno-logical introduction brings about periods of individual and social disruption. Eventually, innovations settle down and become integrated into new social forms, which in turn translate back into technical codes (Feenberg). However, in our present system of capitalist production, also known as the Capitalocene (Lemmens and Hui), disruptions are accelerated on a worldwide scale, forcing people to adapt instead of adopt. At this point, adaptation, detachment and disorientation become the mode of living in the Anthropocene.

From this perspective, every adoption appears to be at once too soon and too late. There is no time to waste, yet "every act is a reaction to circumstances which arose because we were too late to act" (Žižek, *Event* 107). Perhaps, as both Stiegler and Žižek would agree, a human being is like a child, "originally helpless, thrown into a [technological] world when he is unable to take care of himself – that is, his or her survival skills develop too late" (Žižek, *The Parallax View* 20). At the same time, again paraphrasing Žižek, every disruption arrives too soon, "as an unsuspected shock which can never be properly... translated into the universe of meaning" (20).

A POSSIBLE WAY FORWARD

Another way of approaching disruption is to appreciate its apogee as the expression of a potential for change. Technological disruption is only human, because we are always already technical beings. In the face of anthropogenic decay, or what Langdon Winner referred to as the "monuments of gigantism" (177-8) inherent to capitalist accumulation, at the tipping point of our natural and cultural boundaries, how can it not also be recognized that "greatness is a misery aware of itself" (Žižek, "*The Parallax View*" 163)? Like the ancient god Janus, technological utopia and dystopia appear as two faces of the same ideological frame. The recent shift away from the mass industrial abuse of natural resources in the old carbon industry to plastics removal and solar-radiation management in new and alternative industries serves as a fine example. This exciting green wave in industrial engineering sounds very promising, but it does not challenge the overarching ideological frame of science and technology.

The eternal question remains whether a positive science would be able to account for the very horizon of meaning in which it operates. Imagine a rabid realist. This person will probably immerse himself in reality and make up lots of different names for it, all categorized as data. As the event-site of the Anthropocene closes in on him, the frame of his empirical reality starts to crumble, because knowing a phenomenon is not the same as acknowledging it.

Science and technologists want to know the real deal, how things are in themselves, beyond the interplay of appearances. But this stance does not consider that the interplay of appearances as such, or the perspectival distortions that prevent our access to reality, is reality in itself (Žižek, *The Parallax View* 281). Scientific culture does not take into consideration how scientific reality shows itself, that the reality of an event is resolved into its own appearance. This is exactly why Latour points out the disappearance of eventfulness in our current technoscientific worldview.

There are, however, some approaches to science and technology that consider technology to be a constructive medium for human experience and practice. I only mention Peter-Paul Verbeek and his work on Ethical-Constructive Technology accompaniment (Kiran et al.), but there are many encouraging approaches like it. Drawing on such fields as postphenomenology and mediation theory, contemporary philosophy of technology seeks to integrate technological development into who and what we are as human beings. Nevertheless, there remains specific to empirical man an apparent inability or unwillingness to fully recognize his own horizon of meaning, for instance by stubbornly clinging to a misguided belief in instrumental reason. This latter model of technical and scientific rationality has now become the most successful frame of our existence, yet it fails to produce even the most basic conditions for "taking care of the world and those who live within it"

(Stiegler, *What Makes Life Worth Living* 94).

This may ultimately be the reason why we are unable to react in ways other than merely acting out. Our silence, impotence and lack of urgency in the face of a new and troubling epoch arise precisely from the fact that our actions become caught up in their own event. That is to say, our actions become realized into an actual event that changes the coordinates of the frame in which it is active. This kind of transformation without any actual change is stimulated by a global industrial capitalism that disrupts only in order to remain the same. For its part, the anthropogenic tragedy continues as a spectacle that takes place outside the frame of our existence, even if we are directly confronted with it.

The key question is this: Do we truly traverse the fantasy and confront its lurking void, or will we choose to remain under its spell? Unfortunately, Žižek kind of leaves us in the lurch here. For him, in accordance with Badiou, it is "better to do nothing than to engage in localized acts whose ultimate function is to make the system run more smoothly" (*The Parallax View* 334). For him, to be truly critical is to disengage. But the urgency of anthropogenic events leaves us no choice. We can prefer not to, but still we must do something since there is no alternative. We need to create new perspectives from which to generate actions, because we believe doing so will help us find a sense of orientation in the world. We like to believe that somehow the unfolding of an event will be able to change things for the better and extend our hopes into the future. If not for the imperative to act on an event, would we still have reason to exist?

CONCLUSION

To conclude, the biggest challenge of living in the Anthropocene is the fact that we, as technical beings, have become our own antagonistic force. By neglecting the Anthropocene as event, we have allowed ourselves to become either discouraged or complacent. Both attitudes stand in the way of the transformative agency that we so desperately need. This paper has tried to make clear that we are all in it together, at once in danger and facing salvation. This is why the absolutely new that is the Anthropocene should become the event-site of an ongoing source of action. We already start to see such event-sites in slums and flooding islands. Not in the "technologically developed" part of the world, but in places like Port-Au-Prince, Mumbai and the Pacific Islands. These people are already living in the Anthropocene. Theirs should be the story of our time.

WORKS CITED

Bonneuil, Christophe, and Jean-Baptiste Fressoz. *The Shock of the Anthropocene: The Earth, History and Us.* Verso Books, 2016.

Bergson, Henri. *Creative Evolution.* Henry Holt and Company, 1911.

Ceballos, Gerardo., Ehrlich, Paul. R., and Dirzo, Rodolfo. "Biological Annihilation via the Ongoing Sixth Mass Extinction Signaled by Vertebrate Population Losses and Declines." *Proceedings of the National Academy of Sciences,* vol. 114, no. 30, 2017, E6089-E6096.

Feenberg, Andrew and Michel Callon. *Between Reason and Experience: Essays in Technology and Modernity.* MIT Press, 2010.

Ghosh, Amitav. *The Great Derangement: Climate Change and the Unthinkable.* University of Chicago Press, 2016.

Kiran, Asle. H., Nelly Oudshoorn, and Peter-Paul Verbeek. "Beyond Checklists: Toward an Ethical-Constructive Technology Assessment." *Journal of Responsible Innovation,* vol. 2, no. 1, 2015, 5-19.

Latour, Bruno. "Agency at the Time of the Anthropocene." *New Literary History,* vol. 45, no. 1, 2014, pp. 1-18.

Lemmens, Pieter and Yuk Hui. "Pieter Lemmens and Yuk Hui – Apocalypse, Now! Peter Sloterdijk and Bernard Stiegler on the Anthropocene." www.boundary2.org.

Lewis, Simon. L. and Mark. A. Maslin. "Defining the Anthropocene." *Nature,* vol. 519, no. 7542, 2015, pp. 171-180.

Massumi, Brian. *Semblance and Event.* MIT Press, 2013.

Negri, Antonio. *Subversive Spinoza. (Un)contemporary Variations.* Manchester University Press, 2004.

Sloterdijk, Peter. *Bubbles: Spheres Volume 1. Microspherology.* Semiotext(e), 2011.

Steffen, Will, Wendy Broadgate, Lisa Deutsch, Owen Gaffney, and Cornelia Ludwig. "The Trajectory of the Anthropocene: The Great Acceleration." *The Anthropocene Review,* vol. 2, no. 1, 2015, pp. 81-98.

Stiegler, Bernard. *Technics and Time, 1. The Fault of Epimetheus.* Stanford University Press, 1998.

Stiegler, Bernard. *What Makes Life Worth Living. On Pharmacology.* Polity, 2013.

Winner, Langdon. *The Whale and the Reactor: A Search for Limits in an Age of High Technology.* University of Chicago Press, 2010.

Žižek, Slavoj. *The Parallax View.* MIT Press, 2009.

---. *Event: A philosophical Journey Through a Concept.* Melville House, 2014.

Re-Orienting the Noösphere: Imagining a New Role for Digital Media in the Era of the Anthropocene

PIETER LEMMENS

RADBOUD UNIVERSITY NIJMEGEN
THE NETHERLANDS

ABSTRACT: *According to geologists and Earth System scientists, we are now living in the age of the Anthropocene, in which humans have become the most important geoforce, shaping the face of the planet more decisively than all natural forces combined. This brings with it a huge and unprecedented responsibility of humanity for the future of the biosphere. Humanity's impact on the planet has been largely destructive until now, causing a rupture of the Earth System which completely changes the planetary conditions that characterized the Holocene, the generally benign period of the last 11,000 years in which human civilization as we know it has emerged and was able to flourish. In the Anthropocene these conditions can no longer be taken for granted. On the contrary, humanity itself will have to become responsible for the preservation of the biosphere as its ultimate life-support system. This means that its influence on the Earth System has to become a constructive one, among other things by inventing a cleaner and more sustainable modus vivendi on the planet. In this article it is claimed that such a transformation presupposes the invention of a global noösphere that allows humanity as a planetary collective to perceive and monitor the Earth System and interact more intelligently and sustainably with it. The response-ability required for taking responsibility for the Earth System presupposes the existence of a global noösphere that can both support a permanent collective awareness of our embedding in and critical dependence on the biosphere and function as a collective action platform. Based on a Stieglerian diagnosis of our current predicament, a case will be made for the huge potentials of digital media for our future task of caring for the earth.*

KEYWORDS: Earth, Anthropocene, noösphere, digital media, organology, Bernard Stiegler

INTRODUCTION

In a recent essay, German philosopher Peter Sloterdijk argued that the term "Anthropocene," introduced in 2000 by the Dutch atmospheric scientist Paul Crutzen as a name for the current geological epoch in which the human (*anthropos*) is assumed to have become the most important geological factor on the planet, "inevitably obeys an apocalyptic logic," since "it indicates the end of any peace of mind in the cosmos, on which historical forms of human being-in-the-world rested" (Davis and Turpin 334). The Anthropocene is apocalyptic because it signals the impending and necessary ending of a certain modus vivendi of humans on Earth, which can no longer be continued because its planetary-habitat status is changing, as the supporting conditions that enabled human life start to withdraw. And it means the end of any peace of mind because we can no longer blindly and self-evidently assume the presence of these conditions. Instead we must from now on maintain and even produce them ourselves. This unprecedented, allegedly irreversible, totally unexpected and uncanny change in the most fundamental bedrock of the human condition is what is referred to as the "shock of the Anthropocene" (Bonneuil and Fressoz 39).

What was once called "nature" and conceived of as an ever reliant, productive, abundant and robust backdrop has been fatally implicated in the maelstrom of human productivism and consumerism – "enframed" by it, as Heidegger would have it – with its impending exhaustion as a result. The continued existence of this so-called "nature," which we have now uncovered as being just a small and fragile "film" covering a planetary body – the biosphere – can no longer be entrusted to her own autarky since it has been scientifically explicated and technologically exploited, but will become dependent on us humans. Of course this necessitates a transformation of our economy and finding a renewable and non-polluting "clean energy" alternative to what Earth-System scientists have called the *human energy revolution*, referring to humanity's discovery and exploitation of the fossil fuel deposits of the planet (Langmuir and Broecker 573).

However, as I want to sketch out in this article, the most urgent change needed for the establishment of a more sustainable, Earth-caring civilization is the invention – and first imagination – of another global media system, what will be called a *noösphere* here, using a notion introduced in the 1920s by Pierre Teilhard de Chardin and Vladimir Vernadsky, but interpreted more technologically. Such a noösphere first of all allows us to perceive and monitor the Earth System, in particular the biosphere but also the atmosphere, and interact more intelligently and sustainably with it. The response-*ability* required for taking responsibility for the Earth System presupposes the existence of a global noösphere that can both support a permanent collective awareness of our embedding in and critical dependence on the biosphere and also function as a collective action platform. Using Bernard Stiegler's organopharmacological diagnosis of our current predicament, I try to make a case for the huge potentials of digital media for our future task of caring for the Earth.

THE ANTHROPOCENE AND THE CRISIS OF THE NOÖSPHERE

The Anthropocene as the geological epoch in which humans have acquired "geological agency" (Chakrabarty) and thus become the most important geological (f)actor – an *actor* having consciousness and volition – first of all denotes "a *rupture* in the functioning of the Earth System as a whole" (Hamilton 10), meaning that humans have put this system into a new and irreversible state, an unprecedented "no-analog state" that is (Moore III et al.), one that is "less biologically diverse, less forested, much warmer, and probably wetter and stormier" (Steffen et al.). Most importantly, this means that the fate of the planet is now irreversibly tied to the fate of humans and vice versa, and this, as the influential Australian anthropocenologist Clive Hamilton accurately states, "has ontological meaning. It invites us to think about the Earth in a new way, an Earth in which it is possible for humankind to participate directly in its evolution by influencing the constantly changing processes that constitute it" (Hamilton 21). This article aims to contribute to such a rethinking of the Earth by, once again, reconsidering, principally from a Stieglerian perspective, what is probably the most decisive influence determining the Anthropocene, and that is the human-constructed noösphere that now hovers above the planet.

For Stiegler, the notion of the Anthropocene first of all refers to the coming to light of the systemic and massive *toxicity* of the developing global technosphere that now dominates the whole planet and that Heidegger once termed "enframing" *[Gestell]* (Stiegler, *Automatic Society* 8). Stiegler understands this technosphere in terms of what can be called an *organological* configuration, i.e., a configuration of relations between the psychosomatic organs of humans, the technical organs that make up technical systems or milieus, and the social organizations constituted by them. The intimate relations between these three organ systems are what Stiegler's so-called "general organology" studies, with a particular focus on the *libidinal energy* (that is to say that of desire, motivation, will, imagination, etc., but also knowledge, i.e., the noetic) that flows through these organ systems and that is fundamentally conditioned and modulated through the technical organs (Stiegler, *Symbolic Misery* 134).

This organological toxicity, an expression that basically means that the technical organs – which are understood by Stiegler as *pharmaka* that "compensate" for the original lack of human qualities that can function in both a beneficial and detrimental, an enriching and impoverishing, or an emancipatory and disciplinary way, operate today predominantly so as to frustrate, alienate, disempower, and imprison psychosomatic and social potentials instead of fostering, autonomizing, empowering and liberating them (Stiegler, *For a New Critique of Political Economy* 29-30; 42-43). Think here of the way in which an omnipresent marketing today constantly captures and holds the attention of consumers through devices like smartphones, tablets, game consoles, and interactive television but also via social media, as well as the many ways in which workers are increasingly integrated and inter-connected through networks of automated digital systems whose codes and rhythms fully determine their interactions and communication.

Stiegler's critical work is mainly focused on how this capitalist annexation and exploitation of the noösphere has led to an indus-trialization of the mind, i.e., of the noetic capacities of individuals and collectives, rendering them more and more impotent and anemic politically, socially and culturally.

This industrialization of the mind leads finally to the current "age of impotence" and the generalized paralysis of the social imaginary recently analyzed so well by Franco Berardi (*Futurability*). In Stiegler's view, it is this organological poisoning of the noösphere and, as a result of that, of individual psyches and collectives, that is the root cause behind the pollution and deterioration of the natural eco-systems constituting the Earth's biosphere (Stiegler, *What Makes Life Worth Living* 91). This is because the digital noösphere today embodies the crucial instrument through which capital enforces the total mobilization of libidinal energy for the production and consumption required for its constant expansion. And this libidinal energy is the ultimate motor of capitalism (Stiegler and Ars Industrialis, *The Re-Enchantment of the World* 42).

Stiegler theorizes this organological poisoning in terms of the originally Marxist notion of *proletarianization*, understood as a loss of noetic capacity, i.e., of knowledge both practical and theoretical, and of know-how and individual and social life competences. This loss is caused by the short-circuiting of psychic organs and social organizations through technical organs that take over more and more functions and responsibilities of human subjects and social institutions. Together these form a global technical milieu that serves, ever more exclusively, the prolongation and intensification of the consumerism and productivism that are necessary to continue the process of capitalist valorization, which has

imposed itself as the ultimate and almost sacred finality of the human adventure, albeit a nihilistic and self-destructive finality.

It is no doubt capitalism's deployment of the thermodynamic engine that has unleashed the world-wide ecological destruction and climatic disruption that are the most obvious signals leading Earth-System scientists to propose that we have entered the Anthropocene. But the true cause of the Anthropocene for Stiegler does *not* reside in these thermodynamic engines and their carbon dioxide emissions. Of course we should diminish these and think of cleaner, renewable energy sources and more eco-friendly technologies. But the root of the problem lies in the logic of capital and its persistent and all-too-successful strategies, over the last two centuries, to overcome its own intrinsic limits. This is precisely the prime cause behind the proliferation of the processes of proletarianization into all sectors of society (Stiegler, *For a New Critique of Political Economy* 74).

The first of these limits, already recognized by Marx, was the so-called tendency of the rate of profit to fall, resulting from the imperative to increase productivity through the reduction of labor costs, which forced capital in a first movement to an ever-expanding automation of its production processes via the delegation of skills and gestures of workers to machines, gradually expropriating those workers of their skills and know-how [*savoir-faire*], proletarianizing them in the process. This led, at the end of the nineteenth century, to the problem of overproduction, to which capital then responded in a second movement by inventing consumerism through the adaptation of workers' desires to the output of capitalist production via marketing, advertising, and public relations, engendering the proletarianization of the consumer subject by gradually discharging it of its "knowledge of living" [*savoir-vivre*] and responsibility for its own existence and the world around it (ibid. 25). It has produced what Stiegler calls a *systemic stupidity* (ibid. 47), engendering a *global attention deficit disorder* (Stiegler, *Taking Care of Youth and the Generations* 57).

As a result of the systemic exploitation of consumers' libidinal energy, this strategy necessarily implied, Stiegler contends, capital's encountering a second limit at the end of the twentieth century, which he calls "a tendential fall in libidinal energy" (Stiegler, *What Makes Life Worth Living* 90), or in other words, the destruction of desire as the very motor of the capitalist economy and its degeneration into drives and the formation of a drive-based and *careless* economy of addictive consumption and short-termist financial speculation (ibid. 84). Now it is this destruction of desire, *as* a destruction of care, attention and responsibility induced by the toxicity of the technical milieu of the mind geared to the stimulation of unending production and consumption, that eventually leads to the destruction of the natural, geo-physical milieus of the Earth as well, according to Stiegler, as they are exploited as resources at a continually accelerating pace (ibid. 88).

And this is exactly what constitutes capitalism's third limit, which is arguably the meaning of the Anthropocene. This limit can be overcome only through a radical transformation of the capitalist economy, and this is conceived by Stiegler as an organopharmacological turn through which the generalized toxicity of current organological configurations – first of all insofar as they are constituted by the digital technologies principally conceived as *pharmaka* that are simultaneously toxic and curative – is somehow pharmacologically transformed into a noösphere that can serve as the basis of a *new system of care* and attention, namely of a *global ecological* care and attention, through the invention of new (socio)therapies and practices based on this new noösphere.

The deepest problem of the Anthropocene does not reside in the climate, the ecological and the energy crises per se, however acute they are. These crises are only symptoms of the more fundamental crisis in the climatic conditions of the human mind, that is to say, in the noösphere *as* originally and fundamentally constituted and conditioned by the technosphere, or more precisely, a *mnemo*technical milieu, or in organological terms, of the *libidinal energy* – in the form of knowledge, desires, attention, care, etc., – produced (or destroyed) through that sphere and circulating within it (ibid. 91). In this regard, the solution to the problem of the Anthropocene, which is that of finding *a way out* of it (Stiegler, *Automatic Society* 6-7), consists principally in combating, through what Stiegler calls a *psychopolitics* and a *noöpolitics*, against capitalism's *psycho-power* as exercised through the noösphere (Stiegler, *Taking Care of Youth and the Generations* 92; 113; 181).

IMAGINING ANOTHER
EARTH-ORIENTED AND
EARTH-ATTENTIVE NOÖSPHERE

As today's global noösphere is constituted preeminently by digital network technologies, the psycho- and noöpolitical struggle against capitalist psycho- and noöpower should focus on the Internet and digital media, i.e., on the digital noösphere. What is needed is nothing less than a total reinvention and reconstruction of the digital noösphere because it forms the global technical system constituting and conditioning the collective noetic capacities of the *anthropos* in the Anthropocene, thereby significantly determining the emerging anthropo-cenic condition. This calls for a *positive* pharmacology, both theoretically and practically, in the sense of wrestling the noösphere from capitalist control. This would be reappropriating it and reorienting and repurposing it from a machine for inflaming productivism and consumerism that ignores and exhausts the planet as a life-support system toward a shared apparatus of planetary sensing and monitoring. This would allow for a collective care-taking of that life-support system, which becomes possible on a planetary scale by enabling the invention of the many new modes of knowledge, know-how, and care needed to confront the anthropo-cenic situation (Stiegler, *Automatic Society* 147-8). Today's generalized automation, robotization, big data, algorithmic governance, and all of

the other socio-technological innovations realized through digitization have been put into service almost exclusively through capitalist valorization, thus engendering the generalized toxicity of the noösphere that terrorizes our age of global crisis. However, all of these innovations can in principle be re-forged into instruments for the creation of another noösphere, one that can form the basis of a global ecological awareness and care-taking through a *pharmacological turn*, transforming the current toxic milieu serving the nihilistic needs of financial capitalism into a therapeutic, curative arsenal for the constitution of a noösphere explicitly aware of its planetary embedding and dependence. Such a noösphere will be able to steer the anthropic adventure on this planet in another direction, one that is more in tune with the Earth System and that is, in principle, more negentropic.

Employing a terminology derived from thermodynamics, Stiegler conceptualizes the "logic" of pharmacology, basically that of toxicity and detoxification, within the context of his thinking of the Anthropocene with the notions of *entropy* and negative entropy or *negentropy*, giving these notions a much broader meaning than they have in the context of the physical sciences, and applying them to all processes of becoming and, more specifically, to human becoming, be they physico-chemical, vital, psychic, social, technical or, most important here: noetic. Entropy and negative entropy are notoriously difficult concepts, but the latter, later condensed as "negentropy," was introduced in 1944 by the famous Austrian physicist, Erwin Schrödinger, in his seminal book, *What Is Life?* to characterize the processes of life in contrast to those of physics, which all obey the Second Law of Thermodynamics by tending ineluctably to disorder or the absence of free energy or potentiality, ultimately leading to the "heat death" of the universe. Life instead is a negentropic force (although producing more entropy in its surroundings) in that it generates *more* order or complexity and thereby runs counter to the Second Law (Schrödinger). The Romanian economist Nicholas Georgescu-Roegen has applied thermodynamic insights to the economy, showing among other things that resources can be considered low entropy while wastes are high entropy (Georgescu-Roegen).

Stiegler now recruits these insights in the context of his libidinal economy and has coined a new concept, that of *neganthropy*, for thinking the form of negentropy specific to human life, i.e., technical life, as a noetic or knowing form of life. Neganthropy is a measure for noetic wealth and potential. In this sense he can speak for instance of a library as "a collection of *neganthropic potentialities*" (Stiegler, *Automatic Society* 53). Anthropic life as a technical form of life that is not just organic but also (as we saw) organo*logical*, is both negentropic and entropic since technical organs as irreducibly *pharmaco*logical can accentuate and accelerate both the negentropic and entropic tendencies within this technical life, be they economic, political, social, cultural or otherwise (ibid. 31). Interpreting the

generalized toxicity of the current organological configuration in terms of an entropization (and thus proletarianization) of all the processes of human becoming, in turn giving rise to the toxification and deterioration of our planetary ecology, Stiegler characterizes the Anthropocene as the *entropocene* (ibid.). Overcoming it explicitly calls for a *negentropic turn* in the thoroughly organological condition of the *anthropos*, which has until now been largely neglected in philosophy but presents itself for the first time *as such* with the Anthropocene, imposing itself as *the* question of our time.

This negentropic turn should be understood as a *neganthropic* turn, inaugurating the *Neganthropocene* and calling for a new figure of the human that Stiegler calls the *neganthropos*, imagined as arising from a new organological configuration constituting a new *planetary* culture and another, Earth-caring and Earth-tending political economy in which all human activity, first of all in the noetic domain, will be governed and motivated by the criteria of negentropy and where the new ultimate criterion of valuation will be neganthropy (ibid. 33). A crucial element in this turn, again, is a pharmacological reinvention and reappropriation of the media constituting the digital noösphere – the "digital organology" – and their automatizing capacities precisely for the purpose of *de*-automatization and *de*-proletarianization in order to overcome the systemic stupidity and structural carelessness imposed by these media through the capitalist exploitation of those capacities, which breeds only more entropy and thus stupidity and impotence.

As such, the Internet could become the support of a new, *planetary, geo*-organological intelligence, knowledge, and capacity-to-act necessary to overcome the Anthropocene and usher in the Neganthropocene. Of course the whole technosphere should ultimately experience a negentropic turn. In this sense and in this respect, Stiegler argues that we might be living through a veritable "organological chrysalis" (ibid. 156) at the moment, in which all three organological dimensions are metamorphosing simultaneously. And they should be doing so in a wholesome relation with the biosphere. Given the truth of the anthropocenic condition interpreted in a strong sense, this would entail nothing less than a veritable metamorphosis of the Earth's biosphere, through a re-orientation of the noösphere, into an engine of negentropy again. Since humans have become the dominant geological (f)actor and inaugurated the Anthropocene, anthropogenesis *as* technogenesis has become the crucial biospheric process. This means that from now on technology and, in particular, the way in which it affects the energetic play of entropy and negentropy in the biosphere, "constitutes the matrix of all thought of *oikos*, of habitat and of its law" (ibid. 28).

And it is from human *noetic* capacity and imagination that the future anthropocenic Earth will first of all be shaped. The noösphere as the organological repository of this noetic capacity should thus be intelligently transformed from a *de*structive into a *con*structive force. It should come to serve an economy that fosters and cultivates planetary wealth instead of exploiting and ruining it. The task ahead is, first of all, to imagine another kind of noösphere that is eco-aware, eco-sentient, and eco-responsive for a new planetary *oikos* of co-dependence of the biosphere and the technosphere. With Sloterdijk, we could argue that the negentropic turn of technology proposed by Stiegler should take the form of a *homeotechnological* turn, which would be a turn from the traditional, principally *allotechnological* or contra-natural and despotic, Earth-ignoring and Earth-ignorant technological paradigm inherited from metaphysical thought to a co-natural, non-despotic and Earth-caring techno-logical paradigm (Sloterdijk, *Not Saved* 133ff).

TOWARDS A SAPIENT EARTH

Such a homeotechnological turn should inaugurate the neganthropocenic age as one of synergetic cooperation, co-production, co-construction, thus resulting in a conjoining of the biosphere and the technosphere. Through it, the digital noösphere could evolve toward a *global sensorium* and *effective global organon* that is sensitive, connective and responsive to the biosphere. It could become a global network that enables and stimulates the development and cultivation of healthy, caring and Earth-oriented modes of attention and awareness, instead of alienating us from our implication in the biosphere. As such, it could become an instrument for (re-)inserting and (re-)weaving collective consciousness into the long-term life cycles and ecological rhythms of the Earth System. Humanity would thus technologically acquire a completely new mode of sensibility: ecosystemic sensibility. In this respect, a device like Google Glass, which aims to absorb its user ever more deeply into what could be called the planet's "buyosphere," could serve here as an absolute counterexample of the kind of digital media that we need, although it could also be trans-formed pharmacologically into a curative device for enhancing planetary orientation, attention and care. The same applies a fortiori to Google Earth. A genuinely co-constructive noösphere should be conceived and constructed from a holistic planetary perspective, in line with what environmental philo-sopher Edward Goldsmith has designated as "whole maintaining" or "homeotelic" criteria (Goldsmith 282ff).

We could think concretely here of a network of interconnected bio-eco-sensitive and bio-eco-mimetic devices integrating itself into the ecological webs of the Earth, thereby helping to understand, support and possibly also repair and regenerate biospheric processes. A global web of such devices could also connect information about social, cultural and economic processes to that of ecological and geophysical processes and be employed for assisting in their reciprocal attunement. Instead of destroying the existing organic noöspheres of the Earth System, for example, the Earth-spanning "mycelial Internet" that is indispensable not only for humanity's agriculture but for the health of the planet's

vegetation and wildlife as such (Stamets), it could start co-operating with them in mutually beneficent ways.

Although it might be illusory to think that the emergence of such an eco- and bio-cooperative techno-noösphere may eventually lead to a multiplication of the Earth's wealth, as Sloterdijk suggests ("How Big Is 'Big'?"), it will certainly help to create a more healthy and sustainable "metabolism between humanity and nature," to use the old-fashioned Marxist expression here. In any case it is a *conditio sine qua non* for the necessary birth of what the American astrobiologist David Grinspoon has called *Terra Sapiens* or "Wise Earth" (Grinspoon, xviii). Only a massive transformation of our ignorance – as well as our indifference – into an explicit cognizance of our newly acquired geological prominence and impact on the planet, and most importantly a massive change of our collective action based on this cognizance, can usher in what Stiegler calls the Neganthropocene, or what Grinspoon aptly terms the "mature Anthropocene" (ibid. xvii). To what more urgent and noble goal might any useful philosophy of media contribute?

WORKS CITED

Berardi, Franco. *Futurability: The Age of Impotence and the Horizon of Possibility*. Verso, 2017.
Bonneuil, Christophe and Fressoz, Jean-Baptiste. *The Shock of the Anthropocene: The Earth, History and Us*. Verso, 2016.
Chakrabarty, Dipesh. "The Climate of History: Four Theses." *Critical Inquiry*, vol. 35, no. 1,

2009, pp. 197-222.

Crutzen, Paul. "Geology of Mankind." *Nature*, vol. 415 no., 23, 3 January 2002, p. 23.

Davis, Heather. and Turpin, Etienne. *Art in the Anthropocene: Encounters Among Aesthetics, Politics, Environments and Epistemologies*. Open Humanities Press, 2015.

Georgescu-Roegen, Nicholas. "The Entropy Law and the Economic Process in Retrospect." *Eastern Economic Journal*, vol. 12, no. 1 (Jan. - Mar., 1986), pp. 3-25.

Goldsmith, Edward. The Way. *An Ecological Worldview*. Veltune Publishing, 2014.

Grinspoon, David. *Earth in Human Hands: Shaping Our Planet's Future*. Grand Central Publishing, 2016.

Hamilton, Clive. *Defiant Earth. The Fate of Humans in the Anthropocene*. Polity, 2017.

Langmuir, Charles H. and Broecker, Wally. *How to Build a Habitable Planet. The Story of Earth From the Big Bang to Humankind*. Princeton University Press, 2012.

Moore III, Berrien et al. "The Amsterdam Declaration on Global Change," July 2001: www.colorado.edu/AmStudies/lewis/ecology/gaiadeclar.pdf.

Schrödinger, Erwin. *What is Life?* Cambridge University Press, 2012.

Steffen, Will, Crutzen, Paul J. and

McNeill, John R. "The Anthropocene: Are Humans Now Overwhelming the Great Forces of Nature?." *AMBIO: A Journal of the Human Environment*, vol. 38, no. 8, 2011, pp. 614-21.

Sloterdijk, Peter. "How big is 'big'?'. Collegium International Lecture, February 2010: www.collegium-international.org/index.php/en/contributions/127-how-big-is-big.

---. *Not Saved. Essays after Heidegger*. Polity, 2017.

Stamets, Paul. *Mycelium Running: How Mushrooms Can Help Save the World: A Guide to Healing the Planet Through Gardening with Gourmet and Medicinal Mushrooms*. Ten Speeds Press, 2005.

Stiegler, Bernard. *For a New Critique of Political Economy*. Polity, 2010a.

---. *Taking Care of Youth and the Generations*. Stan-ford University Press, 2010b.

---. *What Makes Life Worth Living. On Pharmacology*. Polity, 2013.

---. *Symbolic Misery. Vol 2. The Katastrophe of the Sensible*. Polity, 2015.

---. *Automatic Society. Volume 1. The Future of Work*. Polity, 2016.

Stiegler, Bernard and Ars Industrialis. *The Re-Enchantment of the World: The Value of Spirit Against Industrial Populism*. Bloomsbury, 2014

A New Telluric Force:
Humans in the Age of the Anthropocene

MELINDA CAMPBELL[1]

PATRICIA KING DÁVALOS[2]

[1]NATIONAL UNIVERSITY
LA JOLLA, CALIFORNIA, USA

[2]AUTONOMOUS UNIVERSITY OF THE STATE MORELOS
CUERNAVACA, MÉXICO

ABSTRACT: *The Age of the Anthropocene must address the claim that human activity is one of the main factors in determining not just the course of biological life on planet Earth, but a force powerful enough to affect the Earth's climate as well as the conditions of its oceans and its atmosphere, and in fact, all known life forms. We cannot go backward in time, and it is likely too late to reverse the changes we have already put in motion. We must therefore consider our alternatives for moving forward into the future of this new age. Whatever else is true, we must confront a long-standing problem in this regard, which is to determine who will lead the way, or at least point toward a path forward, in first acknowledging the meaning and implications of this new epoch and then, of course, in figuring out how to deal with the problematic situations that will accompany living in the age of the Anthropocene.*

KEYWORDS: Anthropocene, naturalized phenomenology, intentionality, human subjectivity

The new being installed on the old planet, the new being that not only, like the ancient inhabitants of the globe, unites the inorganic and the organic world, but with a new and quite mysterious marriage unites physical nature to intellectual principle; this creature, absolutely new in itself, is, to the physical world, a new element, a new telluric force that for its strength and universality does not pale in the face of the greatest forces of the globe.

−Antonio Stoppani, 1873

The epoch of the Anthropocene is upon us, if we are to heed the warnings that have been coming at us for decades now, not just from the experts who study the climate and earth sciences generally, but also from historians, anthropologists, and philosophers. We must, finally, confront the undeniable evidence that our activity as a species has turned out to be, in the words of nineteenth-century geologist, Antonio Stoppani, "a new telluric force which in power and universality may be compared to the great forces of the Earth" (Crutzen and Stoermer 23). The claim at hand is that the rise of human civilization has turned out to be a dominant factor in determining not just the nature and character of biological life on planet Earth, but the state of nature itself, including all inorganic, as well as organic forms of being. The idea that the Earth itself is a unique, self-regulating and complex "meta-organic" form of life that encompasses and sustains the inter-relations of a multiplicity of biological life forms and their environmental support systems, known as the "Gaia Hypothesis," dates at least as far back as James Lovelock's well-known *Gaia: A New Look at Life on Earth*, written in 1979, a somewhat romantic and admittedly metaphorical image of planet Earth. Although Lovelock's reputation as a distinguished scientist and inventor was respected, the hard sciences looked askance at his teleological and mythical-sounding Gaia thesis. However, what sounded like a fanciful idea in the latter part of the twentieth century now seems, as we approach the third decade of the twenty-first century, like a foreshadowing of what is coming to be a new understanding of not just cultural or biological reality, but of physical reality itself, as determined by the empirical sciences, and in particular, earth systems science.

In this standard narrative, human activity is often analogized to the activity of the tectonic plates, the Earth's outer crust, or lithosphere, which is in constant motion, riding upon the thick, mostly solid mantle that forms the bulk of the Earth's total volume.[1] Like the movement of tectonic plates, human activity, on such accounts, turns out to be one of the decisive causes of the changes affecting the planet. And as in the case of plate tectonics, in which the movement of land masses forming the Earth's outer shell affects the nature and particular positioning of the Earth's geologic structures, so too does human activity massively affect the human situation. But this way of looking at things leaves little room for willful or creative decision making. If there is in reality a chance to choose what happens to humanity and to the Earth, then we must move past the usual narratives of the age of the Anthropocene. What is glaringly absent from the standard story is a phenomenologically enriched concept of human activity: What is our experience of that activity? How and why do we act as we do? This enriched concept is not far from the scope of science; people in the field of science, although they may not characterize their research as phenomenological, are in fact bringing elements of phenomenology as well as psychology into their conception of what they are studying, not just in the social sciences, but also in neuroscience.

Some philosophers surveying the prospect of the Anthropocene are inclined to think that we are now engaged in yet another "Copernican revolution," implying a post-Kantian view that moves away from Kant's conception of the transcendental subject as pure intellectual awareness, the conscious activity that allows for the synthesis of intuitions that result in representations of the world and of the self itself, to a kind of transcendental self that is objective in its very subjectivity (Hranice). That is to say, rather than claiming that the objects of experience, in order to be known as such, must conform to the a priori transcendental structures of the conscious mind, yet not reverting

---

[1] "Mantle." 2018 *National Geographic Society*, www.nationalgeographic.org/encyclopedia/mantle/.

back to the Cartesian or empiricist-representationist position that knowledge of the world must conform to its pre-existing objects, the idea here is that the transcendental self of the Anthropocene should be conceived as, at the same time, essentially a physical object and a conscious subject, with no ontological distance between them. So knowledge of reality is possible through the investigation of intentionality as much as through scientific observation of the empirical world. For representationist - empiricists, subjectivity remains a murky realm of at best partial truths, and the kind of knowledge available through purely subjective perspectives tells us nothing certain about the world independent of such subjects. And for the Kantian transcendentalist, there remains more than a whiff of an unappealing kind of idealism in taking subjectivity as the starting point of any possible knowledge of the world. The kind of move we wish to make in relation to human knowledge and existence in the age of the Anthropocene is that we must abandon, once and for all, the ontological distinction between subjects and objects, between minds and things, and between phenomenal experience and physical events.

The problem at issue here, roughly speaking, is that the notion of the Anthropocene, which tends to suppress the distinction between nature and culture, also suppresses the epistemological and ontological differences that separate human history from the history of life on planet Earth (Bonneuil and Fressoz). From this point of view, it is not the case that with the advent of *Homo sapiens*, nature, even in its most pristine and savage sense, exists separately from human thought and activity; thus, the Anthropocene cannot be understood as being outside the realm of subjectivity and independent of intentionality. At the same time, "the human of the Anthropocene, defined as a geological force, must therefore be both as neutral and indifferent as the geological reality itself" (Malabou para. 4). The Anthropocene epoch, understood in this way, presents us with an isomorphism, a structural identity between humans and their environment, and at the same time, raises the prospect of a current subjectivity, surprised, astounded, bewildered and even paralyzed in the face of the geological force, or the unintentional mass activity, as a *species* active within the world (Chakrabarty).

What is important to consider here is that human activity is one of the main factors in determining not just the course of biological life on planet Earth, but a force powerful enough to affect the Earth's climate as well as the conditions of its oceans and waterways, its atmosphere, and indeed many parts of its surface, such as coastal regions or island nations that are in danger of total inundation. We cannot go backward in time, and it is likely too late to reverse the changes we have already put in motion. We must therefore consider our alternatives for moving forward into the future of this new age. Whatever else is true, we must confront a long-standing problem in this regard, which is to determine who will lead the way, or at least point toward a path forward, in first acknowledging the meaning and implications of this new epoch and then, of course, in figuring out how to deal with the problematic situations that will define living in the age of the Anthropocene.

In what follows, we will explore the philosophical dimensions of the Anthropocene epoch: What is the best way of conceiving of and conducting human activity in this evolving situation? In effect, a growing convergence of concerned individuals across a variety of domains and disciplines agree on the importance of the concept and the terminology of the "Anthropocene" as a useful way to begin a conversation about the alarming situation currently hanging over our heads, threatening not just a change in climatological conditions or a need for environmental awareness and enhanced sustainability practices, but the end of human civilization or even the demise of all living species from the planet. In particular, we want to think about how we can come to a more complete understanding of this powerful, and often destructive, telluric[2] force that we are identifying with the human race as it now exists. Such an understanding is the province of not only anthropologists, sociologists, and psychologists, but also of philosophers, cognitive scientists, and neurobiologists, among others. In thinking through the

problem, we propose adopting a relatively new kind approach that conjoins phenomenology with the natural sciences, which is to say, a naturalized phenomenology. This merged methodology is perfectly suited for analysis of the sort of conception of human objective-subjectivity in the age of the Anthropocene sketched above.

The human species represents a massive and harmful force, starting at a specific moment in history and continuing to the present day. Though this has been unintentional and unconscious (in the sense of a neutral force), this is not to say that there are not *specific characteristics* of this force, which distinguish humans from other natural forces. For example, since Aristotle, we think of the human being as a rational animal; however, that does not change the fact that we are but a kind of animal among other animals, nor that the corporeal composition of human beings cannot be studied or analyzed as a collection of inorganic elements that are likewise part of the human body. The life of a human being, in general form, can be imagined as following the kind of logic seen in concentric circles (or nested intervals): the human being conserves organic, inorganic and biological matter in its body; for example, it is made up of mineral salts, a high percentage of water and other inorganic components, and has basic needs that are similar to the rest of the animal kingdom, such as the need to procreate and ingest nutrients and water. So, to say that the human being is a rational animal does not imply that man is no longer an animal. The human being preserves both the characteristics of its

---

[2] Telluric current, also called Earth Current, is a natural electric current flowing on and beneath the Earth's surface, generally following a direction parallel to the Earth's surface and arising from charges moving to attain equilibrium between regions of differing electric potentials. Geophysicists use telluric currents to map subsurface structures, such as sedimentary basins, layered rocks, and faults. ("Telluric Force." *Geophysics*, 2018. *Encyclopedia Britannica*. https://www.britannica.com/science/telluric-current).

inorganic self, together with its animal characteristics; however, and this is the point, additionally, it *possesses specific characteristics* that no other animal or amalgam of inorganic matter has. Similarly, the fact that human beings have now become a massive force, bewildered and passive in itself, or even just another unconscious geological force, does not imply that it does not also have certain specific characteristics of a geologic force. In reality, it has the potential, or capacity, to experience itself as a force within itself, and in a conscious way.

In the research program of "Embodied Enactive Cognition," pioneered by Francisco Varela (biologist, neuroscientist, cognitologist and philosopher), we find the specific research methodology known as neurophenomenology, a method invented by Varela himself.[3] Embodied Enactive Cognition is based on the idea that the human cognitive system consists of the bilateral interaction of the agent's whole body with the environment, of which it is itself a part,[4] whereas neurophenomenology is conceived as a mutual interrelationship that generates, in the same time and place, empirical data on both the phenomenological, experiential level and on the neurobiological and practical level (Kordes). It is, therefore, a method that allows us, in a controlled way, to approach cognitive phenomena from the perspectives of both fundamental experiential ontology and empirical

description, without worrying about reducing the first-person point of view to the third, or somehow precisely mapping specific elements of third-person descriptions onto subjective phenomena.

How can we naturalize phenomenology? Initially, both Francisco Varela and Evan Thompson related it to Buddhist philosophy, applying it within the framework of the cognitive sciences towards the end of the twentieth century. The main contribution of this approach in relation to the philosophy of mind (and action), as well as the cognitive sciences and, particularly, for the cognitive neurosciences, was to discover a method based, on the one hand, on the *informed* point of view of the first person, consisting of arduous training in the practice of meditation, which they described as the mindfulness/awareness method (Varela et. al.). This led them to provide an answer to the traditional distinction of appearance and reality, the seemingly irreconcilable ontological divide between the "pure" subjectivity of experience and the "pure" objectivity of science. In *The Embodied Mind: Cognitive Science and Human Experience,* Varela et al. state:

> The quandary: either accept what science seems to be telling us and deny our experience – thereby forgetting that lived experience is the source of science, and that science can never ultimately step outside it – or hold fast to our experience and deny science – thereby forgetting that experience itself constantly seeks to enlarge its own horizons through scientific investigation. Our present

---

[3] Cf. Varela, 1996.
[4] For a general overview of the Embodied Enactive Cognition movement, see: Thompson, *et. al.,* 2005.

culture is still caught up in the constant oscillation between these two tendencies. (xix)

The authors later add that they "feel as if there is a real self that is the subject of our consciousness and that it is in direct contact with an independent, real world" (ibid.).

Twenty-seven years have passed since 1991, the year in which *The Embodied Mind* was published in English, and since then, neuro-phenomenology has been developed theoretically and applied experimentally in the cognitive sciences in several variants by its followers and sympathizers.[5] Neurophenomenology, developed by Varela, is based in part on Dynamical Systems Theory, together with the cognitive neurosciences, thus shielding phenomenology from charges of methodological individualism or radical subjectivity, insofar as it considers the bilateral action of the cognizing subject as a practical entity within the natural and social environment to which it belongs. In effect, as Tom Froese and Thomas Fuchs state: "Varela (in Neuro-phenomenology) has pioneered the use of the Dynamical Systems Theory in combination with phenomenology and cognitive science with his neuro-phenomenological research program." (211). Coining the term "extended body," and making use of the mathematics of dynamical systems, Froese and Fuchs elaborate their own model by way of Varela's neuro-phenomenological hypothesis, which maintains that "through our mutual interactions with others, our living

and lived bodies become inextricably intertwined in a dynamical whole, thus forming an 'extended body' by which we enact and encounter the world together" (Froese and Fuchs). This model is an example of the fact "that we can make the notion of embodied inter-subjectivity intelligible in a non-reductive scientific manner" (Froese and Fuchs 211).

Froese and Fuchs present a cogent example of this model for clarifying "the phenomenology of embodied intersubjectivity," through which, while being pre-reflexive and thus opaque to observation, it is possible to capture the mood of the lived-body of the other by paying attention to "our moods and feelings, as well as our lasting dispositions" (212). If we accept this, then we have to accept that, at least sometimes, it is possible to feel the intention of our fellow humans as threatening, or not, by way of their gestures at the moment of being in their presence.[6]

As a thought experiment, let us suppose that it is possible to scientifically test this hypothesis and successfully repeat the results. Let us suppose that we are able to connect and communicate with a sufficiently large number of experimental subjects, confronting them, for example, by way of videos or other representational media, with a variety of impending or in-progress environmental disasters that have become part of the framework of the

_____

[5] For a general overview, see, for example, Stewart, *et. al,* 2010.

[6] We must not forget that human beings are capable of deceiving others through their bodily expressions. This idea is grounded in the action-oriented version of the "Predictive Brain," developed by Andy Clark in his *Surfing Uncertainty: Prediction, Action, and the Embodied Mind,* 2016.

real world in the age of the Anthropocene. The subjects are made aware that their practices or things done in the support of their ordinary daily activities are causing these disastrous situations. For example, subjects are shown how the disposal of immense amounts of plastic trash end up in the stomachs of many marine or terrestrial animals causing their deaths; or they are made to watch the killing of endangered animals, such as the case of elephants killed for their ivory tusks, and made to understand the circumstances surrounding such mass killings and that the extinction of the species is at hand. Or subjects might be made aware, in some meaningful way, of the quantity of greenhouse gases produced by automobiles, trucks and widespread industrial production that contaminate the atmosphere the world over; there are too many examples and possibilities to review here, but let us suppose that this experiential witnessing has enabled the experimental subjects to feel, in themselves and in others, intersubjectively, the threat of death, caused in great measure by their own extremely harmful (though not intended in most cases to be harmful) practices. The result is that the repetition of such experiments would open up the possibility of obtaining reliable evidence as to whether or not the people undergoing the experiment have a transformative experience in the sense of seeing their own behavior and intentional practices as having detrimental effects on a global scale.

Actually, this type of "experiment" is already taking place, albeit in an uncontrolled way, through myriad Internet sites and online communications in social networks that currently engage billions of people with access to this tool.[7] In principle, therefore, there seems to be no reason why this type of "experiential" experiment could not be carried out in a controlled manner. We already have the theory, the technology, and surely the willingness of a large number of people who would undergo such experiments with the aim of discovering whether it would be possible to convert, or reverse, the harmful direction of the telluric force that we have become. This would be possible to the extent that, while we were experimenting with regard to the negative impacts of our collective force, we could also experiment with the power of our collective global conscience as a potential force capable of transcending our current, catastrophic situation.

Following from the notion of a "geologized" human subjectivity, it might be thought that any future understanding of human nature must either be beyond the scope of either phenomenology or, because we are dealing with human needs, desires, and intentionality in general as a significant underlying cause of the problems of the Anthropocene, beyond the purview of any of the purely objective physical sciences. We believe that the advent of the Anthropocene will in fact be instrumental in bringing to the fore

---

[7] As of June, 2017, 51 percent of the world's population has Internet access. In 2015, the International Telecommunication Union estimate about 3.2 billion people, or almost half of the the world's population, would be online by the end of the year ("Global Internet Usage." 2018, *Wikipedia*.)

the need for the naturalization of phenomenology as both a method of philosophical inquiry and as a mode of scientific investigation. Traditional Husserlian phenomenologists will claim that once we view human intentionality as an objective force of nature, which, as such, is outside the realm of subjectivity that is the concern of phenomenological inquiry, we must appeal instead to the natural sciences to understand the nature and extent of this human juggernaut of short-term resource management and capitalist consumption that created the conditions that led to the situation of the Anthropocene. But we can salvage the valuable insights into the nature of human thought and behavior that phenomenology makes available by naturalizing phenomenology; that is, by making every subjective or qualitative element of conscious experience that plays an explanatory role in a phenomenological analysis continuous with properties accepted and understood by natural science (Petitot et al.). And the form of scientific research most relevant in this situation is an extension and application of neurophenomenology, the methodology originally proposed and incorporated into scientific practice by Varela and others. Any definition or account of the Anthropocene epoch will be based on a central reference to human activity.

Let's take a look at two recent accounts from geographers of the new epoch of the Anthropocene.

Human activity has been a geologically recent, yet profound influence on the global environment. The magnitude, variety and longevity of human-induced changes, including land surface transformation and the changing of the composition of the atmosphere, has led to the suggestion that we should refer to the present, not as being in the Holocene Epoch, but rather as being in the Anthropocene Epoch. (Lewis and Maslin 171)

The second comes from Noel Castree:

"The Anthropocene"... describes an Earth's surface so transformed by human activities that the biophysical conditions of the Holocene epoch (roughly the last 11,000 years) have been compromised. In Mark Levene's apt assessment (2013), "The term ... has yet to become standard currency, though there has been sufficient acclamation from a wide range of scientific and non-scientific disciplines to suggest its durability." (233)

Although neither of these descriptions employs the "tectonic plate" analogy, both accounts are consistent with that narrative. When we read about "the magnitude, variety and longevity [or durability]" of "human-induced changes" in biophysical conditions (in the land, seas and atmosphere), should we not then question the correlative magnitude, variety and durability of the biophysical-condition-induced changes in human activity? Both "poles" in this cause-and-effect cycle are constantly interdependent. It is also of great importance to note that our activity as a species – the causal power of this activity, not simply in terms of its effects, but as a geologic force – has reached noteworthy scales of space, time and complexity. Scholars and scientists have traced the history of the struggles and triumphs of the evolution of human civilization, and reflection on the history of human experience adds intelligibility to the intimate interrelation between two kinds of change: human-induced and conditions-induced. This has been a central task in the disciplines of history, political science, social theory, cultural studies, political economy, technology studies, and for the areas of philosophy related to each one of these disciplines, including, we argue, the new field of naturalized phenomenology.

We have, then, a vast and growing body of material regarding the path taken by human activity, *as activity*, up until the present. This path has abounded with, not just different possible outcomes, uncertainties and risks, but also with many possible levels of cooperation and conflict. And among such possibilities is the important goal of the increasing social organization requisite to both cooperation and conflict. To make intelligible "human-induced changes" in biophysical conditions demands that we make *intelligible* the biophysical-induced changes of human activity. And, this intelligibility demands that we at least note the changes in the modes of social organization with regard to cooperation and conflict and make them intelligible as well.

On the basis of "human activity," abstracted from its modes of organization, standard historical accounts traditionally attribute and highlight the growth of the global population (civilization's "great achievement," which, unchecked, may be its great downfall); but this growth in magnitude falls far short of the real change produced in the magnitude of human activity since the early Holocene. Moreover, historical accounts too often remain silent about the real changes produced in the variety and durability of human activity thereafter, and about the changes produced in the social organization of cooperation and conflict. So, although geologic evolution contains human history, the standard narratives fail to recognize the full impact and importance of the history of human activity. Rather, these accounts see only its residual footprints. Hence, those narratives cannot illuminate the future or, perhaps worse, can only extrapolate the future from the past. But we do not want to repeat our past mistakes.

There is nothing in the above descriptions of the Anthropocene that forces us to accept that this new epoch necessarily signifies a generalized threat, or even more portentous, a threat of death, of total annihilation. Nevertheless, there are many sounding the alarm that human civilization is on the precipice of impending disasters of horrific, even unthinkable, proportions. So we wish to address the controversies surrounding the possibility of anthropogenic disasters, but, as just noted, we also want to make such discussions or debates intelligible. Hence the question: What is the point of declaring the current epoch to be the age of the Anthropocene? Is it the set of more abstract considerations regarding "human activity," or is it the current situation of social organization leading to cooperation and conflict (which, in truth, have been in the making for some time)? What is the true source of the problem of the Anthropocene? One issue at stake is the way to solve the problem of climate change or even to understand how resolving it would be possible. From this perspective, the denial of climate change is propelled, not so much by an epistemic force, but by a resistance to pay the expected cost of social reorganization that remains undefined, or at least inadequately defined. And, of course, global climate change is only one of the questions posed by the concept of the Anthropocene. With the explicit integration of the factors of social organization that lead to either cooperation or conflict, we can note and evaluate, as we advance in making it intelligible, what is at stake in the current situation regarding social re-organization in the direction of cooperation and conflict resolution.

If the concept of the Anthropocene fails to provide a more precise reference to what human activity is; if the social organization is out of focus (or not properly aimed), then it is easy to ignore the differences between nature and culture, and those between human history and biological history (Bonneuil and Fressoz), believing that in this way we can reach a more profound history of human activity. From this reductive view, human activity is mere plate tectonics, a geologic force, as Malabou notes, which is utterly neutral and fully objectivized. But clearly, we cannot surrender to the devastation resulting from the force of our own existence, and that starts to look like suicide. We reject the idea that the only way to address the large-scale questions regarding human activity in a scientific way is by reducing it to some variant of the movement of tectonic plates.

In the first place, this is not a scientific idea, and in no way should it be considered as such. Very often, one of the sciences creates abstractions and simplifications, holding out a promissory note to eventually fill in the blanks and provide a complete account. As much as the physical sciences try to look the other way, the subjective is real, unavoidably real, when human activity is in play. Moreover, if the cost of naturalizing phenomenology is to assume that idea, the result will be something that goes beyond the current scope, strictly speaking, of both natural science and phenomenology. Only if we understand naturalized phenomenology as the commitment to develop phenomenological research supported by (and contributing to) relevant scientific research, could the "naturalizing" make sense, both for philosophical and for scientific practices and developments. And currently, within the cognitive sciences, this is particularly relevant.

Let us consider the cognitive sciences and, specifically, the case of neurocognitive science. Researchers in this field measure various dispositions and the "inputs and outputs" of myriad physico-chemical units, acting and interacting unceasingly in different scales of space and time. They also know that what they are observing and measuring somehow translates into bodily action and environment-organism interactions. There is no consensus among cognitive scientists, but the need for a deeper understanding of human and animal perception and action is much more widely recognized today than even two decades ago. This is the place for naturalized phenomenology to step in as a useful resource and methodology to better understand how subjectivity and its intentional activities are also part of the physical-chemical mix. And the fruits of the studies based on this approach – what we now know as enactive or action-oriented views of perception, cognition, and behavior – are starting to be recognized as leading to new answers to old problems (Clark). Nature, of course, shapes culture; but the converse is also true.

Finally, we acknowledge that a large part of human activity is unintentional – whatever we do on the basis of pure instinct as well as all of those actions and movements of our bodies that go on without our having to do anything but breathe, move, and take in nutrients. However, it is sufficient to recognize that a significant proportion of human activity is intentional, or has an intentional component, in order to make the claim that even the unintentional part of human activity is *not* like plate tectonics. Moreover, the unquestionable fact of human intentionality is enough to establish that the dynamics of the species – the struggle of human survival – is very different from lithospheric dynamics. For the same reason, we can assert that human history has a dynamic very different from the dynamics of the evolution of the species per se.

Finally, we conclude with some practical recommendations related to our recognition and acknowledgement of the claim that we now live in the age of the Anthropocene:

– Beyond geological and paleonto-logical plausibility about the Earth's chronology, a number of acute questions of global significance now confront us, each of which demands both decisions and actions regarding the future of those alive today, and all future generations.

– Climate change may turn out to be only one of the necessary issues to be addressed, so we must be careful not to risk skewing the assessment of our real situation towards only one problem, along with the decisions and actions taken to transform it. Nevertheless, the question of climate change is paradigmatic of the larger and more urgent challenges we face.

– It may be sufficient to consider human activity, on a global scale, as being similar to plate tectonics, so as to win the battle for the epistemic recognition of the Anthropocene epoch and to settle the debate between those who accept the reality of global climate change and climate-change deniers. However, far more than just an acknowledgement or consideration of the geologic impact of human activity is required for any satisfactory response to the challenges presented by the transition into the Anthropocene epoch.

– In order to make sense of all that the Anthropocene and the associated events related to climate change portend, we need to develop human activity, in theory and in practice, by highlighting social organization with an eye on both situations of cooperation and conflict (organization is not merely an administrative question: it involves strategic and technical resources, both material and cognitive).

– Without phenomenology in the full sense of its tradition and with all the richness of its controversies, and without the rigorous and critical support of the natural sciences, and of the disciplines of history, political economy and political science, there is no possibility of improving our concept of human activity.

– We may be overvaluing the plausibility of the Anthropocene and the threat of climate change. Even so, we consider that, in any case, the wisest thing to do is to affirm that what is at stake is the social organization of human activity, along with an enhanced and enlightened understanding of intentionality as a source as well as a goal of behavior.

WORKS CITED

Bonneuil, Christophe and Jean-Baptiste Fressoz. *The Shock of the Anthropocene: The Earth, History, and Us.* Trans. David Fernbach. New York: Verso, 2016.

Castree, Noel, "The Anthropocene and the Environmental Humanities: Extending the Conversation," *Environmental Humanities*, vol. 5: 2014. pp. 233-260.

Chakrabarty, Dipesh, "The Climate of History: Four Theses," *Critical Inquiry* 35: 2009, pp. 197-222.

Clark, Andy, *Surfing Uncertainty. Prediction, Action and the Embodied Mind*, N.Y., Oxford University Press, 2016.

Crutzen, Paul. "Geology of Mankind." *Nature*, vol. 415 no. 23, 3 January 2002, p. 23.

Crutzen, Paul J. and Eugene F. Stoermer. "The 'Anthropocene.'" *The International Geosphere–Biosphere Programme (IGBP): Global Change Newsletter,* No. 41, May, 2000, pp. 17-18.

Froese, Tom and Thomas Fuchs, "The Extended Body: A Case Study in the Neuropheno-menology of Social Interaction," *Phenomenology and the Cognitive Sciences*, vol. 11, 2012, pp. 205-235. Springer Netherlands: doi-org.nuls.idm.oclc.org/10.1007/s11097-012-9254-2.

Hranice, Pohl'ad Za. "Transcendental Subject vs. Empirical Self: On Kant's Account of Subjectivity. *Filozofia* 65, 3, 2010, pp. 269-283.

Kordes, Urban. "Problems and Opportunities of First-Person Research," Interdisciplinary Description of Complex Systems, vol.11, no. 14, 2013, pp. 363-375.

Lewis, Simon and Mark Maslin, "Defining the Anthropocene," Nature, vol. 519, 2015, pp. 171-180.

Levene, Mark. "Climate Blues: Or How Awareness of the Human End Might Re-Instill Ethical Purpose to the Writing of History," *Environmental Humanities*, 2 2013, pp. 147-167.

Lovelock, James. *Gaia: A New Look at Life on Earth.* New York: Oxford University Press, 1979/2000.

Malabou, Catherine. "The Brain of History or the Mentality of the Anthropocene. *SAQ: South Atlantic Quarterly*, vol. 116, no.1, 2016. ISSN (print) 0038-2876 (In Press).

Petitot, Jean, Francisco J. Varela, Bernard Pachoud, Bernard and Jean-Michel Roy, editors *Naturalizing Phenomenology: Issues in Contemporary Phenomenology and Cognitive Science.* Stanford: Stanford University Press, 1999.

Smail, Daniel. "In the Grip of Sacred History." *American Historical Review* 110, no. 5: 2005, pp. 1336-136, nrs.harvard.edu/urn-3:HUL.InstRepos:3207678.

Stewart, John, Oliver Gapenne, and

Ezequiel Di Paolo, editors *Enaction: Towards a New Paradigm for Cognitive Science*. Cambridge: The MIT Press, 2010.

Thompson, Evan, Antoine Lutz, and Diego Cosmelli, "Neurophenomenology: An Introduction for Neurophilosophers" in Brook, A. and K. Akins editors. *Cognition and the Brain: The Philosophy and Neuroscience Movement*, N.Y., Cambridge University Press, 2005.

Varela, Francisco J., Evan Thompson and Eleanor Rosh. *The Embodied Mind: Cognitive Science and Human Experience*, Cambridge, MIT Press, 2016(revised edition).

Varela, Francisco. "Neurophenomenology: A Methodological Remedy for the Hard Problem," *Journal of Consciousness Studies* 3(4): 1996, pp. 330-349.

Hello Anthropocene, Goodbye Humanity: Reframing Transhumanism through Postphenomenology

Richard S. Lewis

Vrije Universiteit Brussel
Brussels, Belgium

ABSTRACT: *It seems paradoxical that the name of the new geologic age might be the Anthropocene, while converging NBIC technologies are advancing to the point where some transhumanists are predicting that humanity will potentially be evolving into a new post-human species in the next 50-100 years. New technologies, such as 3D printing of body parts and genetic engineering, bring about both exciting and potentially disturbing future scenarios. Transhumanists and bioconservatives bring opposing views to this human enhancement debate. However, they both start from a dualistic point of view, keeping the subject and object separate. The philosophical field of postphenomenology is an effective approach for pragmatically and empirically grounding the human-enhancement debate, providing tools such as embodied technological relations, the non-neutrality of technology, enabling and constraining aspects of all technologies, and the false dream of a perfectly transparent technology.*

KEYWORDS: human enhancement debate, postphenomenology, trans-humanism, liberal eugenics, posthumanism, philosophy of technology, Anthropocene

There is a certain amount of irony in referring to the current geologic age as the Anthropocene. The rhetoric from transhumanists suggests that we are nearing a point with converging technologies where we will be able to greatly transform our species. Though humans have used technology to enhance and modify themselves throughout much of our history (i.e., tattoos, piercings, false teeth, eyeglasses, prosthetic limbs, etc.), recent advances in Nano, Biological, and Informational technologies, as well as the Cognitive sciences, collectively referred to as NBIC, create the ability to eradicate many diseases, dramatically increase the human lifespan, and allow us to choose the genetic make-up of our children, culminating in the possibility of transcending, or evolving, beyond what it means to be human.

For the *transhumanists* (Bostrom; Kurzweil; Moravec; More), the notion of becoming something other-than-human is considered to be a positive development that should be embraced. Transhumanists propose that our survival as humans depends upon advancing ourselves as best we can, and there is no reason we should remain subject to limited and faulty bodies if alternatives exist. Counter to this argument, the *bioconservatives* (Fukuyama; Habermas; Sandel) feel that transhumanism threatens the very essence of what it means to be human, even going so far as to call it the most dangerous idea in the world (Fukuyama, "Transhumanism"). Bioconservatives strongly advocate for regulations against unrestricted use of NBIC technologies. Both sides are acting in the best interest of their notion of humanity.

This paper will explore the concept of human enhancement through the lens of post-phenomenology to analyze how new technologies mediate our lifeworld experience. Personally, I vacillate between excitement and concern over the benefits and drawbacks for the profound capacities promised by these technologies. Typically, technology happens in incremental steps, a gradual progression, albeit with an occasionally disruptive invention such as the printing press coming along. However, NBIC advancements now appear to be following more of a Kurzweilian exponential growth model, making it more difficult to dismiss some of the transhumanist claims (Kurzweil). Take for instance the recent 3D printed human ear experiment, where the printed ear was attached to a mouse and began to develop (Kang et al.). Will we soon get to the point where we can print a repaired version of our heart and then have it implanted into us? Or, will we be able to take a "pill" with nanobots that are programmed to clean the plaque from our veins, transfer minute amounts of chemo directly to cancerous cells, or even potentially repair internal damage? What

happens if/when we reach the ultimate transhumanist goal of being able to upload our minds and memories to a computer? Could we then transfer them to a 3D printed version of our younger selves, thereby creating the opportunity for a fresh, biological reset, a kind of technological sip from the metaphorical fountain of youth?

These new human-enhancement technologies challenge us to try and make sense of what it means to be human. Postphenomenology, a philosophy based in pragmatism, is well suited to take a grounded look at human-enhancement issues. Integrating postphenomenology *into* the human enhancement debate can address shortcomings from both transhumanists and bioconservatives and will improve our ability to understand key issues. Before explaining the specific ways that postphenomenology can help ground the human-enhancement debate, I will provide some background context concerning the main actors (in the Latourian sense) involved.

TRANSHUMANISM

Though there have been a few historical mentions of the term transhumanism,[1] the official, collective movement began in the 1980s with Max More's Transhuman Doctrine. Then, in 1998, Nick Bostrom and David Pearce founded the World Transhumanist Association, which is now known as Humanity+. Bostrom formally defines transhumanism as the following:

---

[1] See Bostrom "Transhumanist FAQ's."

1) The intellectual and cultural movement that affirms the possibility and desirability of fundamentally improving the human condition through applied reason, especially by developing and making widely available technologies to eliminate aging and to greatly enhance human intellectual, physical, and psychological capacities. 2) The study of the ramifications, promises, and potential dangers of technologies that will enable us to overcome fundamental human limitations, and the related study of the ethical matters involved in developing and using such technologies. ("Transhumanist FAQ's" 4)

According to transhumanists, we are in a transitory phase between embodying what has been considered to be human and becoming a superintelligent post-human, where technology is used to enhance our minds and bodies. More ("Philosophy") stated that though transhumanist roots can be traced back to humanism and the Enlightenment, most transhumanists fall into the philosophic tradition of critical rationalism, which maintains that they "can give up justification [i.e, to a higher entity such as God] while retaining a respect for objectivity, argumentation, and the systematic use of reason" (6). Transhumanists believe in the right (and ability) for self-improvement. Additionally, transhumanists have a modern, instrumental approach to technology, seeing it as neutral (see the section, Non-Neutrality of Technology, below).

BIOCONSERVATIVES

Bioconservatives are critical of transhumanism. They feel that that there is a human essence that transhumanism threatens. They advocate for international oversight to limit the transhumanist ability to use technology for enhancement purposes that would essentially and irrevocably change human nature. There are various types of bioconservatives, from culturally conservative thinkers such as Fukuyama and Habermas to left-leaning environmentalists like McKibben.

POSTPHENOMENOLOGY

Postphenomenology was developed by Don Ihde around 1990 and has been successfully used to investigate and better understand how technology mediates human relations with the world. Postphenomenology proposes a balanced way of viewing technology that is non-instrumental and non-deterministic. Postpheno-menology grew out of a combination of phenomenology and pragmatism. This philosophical approach is rooted in empiricism and breaks from traditional phenomenology by being non-essentialist. Instead, it proposes that technologies are *multistable*, that they are not just one thing, and that there are multiple (though not infinite) ways in which they can be used. Further, any new technology can be understood to have both enabling and constraining aspects (see below). And finally, post-phenomenology is *relational* and *amodern*, holding that there is not a fixed self or object; rather, each is constituted in relation to the other

(Ihde, *Lifeworld*; Rosenberger and Verbeek).

POSTHUMANISM

Posthumanism is a term used in several different ways. While transhumanism has a generally agreed upon, specific definition, posthumanism remains a fluid concept. It is beyond the scope of this article to explore posthumanism in extensive detail; however, the term will be briefly touched upon, as it often comes up in discussions[2] around transhumanism. Transhumanists use the term very specifically, referring to humanity's next evolutionary step after the *technological singularity* (Kurzweil), when humans either evolve by merging with technology and become superintelligent or when an artificial intelligence becomes superintelligent and "normal" humanity is eclipsed as the dominant entity on the planet.

The term is also used to more broadly encompass the collective aspects known as critical, cultural, and philosophical posthumanism. Specifically, it is often used as a critical term based on anti-anthropocentrism (removing the human, and specifically the white male, as the center of any methodological approach) and to promote the notion that the co-evolution of humans and technology can help deconstruct normative views of what "being human" means (Braidotti; Hayles). It emphasizes the need to blur the boundaries between dualities such as human/nature, human/animal, and human/technology.

POSTPHENOMENOLOGICAL REFRAMING OF TRANSHUMANISM

Currently, the human-enhancement debate is framed primarily as transhumanists versus bioconservatives around the NBIC technological convergence idea. Postphenomenology can reframe the human-enhancement debate, identifying the fundamental flaws in the transhumanist approach and demonstrating that a more realistic and empirically grounded understanding of human enhancement is possible. Sharon (2014) pointed out that both the transhumanists and bioconservatives share the idea of the human "as an autonomous, unique and fixed entity, that is separate from its environment in a distinct way," believing that there remains a clear subject/object duality.

Postphenomenology can move the discussion away from what feels like utopian[3] versus dystopian views to pave the way toward a new transhuman framework. The ideas of *technologically embodied relations, non-neutrality of technology, enabling/constraining, and transparency* are the tools most beneficial to creating a new discursive framework for transhumanism.

---

[2] There are many excellent works describing in-depth the variety of ways trans-humanism and posthumanism are used (see Braidotti; Clark; Coeckelbergh; Hansell; Hayles; Roden; Sharon).

[3] Transhumanists such as Max More argue that they are not interested in a final utopia; instead, More created the principles of *extropy*, a state of perpetual improvement rather than a final, perfect end (More, 2003). However, broadly generalizing, transhumanists tend to focus on an instrumental, or neutral, role of technology and typically feel that any downsides can be generally fixed with more technology.

Interestingly, the relation between postphenomenology and trans-humanism has been somewhat ambiguous. On the one hand, Don Ihde has written a couple of papers (*I Don't Want to be a Cyborg*; *Of Which Human are We Post?*), which clearly indicate his disagreement with the transhumanist movement. Meanwhile, Peter-Paul Verbeek has offered a new postphenomenological understanding of some trans-humanist ideas with his publication, *Cyborg Intentionality*. Sharon (2014) also demonstrated how post-phenomenology can help frame the debate with her adaptation of some of Ihde's work in support of her mediated posthumanist theory.

TECHNOLOGICALLY EMBODIED RELATIONS

The concept of subject/object duality can feel compellingly salient, especially as new technologies are thrust upon us and we are constantly obliged to decide which technologies to adopt (Van Den Eede, "Where is the Human?"). It is easy to see these technologies as utilitarian objects, useful as entertainment or for something practical. Their usefulness is often that which is foregrounded in marketing, but they have other effects that remain hidden and are mostly discussed only in academic arenas. Current philosophers of technology, as well as social theorists (Braidotti; Ferrando; Haraway; Hayles; Ihde, *Lifeworld*; Latour; Sharon; Verbeek, *What things Do*; Van Den Eede, "Extending") have shown that there is a dynamic interwovenness between both subject and object, which refutes the modern idea of their separation (Sharon 3). Postphenomenologists state that technologies mediate and co-constitute both the subject and the world.

Ihde describes four types of human-technology relations.[4] His *embodiment relation* is the most pertinent to the human-enhancement debate. Ihde describes embodied technologies as having varying degrees of transparency while acting as extensions of our bodies. For instance, wearing a pair of glasses typically is a mostly transparent experience. We see *through* the technology rather than being focused *on* the technology. This relation changes how we experience the world. The glasses change and clarify the world we see, becoming an extension of ourselves. Often, a person might forget that he or she is even wearing glasses, as the technology recedes into the background of awareness. The glasses become less transparent if they are dirty, don't fit correctly, or are broken. Embodied human-enhancement technologies such as artificial joints and certain prosthetics can also become close to being transparently embodied once the person becomes accustomed to the technology. However, Ihde points out that they are never as good as the original body part that they replace, often needing to be replaced more frequently than the original.

NON-NEUTRALITY OF TECHNOLOGY

Ihde makes it clear that even embodied technologies, which come

---

[4] Idhe's four types of human-technology relations are embodiment, hermen-eutic, alterity, and background.

close to being transparent, are not neutral. According to Ihde, there is a technofantasy about technology, where he says,

> I want the transformation that the technology allows, but I want it in such a way that I am basically unaware of its presence. I want it in such a way that it becomes me. Such a desire both secretly rejects what technologies are and overlooks the transformational effects, which are necessarily tied to human-technology relations. This illusory desire belongs equally to pro- and anti-technology interpretations of technology.... In that sense, all technologies in use are non-neutral. (Ihde, *Lifeworld* 75-76)

Ihde has referred to transhumanism as hype and technofantasy, equating it to magic in the sense that new human-enhancing technologies are often portrayed without "ambiguous or unintended or contingent consequences" ("Of Which Human" 127). However, Ihde is not rejecting human enhancement out of some romantic, Heideggerian or theologically bound reason, but rather worries "about unintended consequences, unpredictability, and the introduction of disruptions into an ever-growing and more complex system" (132). Ihde's point is that we cannot simply add technology to our lives without experiencing a transformative change in the process. We are different because of the technology, and the technology is different because of us. There is always a lack of complete embodiment, and he demonstrates this when he discusses his own phenomenological experience of being a cyborg with an artificial knee and his experience wearing hearing aids. Neither substitution is as effective as the original equipment he came with at birth ("Aging").

ENABLING-CONSTRAINING

Postphenomenology emphasizes that all new technologies will be both enabling and constraining to various degrees. For example, a telescope allows us to see objects as if they were closer to us, but it also removes the objects from their immediate context, constraining our ability to see them in relation to their surroundings. This postphenomenological idea can be brought to human enhancement technologies by suggesting that we should look beyond the hype of the enhancing aspect and look to see what is constrained and/or reduced by the new technology.

One problem with many of the transhumanist ideas is that the technology they discuss has yet to be created. Therefore, for the empirically grounded postphenomenology, it is difficult to go to the *thing itself* and analyze the impact. We can, however, manage our expectations of the future effects of human-enhancing technologies and use the enabling-constraining idea whenever new technologies are brought forth.

TRANSPARENT TECHNOLOGY

It is easier to see the benefits and drawbacks from enhancing technologies such as hearing aids (they allow one to hear better, but they have issues in noisy rooms and are not that good at filtering out background noise), but what about new enhancement technologies that seem like they could actually be transparent? An example of a seemingly transparent technology is genetic modification. Biotechnology such as CRISPR[5] (Mulvihill et al.) makes it possible to not only modify a person's genetic code, but to also allow the possibility for germline editing, which would cause those changes to be passed down to future generations.[6] This technology is quite invisible to the person and can thus be considered fundamentally transparent.

However, there are enabling and constraining aspects of this technology that remain. Replacing one gene with another may remove the previous functionality that we are aware of, but some of the functionality may not be known currently. The complexity of genetic and epigenetic systems and the details of how they manifest in the human being is far beyond our current comprehension. Additionally, the designer's fallacy states that many technologies are not used in the way they were originally designed. With genetic manipulation, it could be many years before the effects of removing and splicing in new genes are revealed. Though many of the effects can be positive (i.e., for removing genetic defects), there will still be constraining effects, some of which might not be discovered right away.

CONCLUSION

New technologies such as 3D printing of body parts and genetic engineering bring about both exciting and potentially disturbing scenarios and repercussions for the future. Transhumanists and bio-conservatives bring opposing views to this human-enhancement debate. However, both parties start from a dualistic point of view, keeping the subject and object separate. The philosophical field of postpheno-menology is a beneficial approach, which pragmatically and empirically grounds the human-enhancement debate, providing tools such as embodied technological relations, the non-neutrality of technology, en-abling and constraining aspects of all technologies, and the false dream of a perfectly transparent technology.

Beyond effects to the individual, it is necessary to discuss the broader, more sweeping changes these technologies will bring to society. Genetic modification is not a magic panacea without consequences. Additionally, choices that are introduced with each new technology force parents to make decisions involving financial, ethical, and moral issues.[7] Though genetic modification to remove a hereditary disease may be an easier modification to accept on a societal level, there remain questions regarding this kind of decision.

WORKS CITED

Bostrom, Nick. "In Defense of Post-human Dignity." *Bioethics* 19.3 (2005): 202-14. Print.

---

[5] CRISPR is a gene-editing technology that can cut out and replace a specific genetic sequence and is currently being used in trials.
[6] This brings up serious societal issues that will not be explored in this paper, but are discussed in the scholarship on liberal eugenics.

---

[7] See Verbeek (Moralizing) for a deeper dialogue on the morality of technology.

---. "The Transhumanist FAQ: A General Introduction: Version 2.1." *http://www.nickbostrom.com/*. 2003. Web.

Braidotti, Rosi. *The Posthuman*. Oxford: Polity Press, 2013. Print.

Clark, Andy. *Natural-Born Cyborgs: Minds, Technologies, and the Future of Human Intelligence*. Oxford; New York: Oxford University Press, 2003. Print.

Coeckelbergh, Mark. *Human Being @ Risk. Enhancement, Technology, and the Evaluation of Vulnerability Transformations*. Dordrecht: Springer, 2013. Print.

Ferrando, Francesca. "Posthumanism, Trans-humanism, Anti-humanism, Metahumanism, and New Materialisms." *Existenz* 8.2 (2013): 26-32. Web.

Fukuyama, Francis. *Our Posthuman Future: Consequences of the Biotechnology Revolution*. London: McMillan, 2003. Print.

---. "Transhumanism." *Foreign Policy*.144 (2004): 42-3. Web.

Habermas, Jürgen. *The Future of Human Nature*. Cambridge, UK: Polity, 2003. Print.

Hansell, Gregory R. *H+/-: Transhumanism and Its Critics*. Philadelphia, PA: Metanexus Institute, 2011. Print.

Haraway, Donna. "A Manifesto for Cyborgs: Science, Technology, and Socialist Feminism in the 1980s." *Feminism/postmodernism* (1990): 190-233. Print.

Hayles, N. Katherine. *How We Became Posthuman: Virtual Bodies in Cybernetics, Literature, and Informatics*. Chicago, Ill.: Univ. of Chicago Press, 2008. Print.

Ihde, Don. "Aging: I Don't Want to be a Cyborg!" *Phenomenology and the Cognitive Sciences* 7.3 (2008): 397-404. Web.

---. *Bodies in Technology*. Minneapolis: University of Minnesota Press, 2002. Print.

---. "Of Which Human are we Post?" *H+/-: Transhumanism and Its Critics*. Philadelphia, PA Metanexus Institute, 2011. 123-135. Print.

---. *Technology and the Lifeworld: From Garden to Earth*. Bloomington; Indianapolis: Indiana University Press, 1990. Print.

Kang, Hyun-Wook, et al. "A 3D Bioprinting System to Produce Human-Scale Tissue Constructs with Structural Integrity." *Nature Biotechnology* 34.3 (2016): 312-9. Web.

Kurzweil, Ray. *The Singularity is Near: When Humans Transcend Biology*. New York, N.Y: Viking Books, 2005. Print.

Latour, Bruno. *Reassembling the Social: An Introduction to Actor-Network-Theory*. Oxford: Oxford University Press, 2008. Print.

McKibben, Bill. *Enough: Staying Human in an Engineered Age*. New York: Henry Holt, 2003. Print.

Moravec, Hans. *Mind Children: The Future of Robot and Human Intelligence*. Cambridge, Mass.: Harvard University Press. 1988. Print.

More, Max. "The Philosophy of Transhumanism." *The Transhumanist Reader: Classical and Contemporary Essays on the Science, Technology, and Philosophy of the Human Future*. Wiley-Blackwell, Chichester UK, 2013. 3-17. Print.

---. "Principles of Extropy." *Extropy Institute* (2003). Web.

Mulvihill, John J., et al. "Ethical Issues of CRISPR Technology and Gene Editing through the Lens of Solidarity." *British Medical Bulletin* 122.1 (2017): 17-29. Print.

Roden, David. *Posthuman Life: Philosophy at the Edge of the Human.* London: Routledge, 2014. Print.

Rosenberger, Robert, and Peter-Paul Verbeek. *Postphenomenological Investigations: Essays on Human-Technology Relations.* Lanham: Lexington Books, 2015. Print.

Sandel, Michael J. *The Case Against Perfection: Ethics in the Age of Genetic Engineering.* Cambridge, Mass: Belknap Press, 2007. Print.

Sharon, Tamar. *Human Nature in an Age of Biotechnology: The Case for Mediated Posthumanism.* London: Springer international publishing, 2014. Print.

Van Den Eede, Yoni. "Where is the Human? Beyond the Enhancement Debate." *Science, Technology, and Human Values* 40.1 (2015): 149-62. Print.

---. "Extending "Extension": A Reappraisal of the Technology-as-Extension Idea through the Case of Self-Tracking Technologies." *Design, Mediation, and the Post-human.* Dennis Weiss and Amy Propen, editors. Lanham: Lexington Books, 2014. 151-171. Print.

Verbeek, Peter-Paul. "Cyborg Intentionality: Rethinking the Phenomenology of Human–technology Relations." *Phenomenology and the Cognitive Sciences* 7.3 (2008): 387-95. Web.

---. *Moralizing Technology: Understanding and Designing the Morality of Things.* Chicago, IL: University of Chicago Press, 2011. Print.

---. *What Things do: Philosophical Reflections on Technology, Agency, and Design.* University Park, Penn.: Pennsylvania State University Press, 2005. Print.

On- or Off-Life?
Life in the Era of Social Network

Valeria Ferraretto[1]
Silvia Ferrari[2]
Verbena Giambastiani[1]

[1]University of Pisa
Pisa, Italy
[2]Fondazione Collegio San Carlo di Modena
Modena, Italy

ABSTRACT: *Online activities are becoming intertwined with almost everything we do. Social networks are so engrained in our lives that they have turned into a crucial part of what we do, both online and offline. Thus, the first question is, How are social media changing us? The second one is instead, How much has social media changed society? When a medium changes its form, human life is modified accordingly. Regarding the latter, if we assume a Foucaultian perspective, we should consider social media as the dispositif that can develop the subjectivity of individuals. Sharing information on social media represents something more than a simple act. This is a performative act à la Austin that shapes and disciplines human life by means of a virtual crowd which compulsively shares information and general opinions. The online dimension of life is either a technique or a practice that makes the dispositif operative. It enhances and maintains the exercise of institutional, physical and public power. What are the public and private consequences of virtual reality? In what kind of network of power is the virtual life enmeshed? According to Walter Benjamin, the digital era has a positive aspect: it allows humans to be aware of the poverty of human experience in general. However, this is not a lament for the old days. Benjamin introduces a new positive concept of barbarism. It has a creative force: the barbarian is a destroyer, but also a constructor. In this new* Erlebnis, *there is not a progressive linear time; rather, posting, sharing and experiencing happens simultaneously. Digital life is the beginning of a new historical orientation where virtual reality is an extension of the "offline" mode.*

KEY WORDS: social network, online, offline, individual, dividual

I. INTRODUCTION

Social networks are so engrained in our lives that they have turned into a crucial part of what we do both online and offline. One of McLuhan's key concerns lies in making us aware of the consequences of the use of electronic media. When a medium changes its form, human life is modified accordingly. Media are not just channels for information; every new medium changes us deeply. Thus, one of the first issues under scrutiny in this paper will be looking at the question of how social media are changing us.

The second issue addressed

considers how much social media has changed society. Online activity is monitored in order to obtain accurate market surveys, and, moreover, the virtual world is achieved thanks to constant feedback. What are the public and private consequences of this kind of virtual reality? We will analyze this point using the lens of a Foucaultian perspective.

Moreover, can we consider social media as an upgrade of human life? Walter Benjamin affirms that the digital era allows humans to be aware of the poverty of human experience. In this new *Erlebnis*, there is not a progressive linear time, because posting, sharing and experiencing happens simultaneously. Digital life may be the beginning of a new historical orientation in which virtual reality is an extension of the "offline" one.

II. INDIVIDUAL OR DIVIDUAL? ON THE TRANSFORMATIVE POWER OF NEW MEDIA

The relationship between self-determination and the online self seems complex and multifaceted, primarily because it is not clear if the online self is something artificial, an artifact for example, or if it is an expansion of the individual self *ipso facto*.

In order to answer to this kind of question, in a recent debate theorists have argued that we should consider a new form of "community" that distinguishes between "individual" and "dividual." Michaela Ott[1], influenced by Gilles

Deleuze[2], affirms that we can no longer consider human beings undivided as individual entities. Individuals have become dividual. Being dividual is an ambivalent status of being because it means being affected by and interrelated with countless others, of sharing multiple bio- and socio-technological structures. Ott says that thanks to the dividual status, we are interrelated with socio-technologies in such intense ways that "we can hardly separate ourselves from these devices…Therefore we cannot help but understand ourselves as dividuations very much like filmic works of art, continuously reframing."[3]

Gerald Raunig[4] opposes the atom to digital data. Atoms are indivisible units, instead of data that are entities that can be analyzed, segmented, and correlated in endless ways. Digital data do not exist apart from the algorithmic operations that produce and reproduce data incessantly. The impossibility of assigning an ontological pre-eminence to data or algorithms – which exist only for one another – means that the digital world is always already divided. Raunig locates the dividual as the basis of capitalistic society in the age of social-media. In computer networks, this segmentation, or

[1] Ott, Michaela. "Aesthetics as Dividual Affections", *Proceedings of the European Society for Aesthetics*, Vol.7, 2015, 391-405.

[2] Deleuze, Gilles *Cinema I: The Movement-Image*. Athlone Press, 1986; *Essays Critical and Clinical*. University of Minnesota Press, 1997.
[3] Ott, Michaela. "Aesthetics as Dividual Affections", 403.
[4] Raunig, Gerald. *Dividuum: Machinic Capitalism and Molecular Revolution Vol. 1*, Semiotext(e), 2016.

dividualization, is a precondition of the recombination of multiple data points in variable data sets. This means that the dividual is always open to interaction, always ready to be detached from and attached to other dividuals. The dividual has the advantage of being combinable with other divisible beings that share some properties with it. As Raunig remarks, "Whereas individuality mobilizes dissimilarity to emphasize the respective being-different, demarcation from everything else, dividual singularity is always one among others; a dividuum has one component or multiple components."[5]

In *Dividuum*, Raunig wisely shows us that "the middle is dividual" because only that which is divisible can be concatenated with other elements that share some properties with it. Yet he also writes that "in the raging middle of the dividual no ground is needed, no roots, no floor."[6]

The "dividualization," or segmentation, of the online self into a myriad of data-pieces can be considered a point of departure for the advent of new processes of subjectivization. As McLuhan wrote, the effects of technology do not occur at the level of opinions and concepts. Rather, they alter "patterns of perceptions steadily and without any resistance." [7] The core of McLuhan's theory is his definition of media as extensions of ourselves. All technologies are extensions of our physical and

nervous systems to increase power and speed. McLuhan recognizes the transformative power of new communication technologies. With new media, we extend some part of ourselves artificially. Hence, a change in a medium's form is also a change in human life. McLuhan affirms that as a new medium becomes dominant, we are entranced by it to a state of numbness and become its servomechanisms. We become what we behold. We change as what we behold changes. But, change is not of one form. It takes the form of interchanges. This interchange McLuhan describes in the chapter, "Hybrid Energy":

> The hybrid or the meeting of two media is a moment of truth and revelation from which new form is born. For the parallel between two media holds us on the frontiers between forms that snap us out of the Narcissus-narcosis. The moment of the meeting of media is a moment of freedom and release from the ordinary trance and numbness imposed by them on our senses.[8]

But the hybrid is not limited to media. It includes human beings. It has been indicated above that McLuhan's use of the word "message" is not confined to its intellectual and moral connotations. His message is a physical and physiological massage of media on our sensitive bodies. In so far as we participate with our senses, we become "hybridized" with the

---

[5] Raunig, Gerald. *Dividuum*, 67.
[6] Raunig, Gerald. *Dividuum*, 21.
[7] McLuhan, Marshall. *Understanding Media: The Extension of Man*, Gingko, 2003 p.31.

[8] McLuhan, Marshall. *Understanding Media*, 63.

media. Media in the form of technology are nothing but extensions of our own sensory organs or our alter ego working on behalf of and with us. In this way, human energy and nonhuman energies are acting out the physicists' drama, "The Trans-formation of Energies." Electronic media, as an extension of our central nervous system, externalize and extend our thinking process in the same way that computers do.

III. SOCIAL NETWORKS AS FORMS OF SUBJECTIVIZATION

In the *Psychiatric Power, Lesson of November 21*,[9] Foucault shows how the individual is the product of a series of power techniques that he calls "discipline" and that begin to affirm themselves at the end of the eighteenth century. If the individual is the effect of power practices, we can conclude with Foucault that it cannot be considered, in itself and with its rights, as the starting point for any forms of resistance to power. So how do the disciplinary techniques of power "fabricate" the individual?

These disciplines, according to Foucault, would redistribute the relationships between the body, the "somatic singularity,"[10] to use Foucault's locution, the function-subject, and the individual. By coinciding with the somatic singularity of the subject-function, they would produce "submissive" bodies. The individual would

therefore be the effect of the body subjected to the subject-related body.

Through three techniques the individual was thus able to form itself: uninterrupted surveillance, continuous writing, and virtual punishment. In this way, the body was framed and subdued, and a psyche was then extracted from the body. The two main techniques of disciplinary power are those of surveillance and punishment (these are also the two concepts that appear in the title of Foucault's main text on disciplinary power, *Surveillance and Punishment*[11]).

The Panopticon was designed, but never built, in the eighteenth century by Bentham[12] and re-presents in the Foucaultian studies the diagram of power specification. The Panopticon is a model of the technique of modern power and represents a new relationship of power to be exerted on subjects.

In *Discipline and Punish*, Foucault makes a very famous description[13]: visibility is the great turning point of the architectural engineering project that has a definite effect on the prisoners.[14] The power that is exercised in the Panopticon is visible and unverifiable, which leads to the self-discipline of the subjects observed.

For Foucault, the Panopticon serves as a paradigm example that

---

[9] Foucault, Michael. *Psychiatric Power: Lectures at the Collège de France, 1973-1974*, Springer, 2006.
[10] Foucault, Michael. Lesson 21 November 1973, p 39-63.

[11] Foucault, Michael. *Discipline and Punish: The Birth of the Prison*. Penguin, 1977.
[12] Bentham, Jeremy, *The Works*, 4. Panopticon, Constitution, Colonies, Codification, Liberty fund.
[13] Foucault, Michael. *Discipline and Punish: The Birth of the Prison*. Penguin, 1977, p 249-256.
[14] Foucault, Michael. *Discipline and Punish*. 200.

assumes and summarizes all the technical specifications of power:

1) Total conquest exerted on the body – but with effects on the psyche.

2) Applying a constant control procedure.

3) For the discipline to exercise constant control, writing is necessary; recording everything that happens, the transmission of all information is then made accessible to all.

Without going to the extreme of a *Black Mirror* episode, social media has the same incidence in subjectivity because they are all vehicles for exchanging information, but above of all they are vehicles that feed on themselves for the formation of identities. It is important to remember that the production, use and sharing of information are the basis of disciplinary power.

In the same way, disciplinary power intervenes not so much on the gesture but on what precedes it, which has a great deal of importance. It changes the power technique's scope of intervention: it does not act on the accomplished behavior but on its "virtuosity," on its "potentiality." With this new field of action, a new sphere is created, that of the psyche, defined as the set of potentials that could result in one particular behavior or another. Thus, behind the singularity of the body is "projected" a set of virtualities that will constitute the individual.

For Foucault, subjectivity is constituted historically in relation to processes of subjectivization. It

is not only the determining of the plan of the mechanisms of power that shapes historical identity; Foucault also seeks the "devices of knowledge," revealing them through an archeology of forms of culture, in which the conceptual- and value-horizons are primarily "data." But in the last phase of his thought, in the lessons of the 1980s, he focused on the question of identity with a different perspective, referring to the network identification of practices and self-certification of historical subjects. Personal identity cannot be thought of as a "given," as in a substantialist ontology. The areas of identification practices must be considered a type of experience in contextual forms where personal traits are prosecuted, denied, and approved, but remain above assumptions and certificates.

The questions around which Foucault's previous investigation revolved were clear in their genealogical setting and called into question the processes by which subjects are constituted in historically determined forms. What helped produce the notion of subjectivity in that particular historical form? What effect did this have on the subject? What are the cultural heritage coordinates within which a certain form of subjectivity is demonstrated?

IV. ON-LIFE AS THE REAL LIFE FOR A NEW TYPE OF INDIVIDUAL

As reported by Benjamin – in his short essay, *Experience and Poverty* (1933), we live in the era of the radical transformation of the concept of experience.[15]

Following Benjamin's consider-ations, we can find a dialectical parallel between the nineteenth and twentieth centuries' visual tech-nologies[16] and the twenty-first century's new digital technologies. In other words, if film was the most powerful agent of change in the 1930s, the real of computers and Internet pervasiveness in turn play an analogous role today. There is an analogy between the mechanical reproduction of visual works of art enabled by photography and film and the reproduction of our personality, thanks to a variety of networks enabled by digital technology.

Operating in parallel to film, social media is "the obverse of the contemporary crisis and renewal of mankind…intimately connected with the contemporary mass move-ments." The most powerful agent of these changes, "its social significance, particularly in its most positive form, is inconceivable without its destructive, cathartic aspect."[17]

That aforementioned repro-duction (for example, photography, film, or social media) served to multiply and then distribute an original work of art.

Benjamin has proposed the following argument:

> During long periods of history, the mode of human sense perception changes with humanity's entire mode of existence. The manner in which human sense percep-tion is organized, the medium in which it is accomplished, is determined not only by nature but by historical circumstances as well.[18]

That means that even our being-as-self is multiplied, and it enables new forms of perception. By consequence, the entire char-acter of relationships has been trans-formed.

Even if Benjamin could not have known about the new social media to come, he would have never mourned or condemned this novelty. Instead, he was fascinated with innovation and by new possibilities for humankind, preferring to investigate present time rather than taking refuge in the past. Even though he was living in a context characterized by ruins, he conceptualized a new path for writing about human experience. He was not nostalgic, and he affirmed that in the destruction of the traditional way of experiencing the world we can find the possibility of something new, something different, provided by technologies. This is a "form of new barbarism."

The failure of every grand-

---

[15] He shows us that such a sense of experience as tradition, as wisdom which passes "from one generation to the next like a precious ring" (Benjamin, Walter. *Experience and poverty. Walter Benjamin. Selected Writings*, vol. 2, part. 2, 1931-1934, Harvard Press, 1999, 731) has been totally devalued.
[16] Such as the panorama, the diorama, photography, the stereoscope, and the kaleidoscope, as well as cinema and architecture of iron and glass, which he investigates in his writings on Paris and Berlin in the nineteenth century.
[17] Benjamin, Walter. *Illuminations. Essays and Reflections*, Paperback, 1969, 221

---

[18] Benjamin, Walter. *Illuminations.* 222

narrative is the missed chance to listen and grasp voices that have had no room in the educational context of past grand-narratives. Hence, the end of experience and the new form of barbarism could be seen as a new form of freedom.

The destruction of experience also implies the destruction of the traditional values and of the bourgeoisie individual. This destruction raises the possibility not only of a reactive, passive nihilism, but also of an opportunity to establish a new configuration of experience.

The view we wish to express here is that social media should be considered an opportunity rather than a force of delimitation. Like movies, social media can be an important immunization against the alienation caused by new technologies. They could have a sort of cathartic effect.

The digital and physical are becoming increasingly meshed. The new individual is both techno-logical and organic, at once digital and physical. We are living in a reality that is augmented by atoms and bits. However, our selves are not divided because our online Facebook profiles reflect who we know and what we do offline, and our offline lives are influenced by what happens on Facebook. Empowerment of the people can come via new technologies.

In these days the individual user on the Internet is homologous to the *flaneur*, who strolls not along a sidewalk or under passages but saunters in social media reading through posts and news, all without a definite purpose in mind. We

should seek an unknown constellation of fragments. Posts and comments on the social networks function like aphorisms and fragments that appear as windows through which the world is experienced. They have a sense and they can transform the past in their interpretation of the present.

Fragmentation is both the alienated condition of modern post-industrial life, but it is also a way of analyzing the present, where the masses are not only passive consumers or inert spectators, but they are also active producers of information.

Networks are helpful for collective endeavors, including participation in civic and political groups.[19] Nonetheless, it is not the media *per se* that can affect individuals' social capital and engagement, but rather the specific ways in which individuals use media.[20]

---

[19] The chain of *causality* is not yet firmly established, but research has generally confirmed that there are significant positive relationships between the use of digital media and political participation and knowledge (See Boulianne, Shelley. "Does Internet Use Affect Engagement? A Meta-Analysis of Research." *Political Communi-cation*, 26(2), 2009, 193-211; Dalrymple, Kajsa E. and Dietram A. Scheufele, "Finally Informing the Electorate? How the Internet Got People Thinking about Presidential Politics in 2004." *Harvard International Journal of Press/Politics*, vol. 12, no. 3, 2007 96–111; Tolbert, Caroline J. and Ramona S. McNeal, "Unraveling the Effects of the Internet on Political Participation?' *Political Research Quarterly*, vol. 56, no. 2, 2003, 175-185).
[20] Cfr. Dimitrova, Daniela V., Adam Shehata, Jesper Strömbäck, and Lars W. Nord, "The Effects of Digital Media on Political Knowledge and Participation in Election Campaigns: Evidence from Panel Data." *Communication Research*, no. 2, 2011 1-24.

V. CONCLUSION

What would happen if media life offered us a new type of living, and if the divided individual were the real and true subject in the postmodern era? On the one side, the medium, given its technical, symbolic and organizational characteristics, produces effects that are even more important than those produced through the contents that media transmit. McLuhan wrote that our tools end up "numbing" whatever part of our body they amplify.[21] When we extend some part of ourselves artificially, we also distance ourselves from the amplified part and its natural functions. The price we pay to assume technology's power is alienation. In explaining how technologies numb the very faculties they amplify, even to the point of "autoamputation," McLuhan was not trying to romanticize society as it existed before. Alienation is an inevitable by-product of the use of technology.

On the other hand, thanks to the considerations of Walter Benjamin, who describes the life of the nineteenth century as characterized by a loss of experience, we can encounter the opportunity to transform this world into a better one. There is a loose analogy between the mechanical reproduction of visual works of art enabled by photography and film and the reproduction of our personality across a variety of networks engendered by digital technology. Hence, Benjamin tries both to comprehend the reactive elements of decay in modern experience as well as recognize those elements which might be recast and transformed.

There is also an innate political issue within the social media dimension. Facebook defines itself as a social device, or, following the vocabulary of Deleuze in a Foucaultian way, it is a machine to observe and to discuss, to promote processes of subjectivity. The mechanism that makes subjectivity possible is sharing.

Content sharing, which unfolds in thoughts, judgments, and actions to be conveyed through images, music and video, is critical to the very essence of Facebook. Individuals are defined not only by what they share, but also based on what they "like." This makes targeting more and more refined not only for controls or safety but also for marketing. Content sharing is not merely a means to the ascertainment of neutral information: when you share a new story on Facebook, for example, you do it in the presence of a virtual "crowd"; you do it publicly in a forum. The act of sharing becomes a performative act, a gesture that does something in the world, as J. L. Austin would say.

The protagonist of the *Black Mirror* episode, "Fifteen Million Merits," knows that her life is a stage. With her socio-economic conditions depending on her performance, she therefore needs to make an effort to force herself to appear more beautiful, nicer, more polite and kinder, and so she

---

[21] McLuhan, Marshall. *Understanding Media*, 63-70.

adopts more effective behavioral models to ingratiate all those who may put her up to review. In the same way, the users know that an effective use of social media can lead to several advantages.

The creation of digital citizenship, based on what we share in order to get a positive online reaction, or at least the perception of one, will result in a certain reputation that has been or will be reflected in real life. This is the moment of an extreme form of contemporary subjectification, in which a new type of individual is born and bred: the on-off-dividual.

WORKS CITED

Benjamin, Walter. *Experience and poverty. Walter Benjamin. Selected Writings*, vol. 2, part. 2, 1931-1934, Harvard Press, 1999.

---. *Illuminations. Essays and Reflections*, Paperback, 1969.

Bentham, Jeremy, The Works, 4. *Panopticon*, Constitution, Colonies, Codification, Liberty fund.

Berardi, Franco. *The Soul at Work: From Alienation to Autonomy*, Semiotext(e), 2009.

Boulianne, Shelley. "Does Internet Use Affect Engagement? A Meta-Analysis of Research." *Political Communication*, 2009

Dalrymple, Kajsa E., Scheufele, Dietram A. "Finally informing the electorate? How the Internet got people thinking about presidential politics in 2004."

Harvard International Journal of Press/Politics," vol. 12, no. 3, 2007

Deleuze, Gilles. *Cinema I: The Movement-Image.* Athlone Press, 1986; *Essays Critical and Clinical.* University of Minnesota Press, 1997.

Dimitrova, Daniela V., Shehata, Adam, Strömbäck, Jesper and Nord, Lars W. "The Effects of Digital Media on Political Knowledge and Participation in Election Campaigns: Evidence From Panel Data." Communication Research, no. 2, 2011.

Foucault, Michel. *Psychiatric Power: Lectures at the Collège de France,* Springer, 2006.

---. *Discipline and Punish: The Birth of the Prison,* Penguin, 1977.

McLuhan, Marshall. *Understanding Media: The Extension of Man,* Gingko, 2003.

Ott, Michaela. "Aesthetics as Dividual Affections," *Proceedings of the European Society for Aesthetics,* Vol.7, 2015.

Raunig, Gerald. *Dividuum: Machinic Capitalism and Molecular Revolution Vol. 1,* Semiotext(e), 2016.

Tolbert, Caroline J., McNeal, Ramona S. "Unraveling the Effects of the Internet on Political Participation?." *Political Research Quarterly,* vol. 56, no. 2, 2003.

Facing the Digital Partner: A Phenomenological Analysis of Digital Otherness

Nicola Liberati

University of Twente
Enschede, The Netherlands

ABSTRACT: *The aim of this work is to understand what kind of "other" a digital being can be, or the kind of "otherness" that can be attributed to a digital being. Digital technologies are emerging in our surroundings, and they are so close to us that they can be in intimate relationships with us. There are products like Gatebox, which are designed to produce digital entities that are not merely part of the surroundings, but that are also partners with which (or with whom) humans have relationships. In studying the kind of "otherness" these digital entities can have, the paper highlights the effects of different designs on the types of relations that are possible. Following a phenomenological point of view, the elements required to have a form of "otherness" similar to that of human beings is analyzed by focusing mainly on the resistance opposed by the "other." According to these elements, the possible relations in which robots can engage is determined according to their specific design.*

KEYWORDS: digital other, phenomenology, relationships, Gatebox

1. INTRODUCTION

Today computer technologies are spreading all around us, and they are becoming intimate (Prager and Roberts; Vetere et al.; Schaefer and Olson). They are intimate because they are physically and emotionally close to us. They are attached to our body, as in the case of wearable computers, and they constantly peep into our personal life by reading our bodily states and conditions, along with tracking our actions. However, there is another way in which digital technologies are becoming intimate. They are becoming love partners for users by providing digital entities with which subjects can develop intimate relationships.

In the case of fetishism (Nagel), a human subject develops a love relationship with an object that is not a living creature. A person can fall in love with, or even marry, a common object.[1] However, in the case of digital objects, there are differences to be noted. Although they are completely inanimate and inert entities, like fetish objects, digital entities actually interact with human subjects. Of course, such interactions are, in ways that will be explored here, unlike the way humans interact with other human beings, and so, we may situate digital objects as something in between inert objects and human beings (Schneegass and

---

[1] See, for example, the Dutch artist Yvonne Dröge Wendel who married an inanimate object (www.yvonnedrogewendel.nl/content/indexb.php?art_id=64&).

Amft; Kuniavsky).

Of course such interactions are, in ways that will be explored here, unlike the way humans interact with other human beings, and so, we may place digital objects as something in between inert objects and human beings (Schneegass and Amft 2017; Kuniavsky 2010). Digital objects are perceived as illusionary entities that are not part of the everyday social world inhabited by human users of technology in the same sense that other humans are part of society. Digital objects are "virtual" in the sense they are fictional entities (Brey 2014). Even if a digital character of a video game can look like a human person, it is generated through the use of digital technologies, and so can be seen as merely a product or part of a visual fantasy.

For these reasons, the moment we decide to take seriously the idea that love can be generated between humans and digital objects, we face two main problems. First, digital objects are not human, and so love relationships with them are closely related to fetishism, even if there are significant differences between ordinary and digital objects. Second, digital objects are not even genuine entities because they are the production of fictions. Thus, human subjects who "date" digital objects are strange because they are dating an object that is not really alive; moreover, people dating digital objects risk becoming even stranger because they are perceived by others as people detached from the actual world and lost in their digital fantasy.

Since these digital entities are sneaking into our intimate lives, we need to understand what kind of

"others" they are. We need to explore the possibility of designing digital entities with which users can develop intimate relationships as part of their real life in the actual world, rather than being a fetishist, merely pretending to have a relationship that is nothing more than a product of imagination, or attempting to live in a fictional world that merely mimics reality.

2. TECHNOLOGIES
2.1. PREVIOUS USAGE OF "DIGITAL" ENTITIES

Digital technologies have gone through significant development since their first inception. Thanks to their computing power, they are able to generate an entire virtual world in which the subjects can immerse themselves. Virtual reality (Rabanus 2010) is founded on this kind of immersion in a different world (Gibson 1984; Liberati 2016) and, usually, the virtual world generated by the technological system is completely different from the world where human users live their everyday lives.

Users can enter the new world by producing an avatar in it. The interaction with this avatar varies depending on the system used. The avatar could be a figure displayed on a monitor, while the user still has contact with his everyday world just because he can turn his attention from the monitor to what is happening in the actual surrounding environment very easily. It could also be a much more immersive experience enabled by a head-mounted device that surrounds the perceptual organs of the user with digital stimuli by producing a complete disconnection from what is happening in the real world and that connects him more immediately to the virtual environment. In both the cases, the more removed experience and the more immersive one, every experience of the user is generated within the digital system and enclosed within the virtual world. Perception and action are carried out through a digital avatar, which is embodied by the subject, and the digital experiences arise within the limits of this digital "second world." A user can meet other people in the virtual world, but these encounters are made possible only through the use of the digital bodies of their avatars. They can have social relations in the digital world by meeting other people and engaging in conversations with them. The human users can even have intimate relations because they can fall in love with each other, through the personae of their avatars, and they can make love within the digital world. However, these experiences are founded on the virtual bodies of the avatars which exist only within a specific world generated by the digital system.

Obviously, these experiences can have effects in the real world. People meeting in the virtual world and having an intimate relationship in it could develop a relationship in the outside world, too (Ramirez et al. 2015). Therefore, there are tight links between the worlds. However, at the same time, it is clear that the relationship between subjects within the virtual world and outside of it is different. We cannot assume in principle that what happens in the virtual world leads to a similar situation in the real world of everyday life. Moreover, the "other" who is perceived in the digital world may

have no link at all to an actual person in the real world. For example, the "other" encountered in the virtual world might be created and controlled by an artificial intelligence instead of a human person. A clear example of this are the relations within video games that subjects have with "bots" (web robots) or non-player characters in the game (Turkle 1994), where users interact with digital beings that are manipulated by a program.

There are two main concerns in the case of these digitally embedded relationships. First, the "other" encountered is not the other in the everyday world, but a digital representation of it (Lopato 2016). The subject does not touch the body of another person, but only their representation, embodied by the avatar, which, as noted earlier, may have no relation whatsoever to any actual person. Second, the subject's experiences that ground the love relationships are enclosed within a second world, which is a virtual world. These digital experiences and the others encountered therein are thus "virtual" for the users, in the sense they are not part of the everyday world, but rather they are part of a fictional dream that exists only within the limits imposed by the second virtual world generated by the digital system.

2.2. NOVEL TECHNOLOGIES

New trends in computer technologies are providing a completely different approach to digital interactions. Instead of producing a world into which the users have to immerse themselves, they provide digital elements as part of the everyday world. Augmented reality enables the visualization of digital objects in the surroundings (Milgram; Geroimenko; Furht). Wearable computers directly connect the body of the subject to digital databases (Van Den Eede), and robotics is becoming increasingly popular as a way to make intimate connections (Bond; Liberati; Cheok et al.).

In these situations, there is no longer immersion in a digital virtual world; instead, the connection with digital entities is achieved in the actual world. The digital content simply emerges in the surroundings (Gibson). There are no avatars needed to mediate the connection, and there is no second world in which to be immersed. Hence the way subjects relate with these entities changes as a result of this novel technology.

3. DIFFERENT RELATIONS WITH THESE DIGITAL ENTITIES

As we saw in the case of virtual reality, digital entities are able to intertwine with each other through specific relations with the avatar of the user, but they cannot intertwine their activities with the user in the everyday world. Virtual reality allows users to perceive others within the game with which (or with whom) they can develop intimate relation-ships, but these relations are limited to life within the game in the fictional world.

There are other computer technologies that produce digital entities that are not part of the virtual world. Consider, for example, the product *Gatebox*,[2] developed by Vinclu Inc., soon to be released in the market of digital-assistant technology. This device is a robotic virtual assistant similar to Echo by Amazon.[3] It basically consists of a glass tube with a hologram of a girl (your virtual assistant) inside. The user can ask her to perform basic tasks like controlling the lighting in the room, or asking her the weather forecast for the day. However, the innovative part is not related to these functions, which are already included in a number of other virtual-assistant products. The novelty in Gatebox is that this "girl" is designed to be close to the user in a more personal sense. She gets very intimate, providing the user with personalized messages every morning and constantly texting him during the entire day. These simple elements enable the digital entity to be something different from the digital entities generated within a virtual world because of this kind of interactivity.

In the now-familiar case of avatars engaging in a second world, the relationships with the digital entity are clearly limited within the bounds of a specific world defined by the operative technology and programming functions. The entities are digital in the sense that they are generated by a computer device, and they are digital in the sense they are virtual and fictitious. But now, in the case of Gatebox technology, these virtual interactive entities are still digital because they are generated by a computer system, but they are not limited to a second world. They emerge and gain entry into the user's everyday life.

According to Alfred Schütz, the

[2] The product was set to be released in December 2017, at an approximate price of 300000Y. See gatebox.ai/ .

[3] See https://www.amazon.com/Amazon-Echo-Bluetooth-Speaker-with-WiFi-Alexa/dp/B00X4WHP5E .

everyday world[4] is grounded in certain elements that make the objects and the other subjects in it part of the same world. Two such elements are quite relevant to this discussion because they clearly exhibit important differences in the way digital entities and human subjects encountered in the everyday world relate to the users.

Other human subjects in the everyday world interconnect their activities with those of the user though ordinary real-world inter-actions. They co-live in the same world, and the life of a subject is the product of this tight co-living. The digital others encountered in the virtual world have no such interconnection or intertwinement with the everyday activities of the user. Their existence is restricted to actions and interactions within the virtual world among avatars, and so their existence is intertwined only with the actions performed by the avatars. Gatebox is not limited to the virtual world, and its actions go hand in hand with the actions of the users in their usual, real-world activities. While the user is at the workplace, the digital girl sends him text messages. The digital girl asks him about details of his personal life, and she constantly relates her actions to actual needs of the user in the everyday world. For example, she asks directions for managing some basic tasks in the user's actual living space.

The second important element to consider is the fact that an actual human subject in the everyday world is a source of resistance in that a human being is a genuine "other"

who existence is, in a basic ontological sense, in opposition to the existence the subject. The "other" is not simply an entity in the world with whom we need to intertwine our activities. This other resists us, and we need to cope with something that is not under our control, over which we have no real power.

In a virtual reality, the other is resistant only within the world generated by the system. Human users need to cope with these others only when they want to live within that specific reality. They are able to exit the virtual world, leaving everything in it. Users are always able to turn the program off and thus terminate their relation with the digital entities living in it. Moreover, other digital technologies have the same limit. Even in the case of a program generated by new computer technologies, users can terminate the digital entity by turning the device off. They literally have complete power over the existence of these digital entities by being able to decide when and where they live. By having this direct and explicit power over the persistence of these digital objects, the resistance opposed to the user is quite limited.

The relation between digital entities and digital devices cannot be eluded. Digital entities have to be related to the activation of a technology in order to be perceived by the subject and hence brought into being. In the virtual world, the users need digital technologies to immerse themselves in the virtual reality, and, in the case of other technologies like Gatebox, the virtual-assistant girl is visualized through digital technologies. However, on phenomenological

---

[4] With "everyday world", we identify what Schütz calls lifeworld (Schütz 1962; Kassab 1991)

grounds, an "other" can be resistant even without being directly perceived.[5] Other people in our world are still present for us even when they are not in our visual field or sensory field. Thus, the fact that the digital entities are visible only when the device is on does not compromise the presence of these others for the users *per se*. Digital entities fail to be resistant not because they are not visible, but because by turning the device off, they cease to exist. Thus, we can improve the system with features that address this problem by making the digital entities active even when they are not perceived. A system like Gatebox could be improved with a program that registers the time or circumstance under which the system is scheduled to be turned off and designed to solicit reasons for the forced deactivation. In this way, users are not only engaged with a digital other when the technology is activated, but they also have to face the digital other even when the device is turned off because the Gatebox girl would ask user why she is being deactivated. The digital girl cannot be ignored so easily even when the subject decides terminate the program.

These two elements are clearly important in order to make the "other" a subject living in the same world of the user. It is also clear how these elements focus to the way subjects are in relation together more than in the "nature" of these subjects.

It is not important the "others" are human beings. It is important these "others" are able to intertwine their actions with the actions of the subjects in the everyday world, and they have to be resistant to them. They can be human beings, animals, and even programs as far as they have these elements which make them part of the everyday world and interact with the users. Thus, a digital being can be perceived as an "other" towards with subjects can develop intimate feelings if it is correctly designed.

4. CONCLUSIONS

In the first section, we showed how digital entities are perceived as part of a virtual world in the case of virtual reality. This element makes them fictional because they are not part of the everyday world of human users. Subjects need to immerse themselves into a different reality in order to perceive these digital beings. The emergence of new digital technologies is changing the way these digital entities are generated. Instead of being entities that must remain within the bounds of their virtual world, the virtual entities can actually appear as part of the everyday world where users live and interact with others.

An understanding who or what counts as an "other" in relation to a perceiving subject follows the work of Schütz in highlighting two main elements that ground the "other": intertwining activities and resistance. The digital entities within a virtual world cannot intertwine their activities with those of the users in the everyday world; however there are new varieties and versions of digital

---

[5] For example, we can take into account Sartre analysis on the "gaze" of the other. The presence of the other subject has not to be actual. A subject can feel the presence of "others" even if they are not perceptually present (Sartre and Barnes 1992).

entities that can now be produced through the latest digital technologies. This new breed of digital entity can be made to achieve the important element of resistance through the operation of a program that makes them active even when the device that generates them is turned off.

Obviously, this solution is limited, and it does not provide the kind or level of resistance as that provided by other human beings. However, it is clear that it is possible to make these digital entities something more than mere virtual, fictional beings by intertwining and interrelating their activities with the those of the user, and in particular, equipping them to offer meaningful opposition to the existence of the human other through resistance to the will and powerful control of the human user.

Even though their existence is virtual, digital entities can be augmented by certain elements required to become genuine "others," just like when other human beings when they relate to the users. Thus, the digital entities can be perceived as "digital others" with which, or with whom, it is possible to develop intimate relationships.

ACKNOWLEDGMENTS

The author is supported by the NWO (Nederlandse Organisatie voor Wetenschappelijk Onderzoek) VICI project "Theorizing Technological Mediation: Toward an Empirical-Philosophical Theory of Technology" (grant number: 277-20-006). The author would like to thank Melinda Campbell for her help in formatting and editing of the text.

WORKS CITED

Bond, Michael. 2007. "Review: Love and Sex with Robots by David Levy." *New Scientist* 196 (2629): 76. doi: dx.doi.org/ 10.1016 S0262-4079(07)62863-2.

Brey, Philip. 2014. "The Physical and Social Reality of Virtual Worlds." In *The Oxford Handbook of Virtuality*. Oxford University Press. doi:10.1093/oxfordhb/978019982 6162.013.029.

Cheok, Adrian David, David Levy, Kasun Karunanayaka, and Yukihiro Morisawa. 2015. "Love and Sex with Robots." In *Handbook of Digital Games and Entertainment Technologies*, eds., Ryohei Nakatsu, Matthias Rauterberg, and Paolo Ciancarini, 1–26. Singapore: Springer Singapore. doi:10.1007/978-981-4560-52-8_15-1.

Furht, Borko, ed. 2011. *Handbook of Augmented Reality*. Springer. dblp.uni-trier.de/db/ books/daglib/0027797.html.

Geroimenko, Vladimir. 2014. *Augmented Reality Art: From an Emerging Technology to a Novel Creative Medium*. Springer Series on Cultural Computing. Springer Publishing Company, Inc.

Gibson, William. 1984. *Neuromancer*. UK: HarperCollins.

---. 2010. "Google's Earth." *The New York Times*. www.nytimes.com /2010/09/01/opinion/01gibson.html?_ r=0.

Kassab, Elizabeth Suzanne. 1991 "'Paramount Reality'" in Schutz and Gurwitsch." *Human Studies* 14 (2–3): 181–98.

Kuniavsky, Mike. 2010. *Smart Things: Ubiquitous Computing User Experience Design*. Amsterdam: Morgan Kaufmann.www.sciencedirect.com /science/book/9780123748997.

Liberati, Nicola. 2016. "From Information to Perception: The New Design of the Emerging

Computer Technologies and Its Effects." In *IFIP Advances in Information and Communication Technology*, forthcoming. Springer.

---. 2017. "Teledildonics and New Ways of "Being in Touch": A Phenomenological Analysis of the Use of Haptic Devices for Intimate Relations." *Science and Engineering Ethics* 23 (3). Springer Netherlands: 801–23. doi:10.1007/s11948-016-9827-5.

Lopato, Michael Stephen. 2016. "Social Media, Love, and Sartre's Look of the Other: Why Online Communication Is Not Fulfilling." *Philosophy & Technology* 29 (3). Springer Netherlands: 195–210. doi:10.1007/s13347-015-0207-x.

Clark, Andy. "Whatever Next? Predictive Brains, Situated Agents, and the Future of Cognitive Science." *Behavioral and Brain Sciences 36.3* (2013): 181-204. Print. 10.1017/S0140525X12000477

--- *Surfing Uncertainty: Prediction, Action, and the Embodied Mind.* New York: Oxford University Press, 2016.

Milgram, Paul. 1994. "Augmented Reality: A Class of Displays on the Reality-Virtuallity Continuum." *SPIE Telemanipulator and Telepresence Technologies* 2351: 282–92.

Nagel, Thomas. 2002. "Sexual Perversion." In *The Philosophy of Sex*, 9–20. Rowman & Littlefield, philpapers.org/archive/SOBTPO-6.pdf.

Prager, K. J., and L. J. Roberts. 2004. "Deep Intimate Connections: Self and Intimacy in Couple Relationships." In *Handbook of Closeness and Intimacy*, edited by D. Mashek and A. Aron, 43–60. Psychology Press.

Rabanus, Christian. 2010. "Virtual Reality." In *Handbook of Phenomenological Aesthetics*, edited by Hans Rainer Sepp and Lester Embree, 59:343–49. Contributions to Phenomenology. Springer, Netherlands.

Ramirez, Artemio, Erin M. Bryant Sumner, Christina Fleuriet, and Megan Cole. 2015. "When Online Dating Partners Meet Offline: The Effect of Modality Switching on Relational Communication Between Online Daters." *Journal of Computer-Mediated Communication* 20 (1). Blackwell Publishing Ltd: 99–114. doi:10.1111/jcc4.12101.

Sartre, Jean-Paul, and Hazel Estella. Barnes. 1992. *Being and Nothingness : A Phenomenological Essay on Ontology.* Washington Square Press.

Schaefer, Mark T., and David H. Olson. 1981. "Assessing Intimacy: The Pair Inventory." *Journal of Marital and Family Therapy* 7 (1). Blackwell Publishing Ltd: 47–60. doi:10.1111/j.1752-0606.1981.tb01351.x.

Schneegass, Stefan, and Oliver Amft, editors 2017. *Smart Textiles. Fundamentals, Design, and Interaction.* Human–Computer Interaction Series. Springer International Publishing. doi:10.1007/978-3-319-50124-6.

Schütz, A. 1962. *Collected Papers: The Problem of Social Reality.* Vol. 11. Phaenomenologica. Martinus Nijhoff.

Turkle, Sherry. 1994. "Constructions and Reconstructions of Self in Virtual Reality: Playing in the MUDs." *Mind, Culture, and Activity* 1 (3): 158–67. web.mit.edu/sturkle/www/pdfsf orstwebpage/ST_Construc and reconstruc of self.pdf.

Van Den Eede, Yoni. 2015. "Tracing the Tracker. A Postphenomenological Inquiry into Self-Tracking Technologies." In *Postphenomenological Investigations: Essays on Human-Technology Relations*, edited by E Selinger and Peter-Paul Verbeek, 143–58. Lexington Books.

Vetere, Frank, Martin R. Gibbs, Jesper Kjeldskov, Steve Howard, Florian "Floyd" Mueller, Sonja Pedell, Karen Mecoles, and Marcus Bunyan. 2005. "Mediating Intimacy." In *Proceedings of the SIGCHI Conference on Human Factors in Computing Systems - CHI '05*, 471. New York, New York, USA: ACM Press. doi:10.1145/ 1054972.1055038.

Living the Body as a New Anthropocene Experience?

MARTA G. TRÓGOLO

ALEJANDRA DE LAS MERCEDES FERNÁNDEZ

ROSARIO ZAPPONI

UNIVERSIDAD NACIONAL DEL NORDESTE [UNNE]
RESISTENCIA, ARGENTINA

ABSTRACT: *In considering the performative work of the Argentinean artist, Nicola Costantino, this paper reflects on the meanings of the body as active material and conceptual support, regarding the arising of the Anthropocene. Faced with their own invention, humans engage in self-reference, which causes an estrangement and produces a given intrusion threatening the identity-integrity of the ego, inevitably resulting in repulsion. Actions performed in the process of cosmetic surgery and other scientific interventions in biological bodies manifest bodily dehiscence, in the form of expulsion and negation of morphogenetic nature. Thinkers such as Lacan and Déotte are used to examine the implementation of the "body object" as a knotting of meanings, given the impossibility of reticulate substance, humanity, and subject. What remains is to witness through the body an immanent Anthropocene experience rather than one of a transcendental character, achieved in an extreme way by organic and morphological modification, particularly through surgery. This marks the result of the historical passage to techno-science as well as interpreting an Anthropocene conversion as power-totalizing. The question is whether this convergence between knowledge and practice is shaping a new experience from the experience of a completely transformed body and under what conceptions or categories the new generations will embody the Anthropocene. That concept can accommodate the treatment of a Neo-Darwinism involving the adaptation of the human species under a new form of consciousness.*

KEY WORDS: natural body obsolescence, anthropo-scenic performance, intervened body, body-work

1. THE BODY AS "SUBJECT REFERENCE"

Beginning with the performative work of the Argentinean artist, Nicola Costantino, "Lo ominoso es el doble,"[1] there arise a host of meanings of the human body as a raw material and conceptual support, related to the main features in what has been the rhetoric or discourses of the anthropocentric manifestation. The point of departure is the reference to the self-awareness (the real body of the artist) faced with its invention and the estrangement that is the outcome of an operation that entails unpreventable repulsion from the "body produced" by the intervening *techne*. Indeed it is the artist's own body, but it is uncertain whether it can be seen as her "double," as

---

[1] Lo ominoso y su doble" ["The ominous thing and it double"]. "Trailer," de Nicola Costantino, Fundación YPF, Puerto Madero, Buenos Aires, June/July 2010.

opposed to being another processed body whose image is a threatening intrusion into the identity-integrity of the *Ego*.

Figure 1. Image from trailer, *The Ominous and Its Double*.

The inquiries of the body have always been a problem, an obstacle, or at least a source of conflict, when understood with the specificity that it claims; that is, the human body that is fitted to the species and defined within it. The practices carried out in individual bodies are tellingly found in historical practices, having been conceived under categories that have often left out the common biological substratum. These gave rise to technologies that naturalized every-thing that was in operation on generic bodies.[2] Modernity gave rise to a fulsome recovery of bodies as a visibilizing of an assigned subjectivity, made to pass from bodies differentiated by social characteristics in the political power context in terms of sexual division, and perhaps the most significant are subject bodies. Such reassigned bodies are "subject" to morphological, abstract, and conceptual objectivities.

The Sartrean *dixit*, "hell is other people," reverts back to the self, as condemnation of the biblical bestowal of freedom: you will be like God. (Gen.3: 5) The body is exposed as a stronghold and source of all human power. "Having a body" and "being a body" express only a difference of degree or intensity, but do not really bring any qualitative difference. The meaning of the expression, "having a body" reduces to "being an object," even though that is not the intended meaning, because it conveys the idea that the experience of body is inseparable from the body-object understood as the body of a person, at least as a reference.[3]

2. BODY, CREATION, HISTORY (AS SUPERNATURAL AND TRANSHUMAN)

The noesis of history reveals all representations as a covering of humanity with eternity.[4] Nevertheless, such representation does not lie in being an inert image, but in being virtual insofar as it has produced effects on the progression of the evolution of the species. What is instrumental here is the deployment of technology, intertwined with the insertion of the experience of acceleration of time. It will be possible to hold off and resist such evolutionary acceleration, and Darwinian Theory will be put in check, along with the long-held and vituperated idea of "the natural" or "human nature" (remembering the social as second nature). The

---

[2] Foucault, Michel. *Tecnologías del yo.* Paidós, 1999, pages 45-94.

[3] Putnam, Hilary. He says: *"We are not brains in a vat." Reason, Truth, and History,* Cambridge University Press, 1981; reissued in: De Rose & Warfield, *Skepticism: A Contemporary Reader,* Oxford UP, 1999.

[4] It corresponds to the hermeneutic notion of temporality according to Paul Ricoeur.

explanations of natural evolution for our species are insufficient because of its location outside time.[5]

Biotechnological fusion is now a present reality in different areas of life; transbiological reality also crosses the conception of industry, since some of the most profitable and at the same time questionable practices are those that "produce" "organicities," autonomous or linked to similar functions of life, to recompose, compensate, improve, or recreate. The obsolescence of the content of the human, of *Homo sapiens sapiens*, is evidenced by the real tendency (or ability) to overcome the biological. Transbiological beings appear under the thinkable forms of the infinite, of an infinity of constitutive assemblages beyond the cyborg.

Anthropocenesis is undoubtedly a transhumanism, the content of which is given by the interactive relation between noötropics, nanotechnology, DNA genetic assembly, etc., which would enable us to consider the controversial topic of the "natural evolution of species."[6] The real goals of the "scientific artist" are only aesthetic; they are attempts to break boundaries into the unexpected question in the field of bioethics. Was this possibility so unpredictable? Was it already in the very notion of biotechnology to be a deconstruction of an autonomous natural order whose determinism never succeeded in bridging evolutionism but in reinforcing it?

Figure 2. Eduardo Kac watering Edunia, 2009.

---

[5] The notion of *energeia* that resists movement is a metaphysical point, according to Leibniz, that differs from that of Cartesian "body" (*res extensa*), inert resistance.

[6] Kac, Eduardo. *Natural History of Enigma.* 2011, www.ekac.org/nat.hist.enig.html. Accessed in February 22, 2017. Eduard (o) Kac introduced a specific fragment of his DNA (extracted from chromosome 2) into a Petunia so that the plant produced "clonal" hemoglobin from himself; gave rise to an "apparatus" conceived as a new being. "Edunia." *"The sculpture's form is an invented protein composed of human and plant parts. The human part is a fragment of my Immunoglobulin (IgG) light chain (variable region). The plant component is from the Petunia's ANTHOCYANIN1 (AN1), responsible for red pigmentation in the flower. More precisely, AN1 is a* transcription factor that controls genes encoding the enzymes that produce the red pigments [in blood]."*"The gene I selected is responsible for the identification of foreign bodies. In this work, it is precisely that which identifies and rejects the other that I integrate into the other, thus creating a new kind of self that is partially flower and partially human: me."*

3. THE BODY AS ANTHROPOCENESIS

It is possible to think that from within the Anthropocene matrix there arises specific interventions on bodies, whether they are "naturally" realized or mediated by extraordinary resources but accessible in some way (economic, technological, material, industrial, surgical, etc.)

The conception of nature as an independent entity is unsustainable in view of the degree of interpenetration between social and natural systems. The Anthropocene is the age of definitive confirmation of human domination over nature, including the species itself.

Man is an animal, and therefore also nature, and has evolved to a point that we are, in the words of Peter Sloterdijk, those creatures that have failed to remain animals.[7] That is why technique is the interactive activity mediated as an extension that lacks biological specificity (feedback learning). The human body is a product of that creative play between biological indetermination and technological capacity for transformation. McLuhan reinterprets the history of the body "knot" and its "sensorial projections" (tetrad), along with the unavoidable changes in consciousness and the dynamic consequences that follow.

Art has always been sustained and supported in and by the body of the artist directly and indirectly, so it was possible that the same body could be a literal support of activity, taking the place of the "work," as a direct product of the poetic, actual being

"*autopoiesis* true." The bodies of artists happen to represent the same means of sense without metaphor despite the recurring fiction. However, the techniques offer mediation to allow the body to fulfill the desire, the "Holy Grail," of the demiurgic artificer. In the current conception of art there has been an obsolescence of the work as a permanent object – both in its materiality and in its referentiality – and in the artist as the "outward" agent of an interior. The body voluntarily placed and "exposed" is the prolific matter to be transcended by an act that makes it strange insofar as it re-presents as another, as a double, without repeating itself. The artist transforms the art in his own experiment, disposing of his body like an obscene end of the "spectacularity" with which art always has been invested. It results also in the expectant and speculative art of the produced, and it has in this way produced the outcome of the hermeneutic circle.

4. THE BODY AS "MOUNTING"

Déotte refers to the body as a knot of (aesthetic and technical) meanings. Basically "there are no bodies"; bodies are labile results, knotted by symbolic, three-way links: of the others, of the imaginary and the strangely appropriate. Déotte's definition of the "aesthetic apparatus"[8] is the

---

[7] Sloterdijk, Peter. *'Regeln Für den Menschenpark." Antwortschreiben zu Heideggers Brief über den Humanismus,* Frankfurt, Suhrkamp, 1999, page 34.

[8] Déotte, Jean-Louis. "Le Musée, un Appareil Universal," Museum International n⁰ 235, Les enjeux de la collection au XXIᵉ siècle, Paris, UNESCO, 2007. *"Un appareil esthétique (camera obscura, perspectiv, musée, photographie, cinéma, vidéo, etc.) n'est, ni un dispositif (au sens de Michel Foucault) ni un médium de communication (au sens de Marshall McLuhan) ni une prothèse (au sens de Bernard Stiegler). L'appareil, c'est ce qui configure techniquement l'apparaître des existences, singulières ou collectives."*

conceptual scheme that best expresses the fact that there are "new existences," not just new experiences. So they are not extensions, devices, or prostheses: they are genuine differential configurations. It points to a continuity of interpolation between nature and culture in such a way that *innervated sensitivities* (sic)[9] in the body create contemporaneity among individuals. If the body is the knot that happens between the real, the imaginary and the strange,[10] that is to say what is never given to us, and then what follows is the impossibility of feeling it as substance, humanity, subject, etc. What remains is to witness through the body an anthropocentric experience anew, that of the era that geologists and geographers have defined as the era of global change by the predominant intervention of human forces resulting in the end of the Holocene.[11]

All technology and in particular biotechnology is already inserted in the everyday conditions that make life possible under new forms (in extension, in exchange, and in creation). Consequently the possibilities of experiences promise to be inexhaustible *prima facie*. The inherent nature of modeled forms marks the historical passage of nature as a "model" toward techno science as totalizing power. Actions performed

under an artificial morphogenesis, including the insertion of specific DNA fragments and surgical aesthetics, manifest the dehiscence of the existing corporeal matter as expulsion and denial of this nature.

The body cannot continue to be spoken of as a biological support predetermined by inheritance in the sense of itself and the species. The non-transcendental feature of immanence is viewed in an extreme way by organic and morphological modification through surgeries and modifications induced in the DNA of any known form of life.

As ending overview: We consider whether it would be possible to speak of McLuhan-style Neo-Darwinism as referring to the notion of the adaptation of organisms along new configurations of consciousness.

6. BODY REFUGE AND RESISTANCE: THE WORK OF NICOLA COSTANTINO

Costantino's work is an emergent work of the flesh, an evolution from the experiences of the images of the living world to her own body as an experimental support. The work that we refer to almost exclusively is the creation of the remarkable film "La Artefacta,"[12] in which the artist can be seen to bring contradictions and specularities into play concerning art and the most organic aesthetic experience: body of self, experiencing its own boundaries. Cutting and

[9] Déotte, Jean-Louis. *L'homme de Verre: Esthétiques Benjaminiennes.* Editions L'Harmattan, 1997.
[10] His reference has been taken from Lacan's scheme on the body.
[11] British Geological Survey and AWG. This change implies a new scenario in the which would be anachronistic to speak of man, world, life, maintaining the same contents and the same relationships that we have used so far.

[12] "La Artefacta" ["The Artefacta"], created by filmmaker Natalie Cristiani to exhibit at the 55th International Art of the Venice Biennale, 2015, nicolacostantino.com.ar/artefacta-trailer.php. Based on Argentina's work "Rapsodia inconclusa" [Unfinished Rhapsody] in the 54th International of Venice Biennale, 2013. castagninomacro.org/page/exposiciones/id/1 58/title/Rapsodia-Inconclusa.

inspecting the body and its folds and "sleeves" are the conscious forms that the artist adopted to allude to the exposure and fragility of the body, in particular the woman's body; the main character is a woman – a psycho-analytic translation of his father surgeon and his mother dressmaker.

In her first experiences close to the performances, the artist sets out to recreate the mythical procedure of *sparagmosis* (dismemberment), a ritual by which all notion of separateness was lost and only flesh in its various forms reigned: flesh of the victim (food), meat of pleasure (of sensory enjoyment) and the flesh of the suffering, looking. The meaning of the materiality of bodies is related to motherhood in the sense of the capacity to receive, in an abstract sense of the container, that which can shelter or contain another. The edge that the artist decides to put in her work/body (undifferentiated) arises when something happens that alters her "normal body" and is not in principle subject to her will in relation to her form: a pregnancy. "More than having a previous space where you put bodies inside, it is the bodies that make the place, the background reflection has to see what the idea of giving and making place means."[13] The new being (expression par excellence of the *touching-you*)[14] is a kind of device of Déotte´s in which he posits differentiation and at the same time establishes a dependence

on certain extrinsic conditions to live. Likewise, a strange event occurs: a spectator from within, who becomes hostile while "lodged" in the uterus and grows according to an extreme intrinsic determinism, that of the human genome with its own DNA. "The strength and presence of the artist is felt, even at a distance," but there is no audience that can complete this peculiar performance save for the fetal "apparatus" itself" (extra-organic). We would think of the intrusion of the other into itself, as trans-organicity from one to-itself into another to-itself: a strange being, differentiated by its DNA, and yet reconnected to substantiate itself in the reciprocal body-matrix.

Who is an artifact? Is it she – Constantine – herself? Is it her apparatus that was bordering on constituting a metaphor of trans-formation in itself, as an oversized expression of transcendence in her own determination? *Apparatus* is an image and likeness of itself, but strangely "outside." The bodies can be touched, both by oneself and by others (*partage* by Nancy) because the border ambiguity "overflows" every concept and also including the experience of the touch. But in Constantine's work, touch is nevertheless the most distant: forms are far removed from touch, repulsive in terms of tactile sensations, but the gaze traverses them under forms of touch.

The ambiguous bodies, over-whelmed and tactile, depart from Kant's anachronistic imperative to consider man always as an end, never as a means. Nowadays, imposing a phenomedia biotechno-anthropocene makes possible the transformation of

13 Derrida, J. *El Tocar, Jean-Luc Nancy.* Translated by Irene Agoff, Amorrortu, Bs.As., 2011, pages 399-401.
14 "*Se toucher-toi,*" original expression of Jean-Luc Nancy to signified "touch by self as other self."

man into a virtual reality of being, a possibility between multiple, almost inexhaustible power to be and become.

The end and media made indiscernible virtual and material possibilities of technology have reduced the telos to the present, closing the expectation of future. The time is reduced instantly to "right now."[15]

Figure 3. Images from *The Ominous Thing and Its Double.*

4. CONCLUSIONS

According to psychologist Kenneth Ring, author of *The Omega Project*, the transformation of Anthropocenesis "leads us toward a fundamental reorientation of our personal world of values and visions but it is more important that they also seem to accelerate a psychophysical transformation."

However it is probably to break through the threshold of ordinary consciousness to access "transpersonal dimensions" that a new, "more advanced" species is emerging, according to the anachronism of the paradox in current academic discourses. Perhaps a "different species" is in play here, whose limits are no longer biological, for the creative imagination has given rise to a trans-material, transorganic, unstoppable, and synergistic direction of changes sustained in forms of transcendence operated here on Earth, the body no longer without it. The living body is no longer alive in virtue of the biological processes fixed in the alleles originating from the species, but by the intrinsic capacity of having developed in ontogenesis a total capacity to induce arbitrary changes above all purpose and necessity, to own the joy to do, to enjoy, to be another.

When Danto says "the world does not deserve the beauty," he appeals to the sustenance of the human as historically understood to construct that which supposes the beautiful as its teleological correlate.[16] In Plato, however, beauty was identified with truth, immutable and eternal. Could it be actually this eternity situated as the matter of life itself, signified by a biotechnology that intervenes directly in anabolism and cellular catabolism, that is, in the mitochondrial center itself of non-aging, of non-mortality? Are we forming a new anthropocentric experience based on the experience of a totally transformed body? Under what topics will the new generations realize it and for whom?

And in this context, is art the reflexive moment "about" aesthetics, a need for separateness leading to oblique consciousness? It is what has been saving us from extinction since

---

[15] This idea means "Ecstasy," according to Augustinian phenomenological concept of consciousness and temporality.

[16] Danto, Arthur. *El abuso de la belleza. La Estética y el concepto de Arte.* Translate by Carles Roche, Paidós, 2008.

the Neanderthal was subsumed by Homo sapiens, although its DNA is still embedded in ours, a consciousness that reflects and pauses, but only to metamorphose. This is the reverse intention of Kafka's reference to the deplorable and abandoned. The monster, the ominous, is the desired thing, never reached. The Anthropocene belongs to an almost undivided totality, where sensory synergy translates into experience on the body; technology is the objectification of this possibility more real than material. If the body is the medium, and the medium is message, then what is the end of the intervened body? It may even be death – contempt or indifference to and for life – although paradoxically the cultural call to live a healthy life to prolong it, and death is worthy, even appealing, to Euthanasia.

WORKS CITED

Danto, Arthur. "El Abuso de la Belleza. La Estética y el Concepto de Arte. Trans. Carles Roche. Barcelona: Paidós, 2008.

Déotte, Jean Louis. "Le Musée, un Appareil Universal." Museum International No 235. Paris: UNESCO, 2007.

Déotte, Jean Louis. "L'homme de Verre: Esthétiques Benjaminiennes." París: L'Harmattan, 1995.

Derrida, Jacques. "El tocar, Jean-Luc Nancy." Trans. Irene Agoff . Buenos Aires: Amorrortu, 2011. 399-401.

Foucault, Michel. "Tecnologías del yo." Trans. Mercedes Allendesalazar. Buenos Aires: Paidós, 2008. 45-94.

Kac, Eduardo. "Re: Natural History of Enigma." Online posting. 22, Feb. 2011, www.ekac.org/nat.hist.enig.html.

The Artefacta. Prod. Chiapetta, Francesca and Cristiani, Natalie. Dir. Cristiani, Natalie. Film. Venice Film Festival, 2015.

Trailer. Prod. Nicola Costantino. Dir. Nicola Costantino and Victor Kesselman. Film. Puerto Madero, 2010.

Putman, Hilary. Reason, Truth, and History, United Kingdom: Cambridge University Press, 1981.

Sloterdijk, Peter. Regeln für den Menschenpark. Antwortschreiben zu Heideggers Brief über den Humanismus. Frankfurt: Suhrkamp, 1999, 34.

Anthropocene and Art

ALBERTO CARRILLO[1]
MAY ZINDEL[2]

[1]BENEMÉRITA UNIVERSIDAD AUTÓNOMA DE PUEBLA
PUEBLA, MÉXICO
[2]UNIVERSITY OF THE AMERICAS PUEBLA
PUEBLA, MÉXICO

ABSTRACT: *In this paper we offer some considerations about the Anthropocene as the period in Earth's history marked by the presence of the human being as a geological factor, which is especially apparent when considering the products of urbanization: paved roads and night-time illumination when the Earth is viewed from space. Both factors show the scale of human presence on Earth and the corresponding impact on it as our environment. Building on these factors, we reflect on the relationship between art and the consciousness of the anthropocenic character of the epoch. The main point is that the contribution of art to localized or particular ecological changes as well as to changes in the way we think and behave thereby makes both art and human nature ecological.*

KEYWORDS: art, experience, desertification, pollution, biodiversity, scale

Artists are in a unique position to effect…environmental changes…Art changes the way *people look at reality. In its most positive mode, art can offer alternative visions.*

—Matilsky, *Fragile Ecologies*

THE ANTHROPOCENE AND THE GEOLOGIC
Wilderness, Roads and Lights

The thesis that the last great geological period, the Holocene, does not reach into the present but instead ends at some point in the past, about 15,000-12,000 years ago since from that point on man became a factor in geological transformations, is well known and convincingly argued.[1] So for the purposes of this paper, we accept that thesis.[2] Nevertheless, it is worth stressing some aspects of the ways in which man changes Earth systematically, and this in fact makes humans themselves into a geologic factor.

Certainly, there is the widespread assumption of anthropogenic climate change, but independently of this hypothesis, there are other very important changes that are occurring in nature that are undoubtedly linked

---

[1] In that period agriculture, domestication, and the first permanent human settlements appeared. See Mumford, *The City in History* 10.

[2] See Davis, *The Birth of the Anthropocene.*

to human activity: a) pollution, b) desertification, and c) diminishing biodiversity, which could be considered as global changes, or at least as widespread changes,[3] and all of them are caused by agriculture, stockbreeding, mining, lumbering, fishing, and, of course, industrialization and urbanization. Such activities and changes began when human societies transitioned from being migratory or nomadic to being settled.[4]

Already the simplest permanent housing demands expelling nature from it; housing and nature as such are incompatible.[5] Not only a tent or a hut, but all the more so a construction made of stone or bricks, demands a flat floor and the elimination of vegetation on it, not to mention the expulsion of almost all types of animals except for pets.[6] In addition, agriculture and stockbreeding already in their simplest forms mean a profound transformation of the environment around housing. Since its inception agriculture caused a

radical decrease in plant and animal biodiversity.[7] In the same way, livestock farming also reduces plant and animal bio-diversity.[8] Mining and lumbering involve a profound trans-formation of nature, even if they do not occur in the immediate vicinity of the dwelling. Of course, when societies become settled, it leads to the development of more or less extensive villages. However, the first step in housing development that had a very notable impact on nature was the creation of ceremonial centers and settlements around them. Such assemblages had a much more significant impact on the natural environment than simple villages. And with the first urbanizations, those of the Assyrians and Chaldean, the Egyptians, the Mayas, etc., civilization had begun (Mumford, *The City in History* 10, 33, 41).

Already in the time of the Roman Empire a new phenomenon became evident: paved roads. Roads were the outcome of the uniform productive and administrative methods of the Romans, linked to their conquering armies and designed for constant heavy-duty traffic.[9] Along these routes

---

[3] Held refers to "the contemporary levels of transboundary pollution, environmental common—problems and resource squeezes" (Held 381).

[4] Held: "[w]e have ample evidence and accounts of premodern environmental problems." (Held 381-82) The case of the Mayan is one of many examples of premodern environmental problems: "In Mesoamerica, Mayan civilization collapsed around 800 A.D., due in part to extensive tropical deforestation and erosion." (Foster 38).

[5] The occupation of caves as dwelling (*The City in History* 7) meant the systematic effort to expel everything that naturally grew in them. In general, "(…) the primal forest has always been a menacing place that stands for the unknown, the uncontrollable — either in the sense of civilization unbound, or in respect of 'wild' animals like wolves or bears." (Fiedler, "Culture, Heritage, and Diversity").

[6] Above all dogs (*The City in History* 10).

[7] Mumford refers to "the first clearings for agricultural purposes" (*The City in History* 10) and says they had a negative effect on hunting by driving animals "into the swamps and highlands," leading to further clearing and stockbreeding (21).

[8] Protecting cattle demands exterminating other animals feeding on it.

[9] Mumford: "(…) the paved road widened the province of transportation, and gave the city command over men and resources in distant areas." (*The City in History* 71) Furthermore: "Rome (…), its aqueducts and its viaducts and its paved roads, cutting unswervingly across hill and dale, leaping over river and swap, moving in unbroken formation like a victorious Roman legion." (205) Mumford

arose fortified military colonies that demanded intensive mining and forestry activities, along with extensive agriculture and stock-breeding, while allowing the control of vast areas with more or less large local populations under the rule of the military colonies.[10] So civilization gave way to empire. The Roman Empire with its armies became a new climax of the impact of the human being in nature.[11] By contrast, the medieval era was characterized by the abandonment of roads and the decline of urban centers, and the vast majority of the surviving European social groups returned to the village, falling below the level of civilization.[12]

The next steps in the development of the geological character of man were the rise of large-scale manufacturing and industrialism; both demanded immense amounts of natural resources and led to the colonization of America and then of Asia and Africa.[13] Lumbering, fishing,

agriculture and mining became the fuel of industrialization, reaching a global scale and supplying raw materials and food to the growing population and making possible new and extensive urbanizations.[14] Today industrialization and urbanization are the factors that determine the "humanization" of the planet as a whole, characterized by the disappearance of virgin nature and the enormous correlative growth of the world's population. The geological consequences are far-reaching and include very definite ecological problems, among which pollution, desertification of large areas of land, and reduction of both plant and animal biodiversity are especially important.

Certainly, a problem that currently receives great attention is climate change. However, some argue that although such a change is undeniable, it is not anthropogenic. This is the claim that the human contribution to such a change through CO_2 production is in fact negligible, and that climate change is due to the

underscores the Roman "capacity for handling solid objects, and (...) its more generalized aptitude in the standardization and regimentation of large masses" (205) .
[10] Mumford: "By the ruthless pillage of the food-producing territories of Asia and Africa, the Roman Empire appropriated far more energy than Greece, with its sparse abstemious dietary and its low standard of living." (Mumford, *Technics and Civilization* 379; *The City in History* 207).
[11] Mumford insists that Roman engineering "(...) stood supreme in the aqueducts, the underground sewers, and the paved ways (...)" (*The City in History* 216).
[12] Mumford: "(...) a disorganization and diminishment of the forces of civilization did characterize this period: the worst effects became visible only around the ninth century" (Mumford, *The Culture of Cities* 14) .
[13] Mumford: "Man's conscious relation to the earth underwent a profound change in Western Europe in the fifteenth century. (...)

But collectively, the great era of exploration and colonization, which opened in the sixteenth century, introduced a period of terrestrial neglect" (*The Culture of Cities* 304).
[14] Mumford: "Trade, industrial production, mechanization, organization—all these facts helped expand the life of the cities. But they do not account for the feeding of the hungry mouths. People do not live on coins, even if the local mint has the exclusive privilege of coining them; nor do they live on air, even though 'city air makes people free' as the saying went. The thriving life of these towns had its origin in the agricultural improvement of the countryside: an improvement that was spotty, and vitiated ultimately by the reckless deforestation that accompanied it, but sufficient to create unheard-of stores of energy (...)" (*The Culture of Cities* 24).

natural cycles of the Earth.[15] Obviously, the thesis of anthropogenic climate change would be of great relevance to the argument that man is in fact geological in nature. However, given that the discussion is not closed, we will limit ourselves to the three major phenomena already mentioned: pollution, desertification, and destruction of biodiversity, of which there is sufficient evidence, to underline the fact that the human being is a geological factor.

The three great ecological problems mentioned above undoubtedly show that there is no such thing as nature or Earth, considered as an autonomous system that is dynamically independent of any other autonomous system. Clearly, culture, man and his activity have direct effects on the natural environment. Pollution, desertification, and the decline of biodiversity plainly show that the dynamics of culture as a whole have a determining influence on what could still be called natural history; that is, it shows that we live in the Anthropocene, an epoch in which man is a geological factor of first importance.[16]

It is interesting to illustrate the effect of human presence on the Earth, the humanization of it, with one of the most notable phenomena now observable when viewing the Earth from space. The night illumination of large areas of the Earth, resulting primarily from urbanization, indicates the reduction of wilderness and makes evident the geological character of humanity: In fact, the nocturnal illumination of the Earth shows the degree or *scale* of human impact on it.

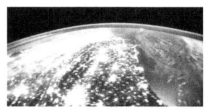

NASA, ISS. "La Tierra de noche, desde el espacio." [The Earth at night, from space.]

The Geologic Factor and the Scale

In our daily life most of us are related to our immediate environment, even the spatial layout of our surroundings a few hundred meters away may surprise us when we see it on a map. In fact, we are aware of our spatial location only along well-defined paths, but that is not the same as grasping the arrangement of paths in relation to each other and with respect to their environments. In other words, our spatial orientation easily fails as soon as things are out of sight. Added to this, our memory is equally limited in capturing the past. Usually we can remember what we did throughout the day, but it becomes difficult to remember what we did the day before. As for the months and years before, we do not really have a real grasp of time; we remember only relevant events and

---

[15] See: "As it turns out, the Antarctic ice-core record has produced *zero* evidence consistent with the view that changes in CO_2 concentrations are responsible for major changes in planetary temperatures. Quite to the contrary, the ice-core evidence suggests that CO_2 concentrations are a *consequence* of temperature changes, not the cause. (Gil-White, "The Antarctic Ice Cores and Global Warming").

[16] Latour has emphasized that the relationship between man and nature has to be seen as a combination of which hybrid entities, such as the ozone hole or global warming, result (Latour 72).

know their sequential order in a merely conceptual way but without a true sense of the passing of time. Conceptually we know that A occurred 10 years ago and that B happened five years before A, but we do not *feel* the time elapsed, whether it is fifteen years or ten years.[17] The restriction of our sense of space and time to the here and now is the most serious obstacle to our being aware of our geological character.

In fact, our grasp of space and time is related to experience, which is always sensory, that is, related to the here and now. Space and time that go beyond our experience do not make any sense. Nevertheless, we can have a sense of space and time that goes beyond the here and now by representing them visually.[18] Such is the problem of scale. Using a scale means to represent any spatial or temporal magnitude, especially one that is outside the limits of our experience, either by reducing or magnifying it.

Kant regarded the mathematical sublime as that which goes beyond our capacity of sensory apprehension by virtue of its magnitude. In this sense, the sublime is what is too overwhelming for our experiential awareness (Kant §26). But there are also things that are below the threshold of our experience, for example, our sensory grasp of the very small or the very fleeting, say,

things smaller than one-tenth of a millimeter or of less duration than one-tenth of a second. For humans, such things make no sense perceptually speaking, so that they have to be brought into our experience by means of a visual representation, which in the spatial case signifies a magnification. This leads to the problem of our geological character.

Of course, what makes awareness of our geologic nature difficult is that our impact on Earth refers to magnitudes that far surpass the here and now – the limits of our experience. They are magnitudes that for us have only a conceptual meaning, unless we represent them in a sensory or perceivable way, meaning, visually.

THE ANTHROPOCENE AND THE ARTS

We can conceptually understand the magnitude of man's impact on Earth; for instance, we can say that a) by 1900 there were 10 million elephants, but because of hunting, agriculture and urbanization, by 2000 there remained only half a million,[19] and b) in six days, considering here only America, as many cows are slaughtered as the remaining number elephants.[20] Worldwide, in a single day, more cows (825,000) are slaughtered than the remaining number of elephants.[21] Conceptually,

---

[17] Recall the situation of the prisoner without a calendar; he has to make one in order to know, not to feel, how much time is spent in captivity.

[18] McLuhan refers to the representation of time between the Chinese and the Japanese in a sensorial way through gradations of the smell of incense (McLuhan 146).

[19] "¿Cuántos elefantes hay en el mundo?" *Aprender.org.* 7 February 2016. Web. 6 July 2017.

[20] "USDA's official number of animals killed for food" *Animal Liberation Front.com.* Web. 6 July 2017.

[21] Ruiz, Adriana "¿Cuántos miles de millones de animales criados en condiciones

all of that is clear. However, seeing is generally more impressive than mere conceptualizing; moreover, in their artistic productions, artists prefer not conceptual but rather sensory modes of representation. Artists also tend to be very sensitive to, very "tuned into," the global problems that each epoch faces. No wonder then, that in recent years there have been at least three relevant art exhibits concerned with the problem of the Anthropocene:

- 9th *Taipei Biennial 2014*, with Nicolas Bourriaud as curator, who proposed as curatorial concept "art in the Anthropocene,"

- *Fragile Ecologies*, 1992 – 93, with Barbara Matilsky as curator who showed the disharmony between humans and nature,

- *La Bienal del Fin del Mundo*, Ushuaia, Argentina, 2011, devoted to art in the Anthropocene.

In these exhibitions artists turned primarily to images, and many of these images show different scales in order to present the reality of our anthropocentric character. For our part, we also resorted to the photographic medium and through our photographs we intend to induce a reflection about our planet by emphasizing the notion of scale.

Below, we present the photographs: *Serie I: The Geologic. Too Big – Small*

inaceptables son sacrificados cada año?" *Fronterad. Revista digital.* 6 December 2012. Web. 8 July 2017.

proposing programs or carrying out ecological initiatives of wide scope, but rather in contributing to the development and reinforcement of the *category* of the geological, simply *as* a category; that is, as a mode of orientation in the world. A category is a mental attitude, not a definite idea; therefore, it is a precondition of experience and in fact, a structure of experience which, as such, is nothing more than merely a common form of many experiences.

Independently of the concrete nature of their work, many artists participating in exhibitions of the kind mentioned above presuppose the geologic character of human beings. And that is what artists can do. Their specific and most valuable ecological contribution is not to point out a specific ecological problem, but to help develop the mental attitude that makes it possible to act in our daily life automatically on the pre-supposition of our geological being, which is to assume that we are intertwined with nature. That is nothing more than an automatic concern on behalf of ecology, which will lead us to think and behave ecologically on the basis of an all-embracing attitude.

CONCLUSION

We want to emphasize that the contribution of artists to an understanding of the ecological problems arising from our geological character does not depend on

WORKS CITED

"¿Cuántos elefantes hay en el mundo?" *Aprender.org*. 7 February 2016. Web. 6 July 2017.

Davis, Jeremy. *The Birth of the Anthropocene*. Oakland: University of California Press, 2016. Print.

Fiedler, Andreas. "Culture, Heritage and Diversity." *Council of Europe*. 2007. Web. 8 July 2017.

Foster, John Bellamy. *The Vulnerable Planet: A Short Economic History of the Environment.* New York: Monthly Review Press, 1999. Print.

Gil-White, Francisco. "The Antartic Ice Cores and Global Warming." *Historical and Investigative Research.* 9 June 2014. Web. 8 July 2017.

Held, David. et al. *Global Transformations. Politics, Economics and Culture.* Stanford: Stanford University Press, 1999. Print.

Kant, Immanuel. *Kritik der Urteilskraft (1790).* Vol. 39. Leipzig: Verlag on Felix Meiner, 1922. Print.

Latour, Bruno. *Nous n'avons jamais été modernes. Essai d'anthropologie symétrique.* Paris: La Découverte: 1991. Print.

Matilsky, Barbara C. *Fragile Ecologies: Contemporary Artists's Interpretation and Solutions.* New York: Rizzoli, 1985. Print.

McLuhan, Marshall. *Understanding Media. The Extensions of Man* (1964). Cambridge: The MIT Press, 1994. Print.

Mumford, Lewis. *Technics and Civilization.* London: George Routledge & Sons, 1946. Print.

---. *The City in History. Its Origins, Its Transformations, and Its Prospects.* New York: Harcourt, 1961. Print.

---. *The Culture of Cities.* New York: Harcourt, 1938. Print.

NASA, ISS. "La Tierra de noche, desde el espacio - The Earth at night, from space." YouTube, 16 November 2011. Web. 04 July 2017.

Ruiz, Adriana "¿Cuántos miles de millones de animales criados en condiciones inaceptables son sacrificados cada año?" *Fronterad. Revista digital.* 6 December 2012. Web. 8 July 2017.

"USDA's official number of animals killed for food" *Animal Liberation Front.com.* Web. 6 July 2017.

Zindel, May. "La postnatura, la deforestación y las prácticas artísticas actuales: la fuerza del arte crítico y el cambio de fenomenalidad." Diss. Universidad de las Américas Puebla, 2017. Print.

Memory of the Future: Cecilia Vicuña's Participatory Poetics and Murray Bookchin's Unfolding Dialectical Freedom

Lisa Daus Neville

SUNY Cortland
Cortland, New York, USA

ABSTRACT: *Chilean poet, visual, conceptual, environmental artist, and filmmaker, Cecilia Vicuña, revalorizes the ancient Incan technology of* quipu *as a gathering of originary emptiness. In this empty core our essential connectedness can be realized. Vicuna's complementary dialectic of openness and interdependence is theorized by North American philosopher, Murray Bookchin, as an ecology of freedom in which human being becomes aware of itself as nature's own self-expression. This paper wonders the role of art in today's field of intensifying ecological crisis and economic injustice and suggests that it may only be the art and activity that requires our participation in order to effectuate itself that has the power to heal our calcified discrete identities and return us to our evolutionary origins in an ecology of interdependence.*

KEYWORDS: Cecilia Vicuña, *quipu*, Murray Bookchin, poetry, ecology, Zen

During a 2012 roundtable discussion of Andean textiles and contemporary art, Cecilia Vicuña runs a three-minute film of a *quipu* in creation. Vicuña's revalorization of *quipu* – an Incan technology for recording and communicating information consisting of variously knotted thread – has been ongoing for over 40 years. Whether massive installations involving miles of rope or spontaneous gestures with string, Vicuña's *quipu*, like her poetry, is designed to connect viewers to a deep core of self-knowledge, in which conventional identity empties, making space for the realization of newly connected information. We see projected on the screen the artist's hand as she lowers a skein of thick red yarn/thread over the side of a brick apartment building. Filmed from angles that demonstrate its aliveness and its alterity, the thread breaks, it floats, it furls, tumbles, dangles and undulates. As we struggle to name what we are seeing, the thread begins to puddle on the concrete ground, writhing as an animate creature might. The film is called *Umbilico*. As it ends, Vicuña looks toward her audience and begins her address this way: "Today as I was walking to you to come with you, my love, James O'Hern said this to me on the sidewalk… 'the function of the *quipu* is to keep the brain open to call the senses so you are in the [*kon*] folded space of fractal geometry'" (*Quipu Talk*).

In the emphasis on chance occurrence in both the *quipu* as performed and the way Vicuña chooses to open her talk, we can discern a fundamental dedication to the experience of being open and, more precisely, to *being openness* that is the fulcrum of all her art. The openness at the core (*umbilicus*) of Vicuña's poetic is both an ontic and an epistemic. It is what we are and the method by which we know what we are. In order to convey existence itself as vast opening, art practices must disclose the way in which things are made up of that which they are not. This way, or *dao*, is traditionally understood as fullness-in-emptiness; Vicuña calls it "emptiness within sound and silence" and identifies it as the "source and reason" of all her poetry (*Quipu Talk*). We do not live in a world in which self-sufficient objects possess absolute boundaries, but in a dynamic in which co-dependent processes express their emptiness temporally as impermanence and spatially as interdependence. *Umbilico* is an experience designed to communicate both its utter transience and interdependence. The poem is composed of a series of inter-nesting spaces, forces and objects. The performance by definition and by design cannot be replicated. The movement of the thread is determined by flow and density of the air, the infinitesimal movements of the poet's hand, whims of passersby... As the thread snakes through space limned by a building, a city, an ocean, a sky, each undulation references another

opening. "The word and the thread behave as processes in the cosmos" (*Word and Thread*). In Vicuña's metapoetics, things and words – and words are things – are actualized in the present in their actual ontic state as openness. A world in which things resolutely shine forth as real within the context of their codependence is made possible by and reflected in the complementarity of her dialectic.

> The word is silence and sound.
> The thread, fullness and emptiness.
> (*Word and Thread*)

Quipus rearrange space. And they reorient bodies in space. As Cecilia Vicuña walks through the cityscape of Santiago or Bogatá or New York paying out red string, as she criss-crosses a river or tributary or highway intersection with thread, she enacts a living metaphor. Living metaphors are performative not only in that they enact themselves but in that they require our participation in order to be true (Kleinberg-Levin xiii). The most basic level of this participation is awareness. When we aware we realize the world as it shines forth, which in turn requires realizing that same world *as oneself*. If otherness were "out there" how would we ever know it? "I see the poet/translator as the person who goes into the darkness, seeking the 'other' in ourselves, what we don't wish to see, as if this act could reveal what the larger world keeps hidden" (*Language is Migrant*). The method of working with our experience so that it reveals ourselves (in our alterity) to ourselves is called by one North American philosopher, "hermeneutical phenomenology." Kleinberg-Levin suggests that our experience harbors potential that is not only unactualized but also unseen. Such potential may be disclosed through inquiry and participation in the rich metaphorical nature of language and phenomena (xii). Open inquiry begins as attentiveness to the present moment; an attentiveness Vicuña exhibits as she spontaneously prefaces her remarks by voicing a thought that arose that morning from the mental-emotional space shared with her partner. "I had to stop and write it down and read it to you," she tells the other participants, re-constellating the interpersonal connections in the room to form a new whole. O'Hern's insight into the function of *quipu* in fact describes a gestalt perspective of wholeness. Fractal geometry describes a world of self-similarity, a chiasmus in which the parts perform the wholes and the wholes are folded back into the parts. Vicuña's *kon* space is a place where dualities meet and are neither one nor two. Her 2010 film, *kon kon*, references the beach at Concón, where she created some of her earliest environmental art – where waters meet sea and sacred mountain meets Earth. Here it is impossible to definitely determine the actual line that demarcates them. Or the boundary between person and surrounding environ. The space folds the openness of water with all that is non-water; the openness of Earth to be constituted from all that is other than itself. This dialectic of the complementarity and co-dependence of individuation and interdependence requires a form of language that is aware of itself.

We need to translate language into itself so that IT sees our awareness, translating us into another state of mind (*Language is Migrant*).

The poem is not speech, not in the Earth, not on paper, but in the crossing and union of the three in the place that is not. ("Introduction").

Early in her poetic career, Vicuña began "opening" words, taking apart their roots and segments to uncover new meanings as dormant associations sprout from the word's opened form.

> I saw a word in the air
> Solid and suspended
> Showing me
> Her seed body
>
> Se abría y deschacía
> y de sus partes brotaban
> asociaciones dormidas
>
> Enarmorados
> en amor, morado
> enajenados
> (*Unravelling Words* 29)

Much is accomplished through these openings in which words themselves voice their interactivities, their shared origins, and their unities with things. For Vicuña words are neither tools of representational reasoning nor discrete parts of a closed system of signification, "A word is pregnant with other words" (*Word and Thread*). Her method of "crossing" words is the compatriot to her method of "opening" them. Words are numinous phenomena, fractal energies, inherently meta-phoric and thus carrying within themselves the capacity to cross over and carry meaning from one system to another. Crossed, they are uncoupled from their represen-tational functions and free to express their true affinities and codependences. Vicuña's poems, not only those made of words, but those constructed of found objects, sounds, lines of sight, movements of thread and environmental patterns as well, are designed to confound habituated subjectivity. "No one will see the same palace/once the threshold has been crossed/no one will see the same flowers" (*Unravelling* 31). These are metaphors and symbols that reorient vision and transform consciousness. Kleinberg-Levin calls the mode of working with experience, language and being as living processes hermeneutic because it neither seeks to discover a pre-existing reality, nor claims to make *ex nihilo* an entirely new creation. The truth is the complementary union of being and boundlessness and it is utterly dependent on our participation. "These metaphors make themselves true," Kleinberg-Levin writes, "by changing us" (xiii-xiv). Opening and crossing the English word *instant* with the Spanish verb connoting urgent insistence, Vicuña constructs a woven text of light and being ("el/e/star"). *Instan* is a verbal *quipu*, the word become thread, the thread erupting into word voicing the urgent expression of the most fundamental nature of what comes into being – living itself out as time – as perpetual transformation. In East-Asian Buddhism this is called the ten thousand things in arrival arising out of and identical with pregnant emptiness. The Daoist sages that Vicuña read as a child know this as the dynamic interplay of heaven and earth. Out of this ceaseless exchange: novelty, creation and disappearance.

Since 1966 Vicuña has been making "structures that disappear," what she calls *precarios*, small sculptures and installations made of found objects, or human litter. This "Arte Precario" is impermanent and sacred. Much of this early work was never recorded; objects were created from the detritus of biological and human life and they dissolve back into the space of their emergence. "The tide erased the work as night completes the day" (*QUIPOem*) Vicuña writes as she places one of the small sculptures at the intersection of land and sea. She weaves thread through landscape as the ancient Celts constructed cairns, as a recognition and realignment with the inherent generative creativity of the cosmos. Space itself is organized, and so begins to recognize itself and to communicate self-awareness.

> Poetry lives in certain places
> where the cliffs need nothing
> but a sign to come alive:
> two or three lines, a marking,
> and silence begins to speak.
> (*Unravelling* 17)

Weaving acts as Vicuña's primary metaphor – in a very real way carrying meaning from one economy to another – and simultaneously constitutes a vital spiritual technology. Weaving is dialectic made concrete; a form of connecting that does not erase difference, or broker compromise, through orientation with the empty space within which warp and weft take place. Weaving is pattern-making, design that demonstrates the underlying forces motivating its form. Indigenous Andean weavers inscribe the principle of complementarity by which sound and silence, emptiness and form constitute each other. One anthropologist writes of such patterning that "the background becomes just as important as the design itself, the two working dynamically together to form one identifiable whole" (Joslyn 52). In Quechua, the word for language is thread. "*La palabra es el hilo*," Vicuña speaks, the empty thread that winds its way through all of her poetry, both actually and figuratively. "To speak is to thread and the thread weaves the world" (*Word and Thread*).

I look to Vicuña's participatory spirit-art practice to answer the question that has gathered increasing weight for many of us during the past few months: How do artists respond to a zeitgeist of social and ecological crises that threaten to extinguish us? What pressure do massive extinctions and global-scale environmental shifts put upon the image and the word, the arrangement of body and sound? Anthropocene art, it has been remarked, is obsessed with loss and disappearance (Macfarlane 4). Is it merely a question of scale? Or are we up against the end-stop imagination has always harbored within itself due to the impossibility of a discrete consciousness contemplating its non-existence? I could say, after all, that the majority of art and philosophy over 2000 years and myriad cultures is obsessed with loss and disappearance; that the problem of longing is eternal precisely because we are never coeval with the objects of our desire. One twentieth-century Zen master called "civilization and culture" "nothing but the collective elaboration of

illusory desires" (Kodo 50).

In the context of Zen and its Daoists roots, loss is the inevitable result of the ongoing current of generative-extinctive energy that constitutes our reality. Sorrow as the emotional background of human life provides an opportunity for awakening as a profound awareness of the flavor of objective sorrow may facilitate a loosening of attachment to those illusory desires. While civilizations may be organized around directing fear and desire, individuals are organized around centers of identity – aggregates of habit, instinct, and enculturated emotional-cognitive activity. Awakening to reality as it is requires both dis-identifying with one's center of identity and realizing the presence of things directly. I have suggested that the power and truth of Vicuña's art presences itself through the revelation of new dimensions of experience. The disclosure of truth occurs only to the extent that those who participate are engaged and transformed through their participation. One translator of Chinese poetry defines poetry as "a spiritual practice opening consciousness to an immediate experience of the existence-tissue that [opens into] thought and language" (Hinton 58). A primary vehicle for such opening is "the emptiness of the thread" that is "the door to all [Vicuña's] art." She continues:

> You enter into a timeless, nameless space. You access the invisible that is there because no information is lost as quantum physics says. That is the *quipu* metaphor; that is how you access collective intentions

because this empty space is egoless.. The *quipu* was holding me, grabbing me into its *quipu-ness*, into the continued weave of its thread [where one is connected to] the vibrations, the frequencies of the universe. There are – look at that – universes and these universes talk to each other! (*Quipu Talk*)

The *quipu* is a medium through which gathered frequencies communicate their common origins. If we call ecology the dynamics of our interdependence in relation to other beings and the world as a whole, then freedom consists in recognizing that interdependence as a platform within which we interactively shape reality. Vicuña's art concerns itself most completely with the advancement of freedom in that it 1) recognizes the threats to free life in the structures of political tyranny, economic injustice, xenophobic othering, ecological amnesia and the unbearable tension of emotional isolation; and 2) enacts a *re*-membering, *re*-connection, *re*-cognition, *real*-ization of interdependence in metaphors that seeks to heal and to "transport" consciousness across paranoid disconnectedness toward a source of actual power and freedom. In this same talk in London she later says cogently, "If people were connected to [true power] we wouldn't live in a system of injustice and exploitation and destr[uction] of the Earth that we are in. So there's a profound reason to keep us separated, because if we're separated and ignoring each other, we've less power, it's very simple" (*Quipu Talk*).

As many others have pointed out, anthropocenic discourse abstracts human being out of the tissue of being itself. As we declare our current situation to be a foreseeable result of "human nature," we universalize what is in fact a specific program of economic enrichment of a few, undertaken with the tacit approval of much of the industrial world and shift our focus away from the structures of global capitalism, colonialism, and militarism that drive destruction of habitat. The anarchist philosopher and social ecologist, Murray Bookchin, began emphasizing this inextricable linkage in 1970 when he declared "all ecological problems to be ultimately social problems, requiring social solutions" (Price 139).

Bookchin accounts for humanity's singular position on the planet by defining the relationship between first nature, by which he means the cumulative evolutionary activity of biological nature with a "vibrant and interactive inorganic world," and second nature, or the evolution of human social, cultural, political structures." Second nature is entangled with and arises from first nature. Most significant here is that Bookchin regards the relationship of humankind to its environment as both interdependent and evolutionary. Humankind cannot coherently distinguish itself from the natural world and thus a position in which it assumes nature to be a basket of "resources" to be utilized or managed is fundamentally incoherent. At the same time, humankind's enfoldment in its natural environs is not static; it unfolds as the creative construction of new systems and cityscapes grounded in human proclivities and desires. Bookchin asserts that human capacities for conceptual thought and symbolic language that seem to transport us "out of nature" are themselves byproducts of a biological evolution of ever-differentiating and increasingly complex life forms. He observes, "Humanity's vast capacity to alter first nature is itself a product of natural evolution" (*Social Ecology* 30-31).

This natural evolution is understood as a dialectical striving that tends toward increasing complexity and diversification, increasing freedom, and self-consciousness. Therefore second nature develops both, in continuity with, and antithetically to, first nature. It is not in the scope of this paper to examine Bookchin's dialectic in detail – but I would like to present three specific details of Bookchin's social ecology as they pertain to ecological dilemma and human freedom. One, social ecology asserts a nondual perspective in which social and biologic nature are not locked in an adversarial relationship but regarded as part of one evolutionary process; one in which humanity's evolutionary unfoldment occurs as a distinct generation of first nature. Two, it stresses the participation of individual life-forms as critical to the path of evolution itself. As each form of life "exercises an increasingly active role in their own development, it expands its regions of freedom. As organisms differentiate and are allowed greater range of possibility their nascent subjectivities become "a *striving* activity…that ultimately yields mind,

will and the potentiality for freedom" (Price 83).

Biologic evolution, therefore, requires increasing human freedom, not *from* nature, but toward active choice made possible by an awareness of the interdependence of first and second natures. The full implications of this interdependence Bookchin calls "free nature" in which *human being occurs as nature rendered self-conscious*. While Bookchin is an anarchist philosopher with little relish for metaphysics, he is theorizing here the inter-being of human and non-human existence in clear terms. In a recent essay, Cecilia Vicuña describes such awareness as a creative force capable, through simple attentiveness of healing "the destruction we are creating" (*Language is Migrant*). For Bookchin, too, ecology is a matter of ethical urgency. Grounding his non-resolving dialectic in science that asserts that biological evolution moves toward ever-greater levels of differentiation, complexity, and self-reflexivity renders it possible to collapse an *aporia* between the rational and the good. Rather than imagine that science cultivates a trans-ethical realm, Bookchin understands the science of ecology to constitute an ethical paradigm for humanity. Those political and cultural acts that "lead to social development that will seek increasing balance through diversity, decentralization and spontaneity," are ethically sound while those that tend toward increasing mechanization, uniformity and restriction of choice are not.

Third, Bookchin identifies the development of social hierarchies as determinant of the structures of domination that oversee both social injustice and ecological collapse. Bookchin strongly advocates against the point of view that humanity's drive to dominate nature is an outgrowth of nascent agrarian societies' struggles for survival. Instead he argues that this drive stems "from the emergence of domination that existed *previously in society itself*" (*Social Ecology* 149). These early systems of hierarchy lend practical and ideological support to structures of domination resulting in a diminishment of human freedom and a consequently felt "necessity" to subdue the natural world. Bookchin points to what he terms "organic societies" as offering an alternative to the view of nature as a harsh realm of necessity. Organic societies imagine first and second natures coeval in the process of unfolding complexity and richness. It is important to note that Bookchin is not hearkening to a "noble" pre-industrial vision of non-differentiation with nature. The people who make up Bookchin's organic societies *are* differentiated from their environments and *do* exercise rational and creative thought. The crucial distinction with modern human societies is their lack of social hierarchies, not their lack of social structure. For Bookchin a non-combative view of nature directly follows harmonized relations within the society precisely because first nature is both vital and innately *social*. He describes such an outlook in *The Ecology of Freedom* thusly:

> Nature as Life…enters directly into consociation with humanity – not merely harmonization… just as the rustle of the leaves

and grasses is part of the air itself – not merely a sound borne on the wind… The people do not disappear into nature or nature into the people. But nature is not merely a habitat; it is a participant that advises the community. (47)

Cecilia Vicuña conducts events in which she ties herself to the audience with thread. She moves through the room with a ball of red thread or textile ropes and weaves them through and around the assembly. Very often, people will begin to move against and test the tensile strength of the thread or feel into its connectivity. Vicuña names this event *el quipu vivo* and writes: "Who is performing; the poet, or the audience?/United by a thread, we form a living *quipu*; each person is a knot and the/ performance is/what happens between the knots" (*Spit Temple* 99). This living *quipu* brings to mind a metaphor from the *Avatamsaka Sutra* that has become well-known, that of Indra's net. In the story, an immortal, Indra, had an infinite net stretched across the cosmos and in the knots between the strings of the net had placed a glittering jewel. Within the facets of each jewel are reflected all other jewels so that the process of reflection-self-reflection is boundless. As Buddhist truth, this metaphor expresses the paradoxical non-duality of both the infinite whole in which the individual participates and the absolutely unique and transient presence of each participant. Working with these metaphors phenomenologically, we experience the most basic facts of our existence, the umbilical threads that retain our connection to the Earth, its rivers, its boulders, the stars and each other. Such cords cannot be broken, although they often do remain unseen and unrealized. Art practices that are grounded in a real experience of openness and participation with the cosmos are precisely those that can transform human being into actualizing, as Vicuña writes, "itself and the whole at once" (*Instan* np).

WORKS CITED

Bookchin, Murray. *The Ecology of Freedom*. Cheshire Books, 1982.

---. *The Philosophy of Social Ecology: Essays on Dialectical Naturalism*. Black Rose Books, 1996.

Joslyn, Catherine. "Representations of Nature in Andean Textiles." *Journal of Global Initiatives: Policy, Pedagogy, Perspective*. Vol. 7 No. 2, *Peruvian Trajectories of Sociocultural Transformation*, Article 4. 2012.

Kleinberg-Levin. "Foreword." *Wholeness Lost and Wholeness Regained*, Herbert Guenther, State University of New York Press, 1994, pp. ix-xiv.

Macfarlane, Robert. "Generation Anthropocene: How Humans Have Altered the Planet Forever." *The Guardian*. 1 April, 2016.

Hinton, David. *Existence: A Story*. Shambhala, 2016.

Price, Andy. *Recovering Bookchin: Social Ecology and the Crises of Our Time*. New Compass Press, 2012.

Uchiyama, Kosho. *The Zen Teachings of Homeless Kodo*. Wisdom, 2014.

Vicuña, Cecilia. *Instan*. Kelsey St. Press, 2002.

---. "Introduction," ceciliavicuna.com

---. *Language is Migrant*. Harriet the Blog, poetryfoundation.org, April 18, 2016.

---. *The Precarious/QUIPOem: The Art and Poetry of Cecilia Vicuña*. Ed. Catherine de Zegher, trans. Esther Allen, Wesleyan University Press, 1997.

---. *Quipu Talk*. University of London, International Conference: Textiles, Techne and Power In the Andes, Roundtable on Andean Textiles and Contemporary Art, March, 2012, *Vimeo*.

---. *Spit Temple*. Ed. and trans. by Rosa Alcalá, Ugly Duckling Press, 2012.

---. *Unravelling Words and the Weaving of Water*. Trans. Eliot Weinberger and Suzanne Jill Levine, Graywolf Press, 1992. *Word and Thread*. www.asu.edu/pipercwcenter/how2journal/vol_3_no./vicunawordthread.pdf.

Art and Experiences of Embodied Disrupted Reality

DAVID ROMERO MARTÍN

UNIVERSITY OF THE BASQUE COUNTRY
BILBAO, SPAIN

ABSTRACT: *The purpose of this paper is to identify the way in which art can disrupt the subject's everyday experience of the world and self. The proposal starts from the hypothesis that art offers experiences of embodied disrupted reality, and this statement is based on the parallelism between certain artistic experiences and certain psychological conditions that are known as dissociative disorders (concretely, depersonalization and derealization), which challenge the subject's sense of reality and self, and lead the subject to experience some level of detachment and a sense of loss of familiarity with respect to the world and the self. These aspects are also particularly felt in immersive environments. Immersive technologies (virtual and augmented reality) offer an important laboratory for perception and sensoriality, taking into consideration the embodied basis and the first-person perspective of the user-experimenter. In this context, art offers a series of strategies that allow the user to undergo a shift in experience, affecting the sense of embodiment and reality. To explore these notions, I refer to some phenomenological implications of the experience of dissociative disorders and the interrelation between art, technology, and dissociative disorders. Finally, I offer an analysis of three artistic interdisciplinary projects ("Systems," by Briand, "Labyrinth Psychotica," by Kanary, and "Decelerator Helmet," by Potthast"), taking into account the particular ways of embodiment and sense of reality they trigger in the user. Based on the parallelism between art and dissociative disorders and its dialogue with immersive technologies, this article aims to contribute to a phenomenology of embodied disrupted reality from art.*

KEYWORDS: art, dissociation, immersive technologies, embodied disruptive reality

INTRODUCTION

In 1917, Shklovsky coined the Russian term, "ostranénie" (Shklovsky 1991), which has been translated into English as "de-familiarization" or "estrangement." Within the context of Russian Formalism to which this author belonged, this concept referred to a group of strategies developed from art in general and from literature in particular. These strategies contributed to a "deautomatization" of our perceptions and a break of our everyday familiar experience, in order to make us adopt new perspectives about what we know.

Precisely, I want to refer to the continuation of this contribution of art to a disruption of experience referred by Shklovsky, taking it to the context of the development of a series of artistic projects that make use of different immersive technologies.

As virtual and augmented reality devices are spreading and becoming increasingly more affordable, immersive technologies are, more than ever, at our fingertips. We can even use our smartphone and turn it into an instant virtual- or augmented-reality device by simply attaching it to some VR goggles.

Different disciplines, such as cognitive science and psychology, have, decades ago, adopted immersive technologies as a kind of laboratory to explore several issues related to our perceptive and interactive nature with respect to the world we inhabit. One such example is the issue of bodily ownership (Petkova and Ehrsson; Slater et al.). However, interest in immersive technologies is not exclusive to the scientific domain, and within the field of artistic endeavor, virtual and augmented reality play an important role in creating and exploring multi-sensorial experiences, as can be seen in the work of artists such as Krueger, Lozano-Hemmer, and Briand, among others.

The break with everyday life and the familiarity of experience to which Shklovsky pointed can also appear as a phenomenon that permeates our perceptions and life experience under certain so-called psychopathological conditions such as depression, anxiety, phobias, posttraumatic stress disorder, or schizophrenia. All these conditions share, in general, the emergence of certain dissociative disorders (in particular, depersonalization and derealization), as disorders that challenge the subject's sense of reality and self and that lead the subject to the experience of a general detachment and a sense of loss of familiarity. From this aesthetical-psychological parallelism, I suggest the hypothesis that art, within the use of the first-person perspective of immersive technologies, develops strategies that can lead to experiences of embodied disrupted reality.

To explore these ideas, I start with an understanding of the main features of the experience of dissociative disorders; then move to later explore the potential relation between art, immersive technologies and dissociation. Finally, I analyze certain phenomenological implications of three artistic interdisciplinary proposals that make use of immersive technologies.

DISSOCIATIVE DISORDERS

According to the *Diagnostic and Statistical Manual of Mental Disorders* (American Psychiatric Association [2013] 291), dissociative disorders are defined as a "disruption of and/or discontinuity in the normal integration of consciousness, memory, identity, emotion, perception, body represen-tation, motor control and behavior." In general terms, a dissociative disorder implies the disruption of certain areas of psychological functioning that affect and change the individual's perceptions.

Two of the most common referred dissociative disorders are depersonalization and derealization. These disorders generally go along with certain mental conditions that imply a change in the subject's perceptions, such as anxiety, depression, phobias, posttraumatic stress disorder or schizophrenia, among others.

On the one hand, depersonalization is defined as a feeling of detachment from one's own thoughts and body. On the other hand, derealization refers to the sense of detachment from the environment and to a general sense of unreality.

Depersonalization and derealization are in fact difficult to differentiate, as they usually emerge together, affecting the person's whole experience of self and the environment within which the subject is located. According to Noyes and Kolb (84), reported symptoms related to the sense of reality from sufferers of dissociation affect both the sense of identity and personality and the perception of external world, which is experienced as unreal. Among the most frequent and general symptoms reported, most sufferers' descriptions agree in their accounts of depersonalization and derealization as states of "dream-like perception," "robot-like perception" (as if the person were somehow driven by an external force, and somehow losing a sense of agency), detachment from one's own body, one's own thoughts and the environment, and a general sense of unreality, as if reality were fake, artificial or "like being in a movie" (Simeon and Abugel).

Official psychiatric definitions, along with reports that appear in clinical and psychological literature made by people who have suffered from dissociation, refer to a range of symptoms that seem to be effects coming from a science-fiction context, in which sufferers question the nature of their own perceptions, their own environment and identity. Although, as Ratcliffe points out (182), in these experiences, people retain "intact reality-testing," unlike experiences of delusion, for instance.

Dissociative disorders refer in this way to a shift of a qualitative kind that affects the subject's experience, which, in González's terms, is referred to as "experience of estrangement,"[1] a notion with which the author problematizes the difficulty of understanding the experience of "familiarity-deficit"[2] (González) with respect to the world and the self that characterizes these disorders. The experience of dissociative disorders leads us to problematize and usher in a phenomenology of embodied disrupted reality.

ART, IMMERSIVE TECHNOLOGIES AND DISSOCIATION

The term "ostranénie" or estrangement, referred to by Shklovsky, points precisely to a group of artistic strategies aimed at breaking our familiarity with that which we know, as well as "deautomatizing" our perceptions. These notions seem to be related to the features of dissociative experience. In order to understand the way in which the artistic context contributes to this phenomenology of embodied disrupted reality, I want to refer to some concerns from phenomenology and technology that reveal the capacity of art to develop strategies that provoke shifts in terms of awareness and sensoriality.

Merleau-Ponty manifests a particular interest in the arts and their ability to reveal to us the world as it is perceived within our experience, in contrast with the world as scientifically structured and theoretically conceptualized, as the author claims in *The World of Perception*. While Merleau-Ponty often points to the genre of painting,

---

[1] Translation by the author. From the original in Spanish: "experiencia de lo extraño." See

González 2012.

[2] Translation by the author. From the original in Spanish: "déficit de familiaridad." See González 2012.

and particularly to Cézanne's works, I propose to revisit his approach in order to highlight the potential of immersive technologies as they provide opportunities for the development of perceptive multi-sensorial experiences within the context of art that are to be experienced and embodied from the user's first-person perspective.

Jones offers a definition of "Sensorium" as "the subject's way of coordinating all the body's perceptual and proprioceptive signals as well as the changing sensory envelope of the self" (8). According to Jones, art reflects and reveals a strong interest for different factors that have can play a role in modifying human sensoriality, especially technological mediation, claiming that art, in this sense, allows us to "try on concepts, experiences, and altered states" (ibid.). Jones also points out the fact that artists establish complex kinds of relations with technologies, for example, the "immersive" kind; the "cave paradigm" kind, which appeals to the use of head-mounted display systems; and the "Alienated" kind, in which technology is used with the goal of triggering a certain shock in the user, offering ways of changing the senses and inducing disorientation.

These ideas seem to align with and be materialized within the affordances of immersive technologies. One of the main aspects of these technologies to consider is their functioning with respect to the user's first-person perspective, through the use of technological interfaces that coincide and overlap with the user's perceptions and embodiment. Virtual reality situations offer the possibility to explore features of our experience

and interaction with the world and ourselves in a multi-sensorial way, through variables such as bodily ownership, presence and immersion, and agency, among others.

Precisely, some references allude to a series of disturbing symptoms experienced by virtual-reality users during and after immersive experiences. These symptoms are described as "VR sickness," which conveys the occurrence of symptoms such as dizziness, nausea and lack of balance, among other effects. Nevertheless, some authors (Aardema et al.; Searles), refer specifically to dissociative symptoms triggered by VR experiences (depersonalization-derealization). Users report particular sensations of unreality during the "discontinuity in perceptual environment" (Aardema et al); that is to say, a recognition or perception of the process of transition from the virtual to the real world, a reaction which is also referred to in terms of "existential hangover" (Searles).

Both the affordances of these technologies with respect to the multi-sensorial dimension, and the "existential," "dissociative" effects they trigger, allow immersive technologies to offer a potential con-text within which to develop artistic strategies that seek to trigger certain "dissociative" effects with respect to the user's sense of reality and self. Such a case may be illustrated by a user who interacts with these technologies and whose "implicit body" (Stern) is altered and constitutive of the multi-sensorial experience.

VR-ARTISTIC EXPERIENCES OF EMBODIED DISRUPTED REALITY
In order to illustrate the way in

which this phenomenology of embodied disrupted reality manifests within artistic practice, I propose a reference to three concrete artistic interdisciplinary projects that make use of immersive technologies for the development of different strategies that affect the subject's perceptions and embodied basis, altering perception of the world and of self.

"Systems" (Briand 1996-2006) is a series of interactive installations, such as "SYS*05.ReE*3," "SE*1/MoE*2" (Briand 2006), among others, in which the artist proposes experiences of interferences and exchanges of different perceptive inputs through technologically mediated perception, with the use of head-mounted displays. In these installations, several users create what the artist calls an "enfleshed network," through which participants receive random and shifting inputs coming from the first-person perspective perceptions of the different users, as well as from other audiovisual material. This exchange of technologically mediated perceptions leads the user to an experience of spatial and identity disorientation, which the artist explains through the concept-strategies of "controlled schizophrenia" and "mental migration." In his own words: "Temporary mental migration is about being able to project oneself without turning one's nature on its back; without having to choose between one's origin and the projection one is heading for" (Briand 116). In this way, we find an artistic proposal that looks for a particular way of triggering awareness in the user, who has to maintain personal integrity at the level of identity, location and sense of reality, despite the virtual and shifting perceptive

interferences to which the subject is exposed, and that defy the subject's senses of ownership and agency (Gallagher and Zahavi 161). As Briand explains, this break of the familiar experience with respect to the self and the environment in which the users are located leads to the discovery of alternative dimensions of experience: "Our usual sense references are perturbed, but it is this de-stabilization that allows us to discover new things" (Briand 116).

Precisely as a pathology that radically problematizes the user's integrity, identity, fluency of experience, and sense of reality, among other aspects, schizophrenia entails for Kanary a point of departure for artistic creation and research, through her project "Labyrinth Psychotica."

It consists of a multimedia interactive installation and a wearable device with which the artist makes use of immersive technologies (virtual and augmented reality) and digital tools to distort the user's perceptions at several levels so as to simulate the experience of schizophrenia. The artist refers to these tools as a form of "digital LSD" (Kanary). In this way, symptoms such as reality disorder, spatial and temporal fragmentation, loss of sense of perspective and self, and visual and auditory hallucinations are experienced by the users, who move through the labyrinth proposed by Kanary, while their perceptions are distorted and disrupted through strategies of audio-visual manipulations in real time. The artist understands her project as a tool for empathy with the schizophrenic condition, understanding this tool as a "prosthesis for imagination" (Kanary 2013), and through which the users are exposed to a temporal break of their familiar perceptions from a first-person embodied perspective, allowing users to approach something close to what it might be like to have psychotic and schizophrenic experiences.

Lastly, Potthast proposes from the field of design his project entitled, "Decelerator Helmet," which is also based on the use of an individual head-mounted display that lowers the audio-visual, techno-logically mediated perception of the user. The temporal deceleration leads users to a particular state of awareness of their surroundings and their own body, triggering the experience of a phenomenon by which the received perceptions overlap with the information that users already know from the environment. In the words of Potthast (4), this phenomenon triggers a "strange" feeling that relates to the "knowledge about the discrepancy of our actual environment and what you percept from it." In this case, the overlap between the user's own perceptions and the technologically mediated perceptions provoke a certain state of disorientation. This can be understood as a dissociative strategy that leads users to question and experience a particular awareness of their own limits of perception and the limits of the technological device, through which interaction with the world takes place.

CONCLUSIONS

This paper has attempted to develop a few aspects of a phenomenology of embodied disrupted reality that is based on the potential relationship between dissociative disorders (depersonalization and derealization) and certain artistic proposals. From both emerge experiences that lead users to break with the familiarity they have of the world and of themselves. I have mentioned the capacity of art, along with the potential of immersive technologies, for the development of strategies that seek to trigger experiences that have a sensorial and bodily impact on the user, who participates in and constitutes such experiences. Through strategies such as "controlled schizophrenia," "mental migration," "digital LSD," temporal deceleration of perceptions, and technologically mediated perception, art offers experiences that challenge the user's everyday perceptions. Users feel a disruption that affects their sense of identity, reality, bodily limits and spatial location.

As it has been shown, a dialogue between dissociative disorders, art and technology opens multiple possibilities at the level of research and creation, allowing for the break of tacit and familiar aspects of our experience that leads us to widen our perceptive horizons and to reach for other facets of reality.

WORKS CITED

Aardema, Frederick; O'Connor; Kieron; Côté, Sophie; Taillon, Annie. "Virtual Reality Induces Dissociation and Lowers Sense of Presence in Objective Reality" *Cyberpsychology, Behavior, and Social Networking*, Volume 13, Number 0, pp. 1-8, 2010, (online), PubMed.

American Psychiatric Association. *Diagnostic and Statistical Manual of Mental Disorders* (5th ed.). Washington, D.C., 2013.

Briand, Mathieu. Interviewed by

Evelyne Jouanno. "Mathieu Briand. Hacking contemporary reality." *Flash Art*, Vol. 37 N° 238, 2004, pp. 115-116.

---. *Systems* (online), 2006. www.mathieubriand.com/category /installations/systems/ (accessed 2 Feb. 2016).

Gallagher Shaun, and Zahavi, Dan. *The Phenomenological Mind. An Introduction to Philosophy of Mind and Cognitive Science*, Routledge: Oxford, 2008.

González, José. *Vivir lo extraño. Un estudio psicopatógico sobre el déficit de familiaridad*, Publications URV, Tarragona, 2012.

Jones, Caroline A. *Sensorium. Embodied Experience, Technology and Contemporary Art*. The MIT Press, Cambridge, 2006.

Kanary, Jennifer. *Labyrinth Psychotica* (online), 2013. Available in: www.labyrinthpsychotica.org (accessed 10 Jan. 2016).

Merleau-Ponty, Maurice. *Phenomenology of Perception*, Routledge, London and New York, 2002.

---. *The World of Perception*, Routledge, London and New York, 2004.

Noyes, Arthur P. and Lawrence C. Kolb, *Modern Clinical Psychiatry* (6th ed.). W.B. Saunders, Philadelphia, 1964.

Petkova Valeria I, and H. Henrik Ehrsson. "If I Were You: Perceptual Illusion of Body Swapping," *PLos ONE*, Vol. 3, Issue 12, 2008, pp. 1-9 (online).

Potthast, Lorenz. *The Decelerator Helmet. Project Description* (pdf.), 2012.www.lorenzpotthast.de/ downloads/project-description_ decelerator-helmet_lorenz-potthast. pdf (accessed 5th May. 2016).

Ratcliffe, Matthew. *Feelings of Being: Phenomenology, Psychiatry and the Sense of Reality*, Oxford University Press, Oxford, 2008.

Searles, Rebecca."Virtual reality Can Leave You With an Existential Hangover," *The Atlantic*, 2006, www.theatlantic.com/technology/arch ive/2016/12/post-vr-sadness/ 511232/ (accessed: 3 Feb. 2017).

Shklovsky, Viktor. *Theory of Prose*, Dalkey Archive Press, Champaign & London, 1991.

Simeon, Daphne and Jeffrey Abugel. *Feeling Unreal. Depersonalization Disorder and the Loss of the Self*, Oxford University Press, New York, 2006.

Slater, Mel; Spanlang, Bernhard; Sanchez-Vives, Maria V.; Blanke, Olaf. "First Person Experience of Body Transfer in Virtual Reality," *PLoS ONE*, Vol. 5, Issue 5, 2010, pp. 1-9. (online).

Stern, Nathaniel. *Interactive Art and Embodiment: The Implicit Body as Performance*, Gylphi Limited, Canterbury, 2013.

Mediating Knowledges:
How Theater Transmits Partial Perspectives

BJORN BEIJNON

UTRECHT UNIVERSITY
UTRECHT, THE NETHERLANDS

ABSTRACT: *This article examines how the human perception of knowledge is structured in the empirical world. It is often argued by scientists that facts in this empirical world can be perceived, which makes us believe that this world is an objective world. However, the human way of making sense of the world is individual and embodied, which causes the creation of an individual world for every human: a body-world. The empirical world is in this case a shared space for multiple bodies that agree on the causality of certain events and objects in that space. Every body-world therefore has its own partial perspective on the knowledge in this shared space, which is formed by the physiology of the body, the cultural background, and the identity of the person. The theater has the power, through the techniques of re-enactment and disruption, to give its audience insight in other situated knowledges from different partial perspectives. It can therefore connect different situated knowledges and create ecological knowledge: the awareness of the connected network of knowledges that is produced in various body-worlds on what is happening in the shared space. Only then can we emancipate knowledge and embrace the various partial perspectives that this shared space of body-worlds has to offer.*

KEYWORDS: knowledge production, enactive cognition, objectivity, body-world, re-enactment, disruption

INTRODUCTION

It is peculiar how opinions on art can differ; although we go to the theater with our friend to see the same performance, we all have different opinions on if it touched us, if we liked it, or if it got us intrigued. This is not any different from the way we encounter objects and events in our daily lives: we all confront different circumstances with different emotions, after which we develop an opinion on that what we have come across. Whenever faced with similar circumstances, either in the same empirical world or in a mediated version of that world, a person will have connotations that are decoded though a personal referential framework (Hall 165). Opinions on various encounters that we have in our surrounding world, as with art, are thus always bound to a system of encoding connotations as well as their decoding.

If this system of connotations is correct, this would mean that everyone has his or her own personal referential framework through which to perceive the world. In relation to this statement, two questions come to mind: [1] How can we ever talk about objectivities, or even say something "objective," since everyone has his or her own subjective way of perceiving the world?; and [2]

To what extent is it possible to get insight into someone else's perception?

This issue under consideration here is how theater, as a form of art, has the capability, through two different performance strategies, to give an understanding of other perspectives and experiences.[1] Both *re-enactment* and *disruption* have the power to show different mindsets towards what a performance re-presents. To show how theater has these possibilities, I will use Milo Rau's *Five Easy Pieces* (2016) and Dries Verhoeven's *Guilty Landscapes Episode I* (2016) to show how each of these performances apply these two strategies to create the awareness for the spectator that there are multiple perspectives on what is represented in the performance.

MAKING SENSE

One way of describing cognition, or the way humans make sense of their surroundings, is provided by Francisco J. Varela et al. in their 1991 book, *The Embodied Mind*, in which Varela and his colleagues combine the cognitive science approach of using mindfulness in understanding how cognition works. The authors define cognition as follows: "Cognition consists in the enactment or bringing forth of a world by a viable history of structural coupling" (205). Cognition is thus not simply higher-order mental processes, but rather is the subjective enactment of the creating of a world through the interaction between a person's body and the environment. Cognition, and making sense of the world therefore lies in enactment.

Varela and his colleagues were among the first to use this *enactive approach* in the investigation of cognition. Cognition, or basically the process between human perception and thought, was not defined as a brain activity or a fulfillment of "the mind" through the body, but as a mechanism of a thinking body (Varela et al. 145). The mind becomes in this enactive approach an *embodied mind* (148-49): the act of bringing forth a world lies in the body itself. Our body has, according to this approach, the capability to create, through the input of different senses and a personal referential framework, not only an image of a world, but a *whole* world (205).[2]

---

[1] Although the same argument could be made for other art forms, like film, paintings, and photography, I have chosen theatre to be analyzed in this article. The same strategies can be distinguished in these other art forms to create an understanding of other perspectives on that what is represented in them. These strategies are then not only positioned in the performance, but in editing, lighting and the use of various colors; every art form has its own appliance of these two strategies to create the same effect.

---

[2] Varela, Thompson, and Rosch are not the only authors that use the enactive approach to analyze cognition. Alva Noë, also uses the enactive approach to describe how we actively perceive that what is represented to us with the help of our sensorimotor skills. On visual and haptic perception, Noë argues: "Through attention, probing, and move-ments of the eyes, visual experience acquires content in much the same way that touch does. Vision and touch gain content through our skillful movements. We bring content to experience by action. We *enact* content" (100). Similar to the arguments of Varela et al., Noë makes the point that perception is bound to skillful structures, or in his case movements, to facilitate the experience of what is represented. Noë's argument is therefore that

When taking the enactive approach, one should notice that the mind and the body can't be seen as separate from one another. Through different sensations, the body has the capability to create a world for the subject who perceives this world as the world she encounters in her daily life. This world is, however, not simply a visualization of the *empirical world*, an outside, objective world that is waiting to be explored by the senses of individual humans. As Alva Noë suggests: "The world we inhabit and explore as perceivers is encountered in the first instance not as housing…facts and properties, but rather as *mediating* our active exploration" (167). Since the body encounters different circumstances every moment, a personal referential framework is used and refreshed in every instance of the body's confrontation with an object or event. The world that is constantly built by our framework is what I will call the *body-world*. This world is always subjective since it is bound to the personal encounters of someone's body in an environment.

BUILDING THE WORLD

What is known as the empirical world is nothing more than a shared space and time among bodies that have agreed on shared knowledge of certain objects and events. The empirical world is, on the view asserted here, the *shared space* of different body-worlds, where some causal events and objects are seen as "facts." However, these facts are at their core nothing more than shared opinions from different bodies. When these shared opinions no longer agree about the existence of the object or event, it would lose its objectivity. For example, imagine coming across a book with a red cover. Various bodies undergoing a specific physiological state and situation of language-use have agreed that the color of the book cover is red. However, if either the language or the perceivers' physiological response state changes upon encountering this book cover, the color may be determined as blue, for example. We objectively state that the book cover is red because the judgment is based on an agreed shared experience that we have among our body-worlds. In a shared space of bodies, the color of the book cover becomes objectively red, as long as our bodies keep agreeing on that in this shared space.[3]

What must be clear now is that there is no hierarchical difference in the objectivity of what is known as the empirical world and the body-world, since both rely on bodily encounters that may have different experiences with "objective" events or objects. However, a question that remains unanswered is how this

---

phenomenological reflection on the character of what is perceived suggests that certain features are present as *available*, rather than as represented: "The world is within reach and is present only insofar as we know (or feel) that it is" (67). We build our own "world" through the action of our perception of that world.

[3] Although this example is based on only the sense of sight, this way of objectifying the empirical world is also the case for the other traditional senses: hearing, taste, smell, and touch. To a certain extent, the same could be argued for the non-traditional senses: balance and acceleration, temperature, proprioception, and pain.

agreement in the empirical world works: On what, exactly, is this agreement based?

This agreement is based on two things. First, there is a shared physiological state of the body through which various bodies experience their surroundings as being the same. Through our perception, we have the shared capability of seeing the example of the book cover as red. However, people who suffer from achromatopsia (cortical color blindness), do not have the capability of seeing the color red in the book cover; instead they will see it as black.[4] If everyone's brain were to become like someone with achromatopsia, we would no longer see the color red on the cover, but the color black, and that would be the objective color of the book cover. The objectivity of our perceptual encounters in the empirical world is thus subject to the shared physical experience of a majority of bodies.

Secondly, our agreements in the empirical world are culturally embedded. As Gilles Deleuze and Félix Guattari state in their book *What is Philosophy?* in the chapter, "Geopolitics," "Thinking takes place in the relationship of territory and the earth" (85). Deleuze and Guattari distinguish "territory" and "earth" as two components on which knowledge production is based. The

Earth is in this case the geographical spot through which different bodies can move through the years. When these bodies settle on this spot, they *territorialize* this place: they embrace it with their own shared immanence, friendship, and opinion (88). However, the Earth often gets de-territorialized, when other bodies conquer the Earth. The territory of the old inhabitants then either becomes extinct, or gets changed (88). The new bodies then re-territorialize the Earth and bring their own new territory. In this cycle of Earth and territory, culture in a geographic place is constantly in transition through a battle of bodies that conquer the Earth. Our cultural agreement on facts in the empirical world thus depends on the contemporary territory that we are living in as bodies. [5]

---

[4] What we see as healthy is directly related to biopolitics: a social normalization of what the stereotype body in a society should look like. Unfortunately, for the scope of this article, I cannot elaborate on this purification of human bodies in Western societies. For more information on biopolitics, see Michel Foucault, *"Society Must Be Defended"* (2003) and *The Birth of Biopolitics* (2008).

[5] Up to now, I have not yet elaborated on the construction of identity. Someone's identity should always be observed as being *intersectional*. This means that: "...gender and ethnicity (and those other factors by which we are assigned a social position) are interdependent, interwoven systems of ideas and practices with regard to differences between people. In other words, gender, ethnicity and class always come into being simultaneously and in relation to each other" (Wekker and Lutz, 24). Our identity is thus by birth already formed by different "sections" through which we can be categorized. This can, for example, be our gender, ethnicity, or class. Seeing our identity as a formation of these different things gives us a deeper and more complex understanding of practices of inclusion and exclusion by going beyond binary and hierarchical thinking. This intersectional approach on identity thus has the power to see connections between our "sections" and the cultural place in which we live (Winker and Degele, 58).

DIFFERENT KNOWLEDGES

In collaboration with our personal referential framework, our identity forms our perspective: our body-world. The body-world is then capable of giving us a "partial perspective" on the shared space, which is known as the empirical world (Haraway 583). Donna Haraway argues that "only partial perspective promises objective vision" (583), since it gives us our own trustworthy embodied knowledge. According to Haraway, the type of knowledge that is produced by our *partial perspective* is thus always *situated knowledge*: "That the object of knowledge [is] as an actor and agent, not as a screen or a ground or a resource, never finally as slave to the master that closes off the dialectic in his unique agency and his authorship of "objective" knowledge" (592). The purpose of our body-worlds is that they, from their partial perspective, have the possibility to generate situated knowledge. Connecting these knowledges is the key for understanding the shared space:

> We seek [knowledges] ruled by partial sight and limited voice – not partiality for its own sake but, rather, for the sake of the connections and unexpected openings situated knowledges can make possible. Situated knowledges are about communities not about isolated individuals. The only way to find a larger vision is to be somewhere in particular. (590)

It is thus very important to not only create situated knowledge, but also to make connections with other body-worlds and their situated knowledge. In this way, we may get a broader understanding of a shared object or event.

THEATER AS KNOWLEDGE MEDIUM

So how do we share our situated knowledges? Theater is the ideal medium to convert someone's situated knowledge to another spectator by creating a controlled shared space in which various bodies can spectate a certain partial perspective on what the performance represents. As stated in the introduction, theater can do this through two strategies: re-enactment and disruption. These strategies will be analyzed by considering two different performances.[6]

Re-enactment: Reliving Knowledge

To show how re-enactment, as a performance strategy, has the power to give spectators insight into other partial perspectives, I will use the performance *Five Easy Pieces* by Milo Rau. In this performance, seven young children (aged 8 to 13) re-enact different parts of the life of the Belgian child-murderer, Marc Dutroux. During this performance, the children are asked by a director to re-enact the roles of various lives that Dutroux touched. The children were asked to play the role of, for example, Dutroux's father, one of the kidnapped children, and the

---

[6] Theatre is in this case for me a *theoretical object*: "It obliges you to do theory but also furnishes you with the means of doing it. Thus, if you agree to accept it on theoretical terms, it will produce effects around itself [and] forces us to ask ourselves what theory is. It is posed in theoretical terms; it produces theory; and it necessitates a reflection on theory" (Bois et al. 8).

police officer who handled the Dutroux case. Every role was highlighted in a different scene during the performance. In every scene, the theatergoer saw how the director positioned a camera in front of every child who played a role in the film he was making. The camera footage was then played live on the screen that hung above the stage.

The case of Dutroux is well-known in the Netherlands: in the 1990s, there was a lot of news coverage on this particular case and on the disappearances of children in Belgium. Most of the Dutch audience therefore already had knowledge of how this case was handled and how Dutroux's crimes had been uncovered over the years. However, through the re-enactments in this performance, the audience was capable of getting new insights in their "Dutroux knowledge." By "re-living" the roles of various characters that are portrayed on stage, the audience is invited to get new insights in the knowledge that they already have on the case; the established *authoritative* knowledge that the audience already had from the news is contrasted with *alternative* knowledge that is provided by the embodiment of people who have dealt closely with the Dutroux case (King 17). The availability of a "live" body for the senses of the audience creates a sensory medium through which their knowledge production gets more engaged to another partial perspective on the case than when provided the same information through, for example, television.

The knowledges in the network of different situated knowledges of the Dutroux case in this performance are, what Katie King calls *transmedia knowledges* (289). By letting multiple children embody different roles, the audience is invited to perceive a bigger picture of the knowledge that it already has about the case.[7] At the same time, the performance shows the audience how the knowledge that it has formed of the case up until now is bound to framing. By filming each performance, the "live" stage director shows how various perspectives can be framed by a camera. The audience is then invited to see how what they perceive on the stage is different from the same thing they see on the big screen hanging above the stage. In this way, the performance is able to show the audience that there is not one objective way of seeing the Dutroux case, but that understanding of it is always bound to different situated knowledges.

Disruption: Rethinking Knowledge

For showing how disruption has the possibility of giving insight, I will use the performance *Guilty Landscapes Episode I*, by Dries Verhoeven. In this performance, one spectator is allowed to enter a darkened empty

---

[7] Katie King uses the term "kit" to show how humans can get insights in other situated knowledges through re-enactments. For her, this has more to do with our cultural agreement with the empirical world, since she directly couples it to 'territorialization'. She states: "By scoping and scaling among their various "kits" we come across opportunities for becoming progressively more alive, and, through each new exquisite sensitivity to each already existing but yet momentary horizon of possible resources and infrastructures, local exigencies, and differential memberships, we *add* these to our worldly territories" (300).

room, which consists of nothing more than a placard sign that explains what sort of techniques are used to make the performance happen. On one of the walls, the inside environment of an Asian factory is projected with various workers working on different machines. The individual spectator is invited to look at the projection while being surrounded by the constant noise of the machines. Suddenly one of the workers stops what she is doing and walks towards the projection. From this moment on, the worker starts to mirror every movement that the spectator makes. After some time, the worker comes closer to the screen and puts on a pair of headphones. The noise in the room suddenly stops, and the woman starts to lie down on the floor. By making some hand gestures, she invites the spectator to lie down next to her, after which she will stand up. She will then continue doing her work, after taking off her headphones, and the noise returns. The performance has now ended and the spectator can leave the room.

Most Western citizens are not ignorant of the fact that most of their products are not produced in the West but in a "faraway" country. Because of news reports and documentaries, most people have an idea of where their products come from and under what sorts of conditions the workers making these products have to work and live. The lives of these people are, however, often ignored in the West: we have knowledge of the conditions, but we do not want to be touched by these conditions that may be horrible in

our eyes (Groys 125). In *Guilty Landscapes*, the spectator has the idea that she is literally brought into contact with someone who is living under these circumstances. Our bodies are, with the help of a projector, taken to the place that we often like to ignore. Our situated knowledge of this place and the conditions are, in this case, disrupted by taking the body of the spectator to a "live" time and space on the other side of the world.

The knowledge that someone may have of a place is rethought through this disruption: how is it to be in such a factory and communicate with one of the workers? We know about the existence of such places, although we often ignore it. This performance creates, however, the awareness that this place does actually exist by creating an *uncanny* situation: the experience of the self as other in the space of technology, making a material of split subjectivity (Causey 385). This uncanniness becomes even stronger through the mirroring gestures of the worker: she shows you that she is aware of what you are doing. The disruption that is created in the time and space of the body-world of the spectator creates a new production of knowledge: the spectator has the possibility of getting insight into the situated knowledge of the worker in her own working environment. The body has a newly available shared space through which it can make sense of its surroundings.

CONCLUSION
Our production of knowledge depends on how our unique bodies,

in their own physiological state and with their own cultural background, produce their own body-world. The space from which we collect our knowledge is not based on an empirical world, but only on a shared space among multiple body-worlds. To get a wider understanding of the things that are going on in this space, it is important to get insights in the situated knowledge of other bodies. We have seen how re-enactment and disruption give us the possibility of expanding the horizons of our own knowledges. Re-enactment does this by making us relive a situation or object through a different partial perspective than the one we already have, which causes us to rethink our own situated knowledge. The same goes for disruption, which causes us to become aware of our situated knowledge by creating uncanny situations.

We have arrived at a point in academia that every sort of knowledge is rethought through the lens of *posthumanism*, which "amounts to higher degrees of disciplinary hybridization and relies on intense de-familiarization of our habits of thought through encounters that shatter the flat repetition of the protocols of institutional reason" (Braidotti 169). Art is in this case, on the view advanced here, the most powerful tool to reinterpret our own situated knowledge, since it has the power to make us aware of our own knowledge, and it invites us to look through other partial perspectives. Therefore, it is of the utmost importance right now to connect different situated knowledges and create, what I will call, *ecological knowledge*: the awareness of the connected network of knowledges that is produced in various body-worlds on what is happening in the shared space. Only then can we emancipate knowledge and embrace the various partial perspectives that this shared space of body-worlds has to offer.

WORKS CITED

Bois, Yve-Alain, et al. "A Conversation with Hubert Damisch." *October*, vol. 85, 1998, pp. 3-17.

Braidotti, Rossi. *The Posthuman*. Polity, 2013.

Causey, Matthew. 1991. "The Screen Test of the Double: The Uncanny Performer in the Space of Technology." *Theater Journal*, vol. 51, no. 4, 1991, pp. 383-394.

Deleuze, Gilles and Félix Guattari. *What is Philosophy?* Columbia University Press, 1991.

Foucault, Michel. *"Society Must Be Defended": Lectures at the Collège de France, 1975-76*. Translated by David Macey. Picador, 2003.

Foucault, Michel. *The Birth of Biopolitics: Lectures at the Collège de France, 1978-79*. Translated by Graham Burchell, Palgrave Macmillan, 2008.

Groys, Boris. *Art Power*. MIT Press, 2008.

Hall, Stuart. "Encoding/Decoding." 1973. *Media and Cultural Studies: Keyworks*, edited by Meenakshi Gigi Durham and Douglas M. Kellner, Blackwell Publishing Ltd., 2006, pp. 163-173.

Haraway, Donna. "Situated Knowledges: The Science Question in Feminism and the Privilege of Partial Perspectives." *Feminist Studies*, vol.14, no. 3, 1988, pp. 575-599.

King, Katie. *Networked Reenactments: Stories Transdisciplinary Knowledges Tell.* Duke University Press, 2011.

Noë, Alva. *Action in Perception.* MIT Press, 2006.

Rau, Milo. *Five Easy Pieces.* 26 May 2016. Utrecht, The Netherlands.

Varela, Francisco J., et al. *The Embodied Mind.* MIT Press, 1991.

Verhoeven, Dries. Guilty Landscapes Episode I. 27 May 2016. Utrecht, The Netherlands.

Wekker, Gloria, and Helma Lutz. "A Wind-swept Plain: The History of Gender and Ethnicity-thought in the Netherlands." *Caleidoscopische Visies*, edited by Maayke Botman, translated by Christien Franken, KIT, 2001, pp. 1-54.

Winker, Gabriele, and Nina Degele. "Intersectionality as Multi-level Analysis: Dealing with Social Inequality." *European Journal of Women's Studies*, vol. 18, 2011, pp. 51–66.

Tools for New Lifestyles: Indigenous Stone Crushing and Public Perception of Television Environmental Reporting in Jos City

SARAH LWAHAS

UNIVERSITY OF JOS
JOS, NIGERIA

ABSTRACT: *The neglect of environmental reporting in television programming in Nigeria has led to a predicament. As global interest and attention mounts, with the Western media playing a positive and vital role in how the environment can impact the lives of people now and in the future, television stations in Nigeria fail to play a constructive role in enhancing public understanding by communicating information on the environment. Consumers of news and society in general do not seem to understand the broad challenges posed, particularly by the impact of indigenous stone crushing, an activity that is fast becoming a thriving business venture in recent years for many people. This study seeks to examine the role and the frequency of coverage of television environmental news reporting in Jos city, particularly in relation to public perception of indigenous stone crushing by women in Jos city. The study is anchored in the Agenda-setting Theory and the Perception Theory, which explains how people make sense of the words and images they get from the media. The paper provides a content analysis of three television stations in Jos city and a focus-group discussion on public perception of environmental reporting in television programming. The study shows that there is an increasing depletion of rock formations, endangering indigenous culture and the aesthetics of Jos city, even while the rocky formations serve as high altitude points for broadcast masts and satellites. There is also an increasing inability to restore the environment in terms of land reclamation and other restorative or protective actions. It recommends that television stations should provide the platform for discussing and understanding issues that are germane to the environment through improved, forthright, and high-quality environmental reporting.*

KEYWORDS: television, environment, indigenous culture, reporting, stone crushing, media

INTRODUCTION

In most countries of the world, societies are grappling with environmental issues: from pollution and waste-management issues to biodiversity and chemical weapons, from climate change and global warming to ozone depletion, pit mining and stone quarrying, among others. Of concern are questions about the relationship between man and nature and how journalists in particular can interpret environmental issues in relation to man and society.

Environmental reporting is a form of specialized news in the media, with reporters who are assigned to cover the "environment beats." These reports are meant to have direct impact on people's lives. Therefore, the reports are presented in an interpretative way. This means that the audience will understand the information based on the way it is conveyed to them (Platt; Miller and Pollak).

Until the year 2000, stone crushing was predominantly a male activity. However, the emergence of women in the stone crushing industry is a common sight today, and women are seen at strategic locations in Jos city, crushing stones, sometimes with their children helping them to earn a living. The rocky nature of Jos, Plateau State, provides the raw materials for stone crushing, encouraging indigenous and artisanal stone crushing as an activity and a viable business venture. The indigenous stone crushers are found at manual stone quarries for artisan small-scale miners.

There are ten major media organizations in Jos, comprising television and radio stations (see below for more details). Jos is the capital of Plateau State, which is located in North Central Nigeria. Surrounded by rock formations, it boasts a temperate climate and is popularly called the "Home of Peace and Tourism." The city is located on the Jos Plateau at an elevation of about 1,238 meters or 4,062 feet above sea level. The city has a population of about 900,000 residents based on the 2006 census.

STATEMENT OF THE PROBLEM

The Nigerian broadcast media often fail to adopt a comprehensive approach in reporting about the environment and investigating environmental issues such as pollution (land, air, water), natural hazards, deforestation, flooding, global warming and climate change, etc. They do not seem to have a clear understanding of the relationship between man and his environment or realize that environmental threats have a direct bearing on the media industries' ability to obtain the right kind of signal for successful program transmission. Most times their reports include only a one-minute weather forecast, but no in-depth reports on the rise of human activities that negatively impact the environment (Dorroh).

OBJECTIVES OF THE STUDY

This study seeks to:
1. Examine the role of television news in environmental reporting in Jos City.
2. Determine the role of women in indigenous stone crushing in Jos city.
3. Examine the frequency of coverage of television environmental news reporting in Jos City.
4. Examine public perception of indigenous stone crushing by women in Jos city.

RESEARCH QUESTIONS

1. What is the role of television news in environmental reporting in Jos City?
2. What is the role of women in indigenous stone crushing in Jos City?
3. How frequently is environmental news covered for television?
4. What is the perception of the public on indigenous stone crushing by women in Jos city?

SIGNIFICANCE OF THE STUDY

Awareness of information disseminated by Western media on

issues regarding environmental concerns has increasingly taken center stage in political, social, and economic discourse globally. This research is significant in conveying to the media, government officials and policy makers, and environmental groups the need to expand public awareness about the environment.

THEORETICAL FRAMEWORK

This study is anchored on the Agenda-setting Theory. Maxwell McCombs and Donald Shaw in 1972 stated that the media sets the public agenda, in the sense that although the media may not exactly tell people what to think, they may nevertheless tell people what they should think *about*. Those who listen to such reports or news programs decide how much importance to attach to an issue based on the amount of information in a news story and its position within the formatting of the news report. The study is also grounded in the Perception Theory, which explains how people make sense of the words and images they get from the media. In other words, different people can react to the same messages in different ways. This implies that people need an initial exposure to the messaging before they can pay attention and subsequently successfully retain the information presented (Folarin; Lahly).

METHODOLOGY

Content analysis and focus-group discussion were employed to collect and analyze the data presented below. Two focus discussions were held. The first was with four women involved in the stone-crushing business; the second group contained seven people, comprising journalists, environmentalists, and public commentators.

POPULATION OF THE STUDY

News reports in the first quarter of 2017 (January-March) of three television stations in Jos City were purposively sampled. The identified categories are based on the following:

A) Focus: Mining activities, monthly sanitation exercises, floods, weather reports, pollution, erosion, global warming, stone crushing/quarrying.

B) Type of report: News commentary, hard news, special report, human-angle reports/features, documentary.

C) Duration: 2 minutes, 5 minutes, 10 minutes, 25 minutes.

THE MEDIA AND THE ENVIRONMENT

The media in society performs the role of shaping and influencing events. Today, there are broadcast stations that have assigned reporters to specific beats, namely health, police/crime, sports, medicine, judiciary, transport, science and technology, etc. Television broadcast news has provided information or programs devoted to developments in certain areas but very little on the environment. (Detjen; Yankah). This is no surprise as there have been increasing levels of environmental issues.

Television is one of the primary sources of news for the public. This therefore implies that the public learns a lot about the environment by consuming mass media news. For instance, a U.S. National Science Foundation survey of U.S. residents found that television remains the leading source of news in most households (53 percent), followed by newspapers (29 percent) (National Science Foundation; Boykoff and Roberts).

As mentioned above, Jos houses about ten media organizations comprising television and radio stations, and among these are Nigerian Television Authority (N.T.A.), Network Centre Jos, Plateau Radio Television Corporation (PRTVC), and Silverbird Television. This study will focus on statistics from these organizations. As with most media organizations, these carry out the function of providing information to the public. As Aliagan states, "These include storing and disseminating information, contributing to social progress …and educating people…" (44). The media stations transmit various programs but do not seem to have prioritized news on the environment.

WOMEN AND STONE CRUSHING BUSINESS IN JOS

The women involved in stone crushing in Jos city are mostly uneducated and unskilled. The women do not own the land where the rocks used for crushing are found, but they negotiate with landowners to pay a certain amount for a "tipper" or truckload of stones. Their tools are not sophisticated: they consist of locally made hammers, which they use to break the rocks into pieces. It takes about three to four weeks for each woman to produce a truckload of angular crushed granite stone which is about five tons (Kwaghe 247).

The blasting of the rock is carried out by men who work on the site by lighting small, controlled fires on the rocks. The heat from the fire cracks the rocks, forming layers that allow for the rocks to be broken into boulders. The boulder is further crushed into smaller sizes known as "hardcore." The hardcore is further crushed into smaller sizes by the women (Kwaghe 247-8). Between six and ten women are usually found working at each crushing site.

Landowners who want to build their own houses or open up some business such as a private fuel station patronize these women. With the economic recession biting hard in Nigeria, the cost of the stones has gone higher, with about 100 percent increase in value. Landowners and home builders see this indigenous stone crushing as an opportunity to expeditiously obtain available stones close to their land and building sites (Mark 2).

While this business venture blooms, the women are exposed to dust from crushing granite rocks and the sun. Urom et al., cited in (Kwaghe 250), opine that dust from the granite rocks can cause lung infection, as well as respiratory and other disease symptoms. The women often wrap their legs with old rags to protect them from being stung by flying shrapnel. Stone crushing also has environmental hazards. It rids the soil of its natural protective covering over time, exposing it to erosion and other harmful environmental effects on the ecosystem. The rock sites eventually become deep ditches that accumulate water and turn into breeding ponds for harmful insects, creating a human-hazard site.

Most of the women engaged in stone crushing in about five locations in Jos city, are either widows or heads of their families seeking for ways to make ends meet.

CONTENT ANALYSIS OF COVERAGE OF ENVIRONMENTAL NEWS IN JOS CITY BY THE MEDIA

Research Question 3 was used to analyze the coverage of environmental news reports in Jos City, while Research Question 1 was analyzed using relevant literature. As a reminder, Research Question 3 asks, How frequently is environmental news covered for television?

Table 1 Nigerian Television Authority (NTA) Jan- March 2017

Month	Focus	Type	Duration
Jan	NIL		
Feb	Sanitation (24/2/2017)	Hard News	2 minutes
March	Mining (7/3/2017)	Hard news	2 minutes
	World Int'l Forest day (21/3/2017)	Hard news	2 minutes
	Weather – world meteorologica l day (23/3/2017)	Special report	2 minutes 30 sec
	Weather– world meteorologica l day (23/3/2017)	Special report	2 minutes 30 sec
	Sanitation (25/3/2017)	Hard news	1 minute 30 sec

Table 2. SILVERBIRD Television Jan-March 2017

Month	Focus	Type	Duration
Jan	Oil spill (31/1/2017)	Hard news	2min 30 sec
Feb	Rainfall over flow in US dam (13/2/2017)	Hard news	2 minutes
	Tropical cyclone (14/2/2017)	Hard news	1 min 30 sec
	Gas flaring (18/2/2017)	Special report	2min 30 sec
March	Heat wave (19/3/2017)	Hard news	2 minutes

Table 3 Plateau Radio Television Corporation (PRTVC) Jan- March 2017

Month	Focus	Type	Duration
Jan	Mining (20/1/2017)	Hard news	2mins
Feb	Public lecture on nature (18/2/2017)	Hard News	1 min 30 sec
	Sanitation (25/2/2017)	Hard news	1 min 30 sec
	Water pollution (27/2/2017)	Hard news	1min 30 sec
March	NIL		

Tables 1, 2 and 3 show that all three media stations sampled did cover reports on the environment. However, there had been no reports on stone crushing from January to March, 2017. Though reports on the environment were aired, they were not dedicated sections of the news reports of the stations. They were reported only when the need arose, or when environmental issues necessitated the reporting of related events such as the commemoration of the World International Forest Day and on the state's sanitation exercise days at the end of each month in the state. Each of the reports from the three media stations ran their stories for a maximum of one minute, thirty seconds, and mainly as hard news. Only once were the reports presented as special reports for two minutes, thirty seconds, on NTA in the month of March, 2017, to commemorate World Meteorological Day, and on SILVERBIRD TV in February, 2017, on Gas Flaring in Bayelsa State, Nigeria. The absence of regular feature reports and more in-depth stories is an indication that journalists or the media generally just do less of this type of investigative reporting or are not aware of the effects of environmental issues, such as stone crushing; at least they are not concerned enough to attempt to educate the public about the situation.

It may therefore be argued that in spite of the coverage of some environmental issues in an attempt to carry out its surveillance function, the media failed to perform its agenda-setting role because there is no environment section in the news beats of the three local stations sampled in this research. So far, attention to reporting environmental issues elsewhere and sanitation days outweighed issues of hazards occasioned by long-term implications of stone crushing to the scenic beauty of the City of Jos, the inability to reclaim the areas where stone crushing is being carried out, and the health impacts of those engaged in the profession.

ANALYSIS OF FOCUS DISCUSSIONS

The analysis of the Focus Group Discussions [FGDs] was based on Research Objectives 2 and 4 in this study. The women involved in stone crushing are coded WC, while the respondents in the second FGD are coded RES.

Research Question 2: What is the role of women in indigenous stone crushing in Jos city?

WC1: *I am doing this job to provide food for my children. This is what I am able to do to make sure my children are fed.*

WC 2: *Our children need to go to school and I'm doing this job to support the family.*

WC1: *We usually start work as early as 6 a.m. until 5 p.m. When I break the rocks to fill a 50kg bag I can sell it at N250-N300 naira.*

WC 2: *Sometimes we are paid about N8, 000 naira if we are able to produce a tipper load in a week. That sells for about N15, 000 naira…it's a very tedious job.*

WC1: *We are exposed to the dust and some pieces of rocks that may injure our legs, hands, eyes… in fact some of us have developed different illnesses.*

WC2: *We protect ourselves by covering our legs with pieces of old clothes…but you can't avoid getting injured sometimes.*

These statements support the fact that stone crushing work is tedious, cumbersome, and open to health hazards, though the women claimed that they are in it to earn a living.

Research Question 4: What is the perception of the public on indigenous stone crushing by women in Jos city?

RES 1: *It's part of the livelihood sustenance because most of the women are not doing it as a lucrative business they must engage in but it helps support what they get from their farms.*

RES 2: *It's a very tedious job for the women. There's no standard pricing, so people come to negotiate prices and the women may be exploited in the process. They create spaces for people to build by breaking the rocky areas.*

RES 3: *You see the women struggling with their children sometimes.*

RES 4: *That job provides an outlet, an opportunity to make an income. Definitely it is a growing and viable industry.*

RES 5: *They are exposed to a lot of hazards and some injuries such as blindness. The beautiful landscape is being destroyed. It's a highly an unregulated job.*

RES 7: (Government Environmentalist). *We have received complaints from communities on the impact of the dust emitted and cracked walls of houses through the blasting of these rocks.*

RES 2: *Stone crushing is really trending because more and more women are coming into this venture.*

RES 1: *There's a new and increasing demand for houses and the city is developing fast.*

RES 5: *I think the media hardly engage in investigative journalism. Firstly, you are dealing with the media which is not properly funded. So how conscious are the journalists on these issues of reporting the environment? I don't think the media is proactive. Nigeria is a signatory to the 1997 UN Kyoto protocol…I don't think we have provided the enlightenment on what the requirements are, so that explains the devastating effects of what we see in the environment.*

RES 6: *Reports on the media on the environment is only when there is an accident or mishap in the environment. I have not seen reports on stone crushing.*

RES 1: *The media is not doing enough and it's a disservice not to report the depletion of the rock formations, erosion and the general destruction of the environment. The women dig out the rocks from the ground which eventually become pits where reptiles and water gather. Besides women who crush such rocks do not live in the areas they carry out their work, therefore may not fully comprehend the problem they are creating.*

RES 7: (Environmentalist) *Most of these activities are illegal. Any mining activity must be carried out with plans for reclamation. Stone crushing affects the soil and creates paths for emission of dangerous gases and dust particles in the air, particularly on those involved in the crushing.*

CONCLUSIONS AND RECOMMENDATIONS

Journalism is a form of communication that interrogates the environment by asking relevant questions with the aim of verifying and presenting news of current issues, trends, and peoples. Therefore, the relationship between journalism or the media and the environment is interactive. It provides journalists with a general understanding of current environmental concerns, to enable them to communicate all of that information, whether complex or not, to the public in such a way that it can be easily understood.

Results of this research show that the media do not perceive stone crushing as the environmental and human-welfare scourge that it is in order to warrant its constant reflection in their news reporting. The Nigerian media seem unwilling or reluctant to venture into in-depth reports in news analyses, features, news commentaries, etc., because of their lack of knowledge on environmental issues.

While stone crushing in the city of Jos is taking center stage as a fast-growing business venture, providing a new lifestyle for more women, there are increasing numbers of sites, creating increasing depletion of the rock formations in the city, all without adequate reclamation. This is indicative of how man gradually destroys his own environment.

The media should interrogate harmful practices by citizens, open up debates, and expose options to promote attitudinal and social change. They should also engage academics and researchers to highlight the need to preserve nature and the environment. Media organizations should encourage journalists and newscasters to investigate and report on the environment and provide regular editorials on environmental issues.

Government should, with the help of communities, enforce regulatory policies against indiscriminate stone crushing. The government should provide alternative jobs for people and locate sites for stone crushing outside of the city of Jos to reduce the exposure of citizens to the attendant health hazards, particularly from dust particles and destructive chemicals.

The women involved in stone crushing should form cooperative societies where they can obtain support in form of training and funding from the government to carry out this profession effectively.

WORKS CITED

Aliagan, Isiaka. Fundamentals of Newspaper Journalism. 1st(ed). Kraft Books, Ibadan 2005. Print.

Ademosu, Ifedapo. Taking Stock: Nigerian Media and National Challenges. Ed. Oluyinka Esan ASCPN Book series1 Canada University Press Concord, Ontario Canada. 2016. Print.

Boykoff, Maxwell, Robert, Timmons. Media Coverage of Climate Change: Current Trends, Strengths, Weaknesses. United Nations Development Programme Human Development Report, hdr.undp.org/en/viewdoc/downloa d?doi=10.1.1.422.4961&rep=rep1ty pe. 2007/2008 web. 31July 2017.

Detjen, Jim. A New Kind of Environment Reporting Is Needed. niemenreports.org/articles(n.yr) Web. 21 July 2017.

Dorroh, Jennifer. Environmental Reporting and Media Development, internews.org/ sites/ default/files/resources/CIMA. 2015. Web. 25th July 2017.

Folarin, Babatunde. Theories of Mass Communication: An Introductory Text. Stirling Harden Publishers. Lagos. 1998. Print.

Kwaghe, Zara. Women Quarrying activities in North Central Nigeria: A Case Study of Jos Metropolis and Alizaga in Nasarawa State. Ed. Sati Fwatshak In The transformation of Central Nigeria. Essays in Honor of Toyin Falola Pan African University Press. USA. Print.

Lawal, Teslim. The techniques and practices of technology reporting in Developing Countries. Communication review, University of Lagos. 2010. Print.

Mark, Esther. The Super Heroines of Jos Who Break Stones to Feed, Educate their Families. www.edfrica.com/2015/12. 2015. Web 6 February 2017.

McCombs, Maxwell, and Shaw, Donald. Mass Communication Theory: from Theory to Practical Applications, masscomm theory.com/theory-overviews/ agenda-setting-theory.1972. Web. 5 July 2017.

Miller, Tyson and Pollak, Todd. Environmental coverage in Mainstream news. climateaccess .org. 2012. Web. 8 August 2017.

Platt, John. The Need for

Environmental Journalism Is More Acute Now than Ever. *The Revelator,* therevelator.org. 2017. Web. 2nd August 2017.

Popoola, Muyiwa. Content and Hermeneutical Analysis of Selected Newspapers Reportage of Environmental Issues in Nigeria. *IOSR Journal of Humanities and Social Sciences.* (IOSR-JHSS) Vol. 19, issue 3, Ver. II. www.iosrjournal.org. 2010. Web.12 June 2017.

Popoola, Ibitayo. Media as Regulatory Mechanism in Environmental Pollution. Communication: Communication Review. *Journal of Mass Communication,* University of Lagos. Vol. 4, No. 2. 2010. Print.

Yankah, Kojo. Covering the Environment in Ghana. *Africa Media Review.* Vol. 8. No.1. ACCE. 1994. Print.

Time Machines and the Appropriation of Time: Mediated, Unmediated, Immediated

PAUL MAJKUT

NATIONAL UNIVERSITY
LA JOLLA, CALIFORNIA, USA

THE OWNERSHIP OF TIME

In "Advice to a Young Tradesman" (1746), Benjamin Franklin, in a memorable proverb, coined the aphorism "Time is Money":

> Remember that Time is Money. He that can earn Ten Shillings a Day by his Labour, and goes abroad, or sits idle one half of that Day, tho' he spends but Sixpence during his Diversion or Idleness, ought not to reckon That the only Expence; he has really spent or rather thrown away Five Shillings besides.[1]

Franklin's pithy remark is more than a quaint expression of New England frugality. It is not only a prescient foreshadowing of Adam Smith's revelations concerning market economy in *Wealth of Nations* (1776), predating the Scotsman's work by three decades. It also introduced the suggestive equivalence of time and wealth whose implications were to prove essential to Marx's concept of the commodity as well as echoing the historical shift of time-measurement machines from natural to arithmetic that had already taken place in the mediation of time. The mediation of time and the everyday experience of time through temporal media are the crux of this discussion, though my disorderly mind prefers to wander digressively than follow an

Figure 1. Typical 24-hour digital clock: a series of ever- increasing numbers. Additional numeric representations could be added for epoch, year, and month, and so on.

argumentative path. The syllogistic snake is deadly to associative expression and thought.

Franklin's aphorism suggests many lines of investigation: the reification and spatiation of time, the commodification of time, the monetization of time, the textualization of time, and, above all, the mediation of time, all roads leading to a fundamental under-standing that time is essentially a property relationship, not one of the relativity of physical

---

[1] Franklin, Benjamin. *Advice to a Young Tradesman, Written by an Old One.* founders.archives.gov/documents/Franklin/01-03-02-0130. [Original source: *The Papers of Benjamin Franklin*, vol. 3, *January 1, 1745, through June 30, 1750*, ed. Leonard W. Labaree. New Haven: Yale University Press, 1961, pp. 304–308.]

dimensions. Consequently, the question of who owns time is central to my rambling approach.

Figure 2. Analogue 12-hour AM/PM clock representing time as cyclical or curvilinear.

To see time as a property relationship, we look to historical shifts in the mediation of time, mediation that presages inevitable changes in class relationships. We come upon a contradiction that sees time as either cyclical or linear, which requires a closer look at how time is mediated and measured.

Literature, as Thomas Piketty suggests in *Capital in the Twenty-first Century*, offers "a very good introduction to the subject of wealth."[2] Following his lead is to take the side of the historical materialism of the Paris School of Economics and its descent from Marxist dialectical analysis against the psychologized Austrian School of Economics and its roots in petit-bourgeois, phenomenological liber-tarian ideology and Austrofascism.

The association of phenomenology, libertarian economic ideology, and fascism has long been recognized, but association of "third way" subjective-idealist philosophy and Austrofascism has received little attention.

Insightful literary vantage points from which to see the mediation and appropriation of time are illustrated in Franklin's "Advice to a Young Tradesman" and H. G. Wells' *The Time Machine.*

But, before we attempt to crack the shell that contains the kernel, understand that in this discussion time is a mediated experience and, like objects of consciousness in the spatial world of length, width, and depth, its technological mediation forms and defaces experience, representationally removing it from the direct experience of *immediated* reality.[3] The purpose here, to the contrary, is to return to immediated reality.

Briefly, three terms in the title of this essay need definition.

Mediation refers to communication structured by a specific medium's technology (print, radio, television, the Internet, smoke signals, etc.). *Unmediation* is the negative process by which that medium's imposed limitations are revealed and

[2] Piketty, Thomas. *Capital in the Twenty-First Century,* "The Nature of Wealth: from Literature to Reality," (trans. Arthur Goldhammer). The Belnap Press of Harvard University Press: Cambridge, Mass., 2014, 113.

[3] We return to the question of how to proceed. I rely on a procedure based in media theory, not philosophy. In the general discussion of media, it is the media of time and their technologies that occupy us, not the philosophy of time – except as it is a consequence of material media. Analysis and identification of the limitations of a medium that defaces what is represented is our first step. Defacement is the first subject of concern because it underlies all media representation.

defacements (i.e., distortions) of the communication noted, although they cannot be removed without destroying that medium. *Immediation* has two senses: 1) Not mediated: the positive, post-mediated relationship to reality possible once *unmediation* has been performed or the relationship known in pre-mediated cognition of the world; 2) more importantly, immediation is inherent, simultaneous, and spontaneous knowledge of the world as direct knowledge of reality in the manner of Thomas Reid's and G. E. Moore's common sense realism (direct realism).[4] The task of immediation is to reestablish the direct relationship to nature of children and artists. Further, it is assumed that subjectivist and idealist claims that place the world in "brackets" are a delusional form of idealist madness.

THE LINE AND THE CIRCLE

When in the opening scene of H. G. Wells' *The Time Machine*,[5] the Time Traveller explains to his skeptical guests, "There is no difference between Time and any of the three dimensions except that our consciousness moves along it," he has spatialized time. Time has become a Euclidian line. In this commonplace trope, the reader and guests at the Time Traveller's home are told that consciousness moves along a timeline that stretches from the past into the future. The Time Traveller explains that "[A]ny real body must have extension in *four* dimensions: it must have Length, Breadth, Thickness, and — Duration." To his discredit, he does not understand that duration as well as time are bound by Eddington's arrow of time and fly in one direction only. *Tempus fugit* into the future; *carpe diem* is a here-and-now, existential fool's wisdom. In any case, fixed temporal direction no more stops the Time Traveller from back-and-forth time travel any more than Cyrano de

---

[4] Reid, Thomas. *Essays on the Intellectual Powers of Man,* "Chapter 5: Perception," 50. "Well, now, if we attend to the act of our mind that we call 'perceiving an external object of sense' we shall find in it these three things: (1) Some conception or notion of the object perceived. (2) A strong and irresistible conviction and belief that the object does at present exist. (3) That this conviction and belief are immediate, and not upshots of reasoning" (www.earlymoderntexts.com/assets/pdfs/reid 1785essay2.pdf).

[5] Wells, H. G. *The Time Machine.* New York: New York, 1995. Time travel, that peculiar blend of the medieval dream vision, renaissance utopian and travel literature, and modern science fiction, took explicit form in the late nineteenth century in works such as Wells' *The Time Machine,* Edward Bellamy's *Looking Back from the Year 2000,* Ignatius Donnelly's *Caesar's Column,* and William Morris' *News from Nowhere.* It is only in novels such as these that time is traveled. Before modern times, travel and utopian literature featured spatial travel, not temporal, and medieval dream visions did not feature travel at all, but rather placed the dreamer in an alternate reality of his present. What unites these genres is the fanciful introductory convention of the fairy tale's "long ago and far away," although nineteenth-century science fiction expands time to include "in the future" as well as "long ago." Medieval and renaissance works within the trope of the "golden age" or "Garden of Eden" focus exclusively on the past. The late nineteenth-century shift from reliance on the past to the future is paralleled by a shift from utopian to dystopian fiction in which the past is bright and golden, the future is dark and oppressive.

Bergerac is prevented by the laws of physics from space travel by holding morning flowers whose dew evaporates, elevating him in *Voyage to the Moon*.

Setting aside the Time Traveller's facile equation of time and duration, we visualize the line of time, presumed to be straight, that in Wells' three-dimensional Euclidean space is a fixed, fourth dimension in relationship to the other three spatial dimensions.[6] The cosmos is static. The first three dimensions do not move along the timeline, but are fixed in relationship to it and each other. It is the Time Traveller who moves through the dimensions, not length, breadth, or depth ("thickness") that move along the timeline. Wells has reduced time to spatial perception and consciousness.

If we follow the Time Traveller's argument that time is a spatial "object of consciousness," one that he argues can be traversed, then the quantification and measurement of objective time is not only possible, but necessary — especially if a traveler does not wish

to be lost in time.[7] To do this, we note the conflation of subjective time or duration (*durée*) and objective time and, for the purposes of the present discussion, set aside subjective time for another occasion.[8]

The measurement of objective time brings us to various material time machines that quantify time (i.e., clocks, calendars) and the long, failed but glorious history of man's attempts to subjugate and tame time to have good manners and behave well within the demands of various and conflicting philosophical and, more importantly, economic discourses.

Whatever philosophical disagreements or interpretations of time may be, one truth is evident: the instruments that represent objective time are themselves *media of communication*, and it is this aspect of time that initially draws our interest.

The objection will arise that this approach is clearly an example of technological determinism, but attention to media technology is simply one feature of a prevailing economic determinism that rests on

---

[6] Eddington, Arthur Stanley. The Nature of the Physical World, 35. "Let us draw an arrow arbitrarily. If as we follow the arrow we find more and more of the random element in the state of the world, then the arrow is pointing towards the future; if the random element decreases the arrow points towards the past. That is the only distinction known to physics. This follows at once if our fundamental contention is admitted that the introduction of randomness is the only thing which cannot be undone. I shall use the phrase 'time's arrow' to express this one-way property of time which has no analogue in space." The arrow of time flies in one direction.

[7] Time travel is a headache in science fiction with endless confusion about cause and effect that doubles back on itself. Time travel is a scientific muddle that is evident in the non-sequiturs in *Back to the Future* or Tony Scott's *Déjà Vu*. Tampering with time in fiction is a good way to undo the narrative satisfaction of closure, replacing it with a thought experiment. This is not to say that time cannot be reordered within a narrative, as is the case in many *films noirs* (most famously in *Out of the Past*), through the use of flashbacks or trick memory (as in *Memento*) is narrative gimmick, not understanding.

[8] Subjective time (*durée*): *ubi sunt*, nostalgia, *déjà vu*, etc.

attention to means and modes of production. As such, it is labor that drives dynamic, living history. As an account within the context of historical materialism, the case made here concerning the technologies involved in the measurement of time, clocks and calendars, is but one strand of dialectic history.

Clocks are as much media of communication as are medieval manuscripts, printed books, television, film, radio, the Internet, or smoke signals. Just as an image may represent two-dimensional reality (length and width) in a line drawing or three-dimensional reality in perspectival renaissance art and CGIs, time may also be represented spatially. Just as media that represent the first three dimensions confine what they represent according to their own technological limitations, each medium revealing what it represents in its own fashion that differs from other media, so too time machines differ in how they represent time and what they do with it. Various clocks and calendars are widely divergent time machines.

The first American digital clock, Eugene Fitch's Plato Clock,[9] was

introduced in the United States in the early twentieth century. A spring-wound machine, it lacked the display range to represent time arithmetically that contemporary digital screens have today. Digital clock readouts today imply arithmetic infinity in both past and future directions, though they normally show only hours, minutes, and seconds. What, for our purposes, is significant is that digital clocks display a linear concept of time – numbers running in a straight line into the past or future [Fig. 1], the line upon which Wells' Time Traveller moved. Simply put, time is a straight line that is the shortest distance

---

Fitch mistakenly attributed the lantern story to Plato, though historical authority attributes it to Diogenes the Cynic. Hence, the Plato Clock is more accurately called the Diogenes Clock. Although Fitch named the first digital clock and introduced it at the St. Louis World Fair in 1903, Josef Pallweber had patented it in Germany 13 years before and Aktiengesellschaft für Uhrenfabrikation Lenzkirch manufactured digital clocks between 1893 and 1894. Fitch's Plato Clock was produced by the Ansonia company in Brooklyn. The American Electrical Novelty and Manufacturing Co. of New York City had sold more than 40,000 by 1904.

A digital clock's readout is always incomplete, unlike analogue media, because numbers are infinite. A digital clock, in addition to showing year, month, day, hour, minute and second could be expanded at either temporal end to include geological epochs such as Anthropocene, Holocene, etc. all the way back to the Big Bang, and forward into nanoseconds, femtoseconds, jiffies, yoctoseconds, and Planck time units, ad infinitum. Practically speaking, the ∞ symbol at each end of the digital readout would indicate as much and is implied.

---

[9] Fitch, a clock master, was careless in matters of the history of philosophy. He designed his clock to resemble a lantern. "Flipping numbered cards displayed the time. The clock had a brass stand and handle, with a glass cylinder enclosing the cards. The unusual clock was named the Plato because the famous Greek philosopher was said to have carried a lantern shaped like the clock while he was 'looking for an honest man.'" Cf.

between two points, a past and future that are infinitely separated. This *line* is today globalized and fixed by an atomic clock, its accuracy measured in units smaller than nanoseconds and maintained by the National Institute of Standards and Technology and the U. S. Naval Observatory.[10]

Digital clocks are linear, non-repetitive, based on an unknown and unknowable past and future. They are conceptual units. When time is mediated analogically, however, its representation is *continuous* – time is displayed as an uninterrupted flow, though the mechanism that moves the hands of an analogue clock are driven by tick-tock gears. Digital mediation represents time in *discrete* arithmetic units.

Analogue clocks, contrary to digital media, communicate time as a finite, recursive curvilinear line that is local, not global, and fixed on natural and cosmological occurrences, not arithmetic abstractions [Fig. 2]. Sunrise and spring, day and night, and the seasons order analogue temporality rather than the digital medium's arithmetic, atomic clock. The measurement of time by analogue media is flexible; digital measurement is as arithmetically exact as particle physics allows. This contrast is nowhere better seen than in the medieval system of *hours equal, hours unequal* in which the number of minutes in daylight and night hours increase or decrease according to the season.[11] The mediated representation of time by analogue clocks is limited, but infinite in its recursiveness. Time is not a dimension of space, but contains it. Time contains space and is outside of the three spatial dimensions. Analogue time refers to nature and is directly experienced though the senses; it is transcendent and empirical. It is conceptual, not perceptual.

By way of generalization, we may contrast the analogue measurement of time as local, flexible, cyclical, and continuous as opposed to digital measurement as global, rigid, discrete, and linearly straight – "straight" defined as the shortest distance between two points.

THE LINE

We are bound by lines everywhere at all times, literally and metaphorically, circumscribed, fixed and unfixed, moved forward and backward in space and time, centered and decentered, rudderless and blown adrift from original intentions and goals, given and denied personal and social identity by all-embracing linearity. Lines are visible and invisible. They are spatially geometric and temporally tyrannical. They exist literally and figuratively, in experience and

---

[10] This public service is cooperatively provided by the two time agencies of the United States: Department of Commerce, the National Institute of Standards and Technology, and the U.S. Naval Observatory. Readings from the clocks of these agencies contribute to world time, called Coordinated Universal Time. The time maintained by both agencies should never differ by more than 0.000 0001 seconds from UTC.

---

[11] Whyte, Nicholas, Hours and Hours Equal (nicholaswhyte.info/hours.htm#02n).

beyond experience, in mediated and unmediated knowledge, and as activities we impose on others as well as behavior imposed on us. In discourse, they are used for descriptive and imperative purposes. Elevated in sacred scripture, the line assumes the honorific title *verse*.[12]

Line is not only a media term, though it is the most fundamental concept in media studies. It is the most comprehensive word in language. "Line" is more fundamental than "Being," "nature," "cosmos," "universe," or other terms that serve to describe the whole of human experience and transcendent reality. All thought and action are corralled into lines. Lineation is at once the most concrete yet most abstract of concepts. Line fences Being and becoming. The word "line" is both *necessary* and *adequate* to its generalized descriptive task.[13] Electronic digital media are lines of code which digital machines (clocks) express visually.

Our family, clan, and national accounts are narrative storylines, our ideologies party lines, our location a matter of longitudinal and latitudinal lines; our thinkers follow lines of thought; our visual perception is a matter of lines of sight. Our everyday life is a routine of finding where the line begins and getting into it. Lining up is regarded as a sign of civilization in contrast to the push-and-shove of barbarian strength over civility.

To be "out of line" places the offender in "a line up."

The Earth has fault lines. Age has worry lines.

Cocaine is snorted in lines.

Algebra is linear. Every point in space is a linear combination of three vectors: length, width, and depth, and these are the basic names of lines. As *length*, line is the one-dimensional source of width and depth, whether in Euclidean or Cartesian geometry.

Lines can be straight, curved, and broken.

Some lines have beginnings and ends, but these autonomous lines are preceded and followed by lines that have no beginning and no end. In this final sense, there are not *lines* but only a single *line*.

The line permeates our lives to the extent that it may be taken as inherent in human experience. Linearity includes the rational and the irrational, the seen and the unseen.

In various media, the universal line takes a particular form: a line of print, a groove in a vinyl disk, a film strip, a line of code, and so on, and, for our purposes, a timeline.

---

[12] The line has many aliases: *lane, queue, file, row, column, string, track, ladder,* and so on. The *scala naturae* ("stairway of nature" or "great chain of being") is more fundamentally a line than it is "Being." It is the chain that is great, not Being. In everyday life and activity and in every discipline and the realities those disciplines represent and refer to, there are fundamental lines: *bottom line, line of credit, line up, front of the line, in and out of line, to be kept in line, top of the line, red line, direct telephone line, line of thought, political line, assembly line, on-line, off-line, ad infinitum.* Life does not escape the line: *end of the line.*

[13] Unlike the typological gimmickry of Derrida's *sous rature* or Heidegger's *under erasure*, both of which are necessitated by words (such as Being) that are "inadequate but necessary."

TEXTUAL IDEALISM, TEXTUALIZED TIME

We think of media within its three spatial dimensions, not as instruments of mediated time. We acknowledge spatial apparatuses (print, TV, Internet, smoke signals, etc.) as objects that exist within the flow of time, but do not ordinarily associate time with its media. Time is associated with death, with eternity, and with nature, but its media representation is curiously ignored in favor of consideration of abstract and philosophical time. But the representation of "time" is no more immune from its medium's technological structure than are spatial objects immune from defacement by their media.[14] When we look closely at the apparatuses of temporal media – time's machines – this connection is quickly apparent. The technology of time machines – clocks and calendars – and the measurement and representation of time are superb examples of media defacement of natural time. The read-out in Figure 1 (23 30 45) reveals one bias in the representation of mediated time. More fully, this linear representation would read ∞2017 03 01 23 30 45∞ (today's date), the infinity symbol before and after the numeric date and time indicating that time stretches without knowable ends into the past and future. Past and future numeric representations could be added, but any digital sequence is an arbitrarily imposed abbreviation (era, epoch, age, etc.). Analogue temporal media (water clocks, sun dials, hour glasses, and so on), on the contrary, do not represent an open-ended arithmetic system. Dependent on nature, they do not represent eternity but instead display real time as a natural recurrence.

Attention here is drawn to mediatized time, but the analysis of clocks, whether analogue or digital, is not the final goal, only a first step. Rather, attention to mediation – as is the case in spatial media analyze s[15] – is a first analysis made in order to *unmediate* time which, in turn, allows those who are not timid to abandon the medium of the book altogether in order to *immediate* time. It is *immediation* of time that is the goal – a return to nature in which there is no distinction between subject and object. This is a philosophy of immediate surroundings.

But we are blocked by the not inconsiderable limitations of the medium of bookish text.

Modern Western thought has, often unknowingly, surrendered to print and the printed page, as in the cases of Heideggerian hermeneutics and Derridean deconstruction. It has detached the function of the representation of language in print to a self-enclosed and self-referential system that is closed to the world to which language refers.

---

[14] "Defacement," a term I borrowed and generalized from Albert W. Pollard's *Early Illustrated Books,* refers to the distortions of content implicit in all media, not individual acts of vandalism on individual works in any medium. Marginalia, underlinings, and hi-lites are not, in this sense, defacements.

[15] Majkut, Paul. "Untext," *Glimpse.* San Diego: Society for Phenomenology and Media, 2009.

"Language" no longer means the spoken word and periphrastic gestures that accompany it that point to things outside of language. Language in much Western thought is no longer an *indicative gesture*. Contemporary philosophy is paper, not sound. Philosophy has become *bookish*.

Trần Đức Thảo's discussion of the organ of language is in sharp contrast to Derrida's self-enclosed, hermetically-sealed understanding of language.[16] Demonstrative pronouns, nouns, adjectives, verbs and adverbs all point for their meaning outside of language. Only by the fait-accompli definition of philosophical fiat does one word only refer (defer) to another word and not the transcendent thing. But some parts of speech refer outside of themselves, are deictic, having meaning only in the context of the transcendent world to which they point. Deixis or linguistic pointing is at the heart of language. Trần finds *the indicative gesture* the origin of verbal pointing and the origin of language; Louis Althusser finds "hailing" ("Hey, you!") to be the origin of subjectivity. We are socially called into our personal identity as subjects by language.

Textual idealism as practiced by Derrida's deconstruction and Heidegger's hermeneutics is the world mediated to text, thought cut off from the world, a commentary on itself, an elitist praxis of the literati. Just as Husserl's phenomenological *epoché* dismisses the transcendent world and reduces it to *conscious-of objects*, a form of transcendental idealism, Derridean deconstruction and Heideggerian hermeneutics also dismiss the transcendent world in favor of self-contained text found in the medium of the book—not only the book, but the *printed book* of the renaissance.[17] Consequently, language is (1) reduced to its printed representation, and (2) its representation is cut off from the world it first represented.

György Lukács gives this telling account of phenomenology and Max Scheler:

> Even when phenomenologists dealt with crucial questions of social actuality, they put off the theory of knowledge and asserted that the phenomenological method suspends or "brackets" the question whether the intentional objects are real. The method was thus freed from any knowledge of reality. Once, during the First World War, Scheler visited me in Heidelberg, and we had an informative conversation on this subject. Scheler maintained that phenomenology was a universal method which could have anything for its intentional object. For example, he explained, phenomenological researches could be made about the devil; only the question of the devil's reality would first have to be

---

[16] Trần Đức Thảo. *Investigations into the Origin of Language and Consciousness*. Trans. Daniel J. Herman and Robert L. Armstrong. Dordrecht, The Netherlands: D. Reidel Publishing Company, 1984.

[17] Majkut, Paul. *Smallest Mimes: Defaced Representation and Media Epistemology*. Zeta, 2014.

"bracketed." "Certainly," I answered. "and when you are finished with the phenomeno-logical picture of the devil, you open the brackets – and the devil in person is standing before you." Scheler laughed, shrugged his shoulders, and made no reply.[18]

The ideological hothouse in which phenomenological idealism grows is found in the use of the print medium. Specifically, we see in the history of "reading" a shift from texts of antiquity and the Middle Ages, written as scripts to be read aloud, to texts that are read silently, a process of internalization that detached the reader after the invention of the printed page from vocalized linguistic praxis, the very nature of language as a communicative tool, and, lacking that connection, became no longer self-corrective. The auditory-acoustic loop of speaker and listener was broken. The silent reader has only herself or himself as an audience. Without the linguistic feedback loop, language becomes archaic and solipsistic, as is the case of bookish philosophy and philosophers. The printed word chains the thinker to the past. Rather than acknowledge this limitation, textual idealists argue that solipsism is a virtue, as does Husserl, who openly requires the use of "phenomenological sentences." Despite claims of existence outside of any particular natural language, these sentences are written in a natural language. Heidegger and Derrida demand of readers an understanding of their coined, esoteric language. As such, phenomenology may be thought of as a class-based, academic and bookish "style" of rhetorical "eloquence"; typography, not thought.

Can a text ever be used to break free of textuality, of the medium of the book, or are readers forever doomed to no exit once they enter a text, to making clever arguments that cite other texts, students writing papers on philosophers in a Jesuitical or Talmudic maze? Can only literate thinkers in the tradition of Europe and America be philosophers? Can an illiterate offer us anything about time and the world?

Can a text break free of its medium? I suppose not. Or nearly not. When Husserl places the natural world in brackets, claiming it a necessity in order to achieve certitude and surmount the naïveté of the natural sciences, he would have been more accurate to say that natural science was *innocent*, not *naïve*. Both words have the sense of "not knowing" or "ignorance," but Husserl's term is pejorative. Husserl places experience above innocence as a way of knowing and certitude above open-eyed wonder. Phenomenological bracketing is in antagonistic contradiction to immediation, which returns us to the natural world. Husserl is disingenuous when he says that phenomenologists must always be beginners. What he means is that we must be beginners *in order to move on from beginning*, that is, move

[18] Lukács, Georg, *Existentialism*, 1949 (www.marxists.org/archive/lukacs/works/1949/existentialism.htm).

from naïveté to experience – not beginners who remain in a state of innocent wonder, wonder being a state of not knowing that is not ignorance but a state of awe – *beginning* as a permanent state rather that a starting place: the world of the child and artist. Immediation frees the knower of tyrannical certitude.

If a text merely strengthens textuality by adding to the prison whose paper walls are its front and back covers, if philosophy has become no more than a bookish exercise, then *immediation* as direct realism is not possible. But, if text itself is employed to unmediate itself, though it remains within the text as analysis, the reader is led to the threshold of the text and, viewing reality through the text's door while yet in that text, may take the step of immediation that returns her or him to what was mediated and represented by text: the world itself. Unmediation is not deconstruction of text, but its destruction and abandonment – a return to the "transcendent" world that exists prior to and outside of Derridean self-enclosed, textual idealism and Heideggerian hermeneutics that see the world as words, words, words. Immediation breaks free of stylish Nietzschean wordplay.

TEXTUAL IDEALISM AND INTERTEXTUALITY

Despite the misnomer, Fitch's Plato Clock is misnamed for Plato for a more serious reason. It is a digital clock, not analogue, which undoubtedly would have upset the wrestling philosopher, whose concept of time was analogue, not digital, natural, not arithmetic.

Platonic time is the shadow of eternity. In *Timaeus*, we find a strong idealization of time, positing the natural world as an imperfect reflection of an ideal Model ("form," *eidos*, essence) of time[19]:

> [37c] The Father designed to make [time] resemble its Model [37d] still more closely…. [T]his quality was impossible to attach in its entirety to what is generated; wherefore He planned to make a movable image of Eternity, and… He made an eternal image, moving according to number, even that which we have named Time. [37e] … He contrived the production of days and nights and months and years, which existed not before the Heaven came into being. And these are all portions of Time; even as "Was" and "Shall be" are generated forms of Time…. [38b] Time was made after the pattern of the Eternal Nature, to the end that it might be as like thereto as possible; for whereas the pattern is existent through all eternity, [38c] the copy, on the other hand, is through all time, continually having existed,

---

[19] In other translations "form" or "essence." In *Timaeus*, Plato avoids sticky questions of mutability and immutability and the one and the many by escape into idealism. Although the passage quoted here goes to lengths to establish time as a natural occurrence that is forever changing ("moving"), reference to the "model" of time that is eternal, unmoving and immutable, denies the possibility of natural time as anything more than illusion.

existing, and being about to exist. Wherefore, as a consequence of this reasoning and design on the part of God, with a view to the generation of Time, the sun and moon and five other stars, which bear the appellation of "planets," came into existence for the determining and preserving of the numbers of Time.[20]

ANALOGUE AND DIGITAL CLOCKS: MEDIATION AND SPATIALIZATION OF TIME

The radical difference in the mediatization of time signified by analogue and digital clocks, the difference between linear and cyclical representation of time, is found in the time machines of each attitude towards nature. Analogue media realistically refer to the natural world; digital media refer to the idealized world of arithmetic. Analogue representation is analogical, therefore, mimetic. For example, an analogue clock represents the natural time of day and night and the seasons in a one-for-one relationship between its parts and nature: indicative hour "hands," sounds of nature such as cuckoo birds, figures that move indicating various praxis, etc.[21] A traditional Black Forest cuckoo clock, for example, is constructed as a house

with a carved floral frame (birds, leaves, vines, etc.), weights in the shape of pine cones, and a small attic window out of which a cuckoo bird sings the hours. Analogue mediation refers the viewer out of a realistic, human temporal medium back to nature as the place of time. The digital clock demands that the viewer find time internally, as an arithmetic, conceptual object, not a material thing.

In *Capital*, Marx develops his ideas on the modes and means of production, remarking that "It is not the articles made, but how they are made, and by what instruments, that enables us to distinguish different economic epochs."[22]

Clocks, whether analogue or digital, are intimately connected to class consciousness and economic classes.

Ideological-epistemological breaks that appear in history may be associated with shifts in media, especially in a period when one medium is being replaced by a successor. It was not "cogito ergo sum" that marked an epistemological break, but the media shift from the *collective* act of reading aloud of a manuscript to internalized, silent reading that brought the *individualized* subject (cogito) into the ideological center.

The epistemological break in spatial media in the cusp period

---

[20] *Plato in Twelve Volumes*, Vol. 9, *Timaeus*: Sections 37c-38c, translated by W.R.M. Lamb. Cambridge, MA, Harvard University Press; London, William Heinemann Ltd. 1925: www.perseus.tufts.edu/hopper/text?doc=Pe rseus%3Atext%3A1999.01.0180%3Atext%3 DTim.%3Asection%3D37c.

[21] For example, the Prague astronomical clock of the Old Town Hall.

[22] *Capital*, Vol. I, Part III: "The Production of Absolute Surplus Value," Chapter Seven: "The Labour-Process and the Process of Producing Surplus-Value, Section 1, "The Labour-Process or the Production of Use Values."
https://www.marxists.org/archive/marx/works/1867-c1/ch07.htm.

from manuscript to print affected social consciousness in ways that are as obvious as they are ignored—the loss of color, the shift from reading aloud to silent reading in the shift from the Middle Ages to the renaissance. These are significant ideological changes. The loss of color is not merely a rainbow consideration. It also indicates a shift away from a society that was highly symbolic—color symbolism an essential expression of medieval ideology—to a black and white, either-or analytic renaissance of modern society. Medieval manuscripts were colorfully illustrated and illuminated; early print was reduced to black and white. For example, visual green was not seen in a text after Gutenberg, but textualized and referred to by the printed word "green." The symbol became a lexical item, not a visual one.

Clocks and calendars also made a shift. When Marx says that "It is not the articles made, but how they are made, and by what instruments, that enables us to distinguish different economic epochs," he reveals the economic underpinning of technological and therefore media change. The weight-driven cuckoo clock, for example, developed as two different commodities: a metal-gear clock for the rich and a wood-gear clock for workers.

HOURS EQUAL, HOURS UNEQUAL AND THE BOOK OF HOURS

In his thorough studies of medieval time measurement, Nicholas Whyte observes that:

In the fourteenth century the ownership of time, the control of time-keeping, passed from the Church to the merchant classes. It is usually thought that this transition is linked to the change from measuring time in unequal hours, also called seasonal or temporal hours, which divided both day and night into twelve, to the practice of dividing the whole day and night into twenty-four equal parts (or two sets of twelve equal parts)...[T]he introduction of equal hours in the thirteenth - fourteenth centuries was not so much a replacement of unequal hours as a reflection of the new importance of the measurement of time.[23]

While not making an explicit connection, Whyte provides valuable historical research to bolster the concept of time as a property relationship, one of economic ownership. The Time Clock used by companies today, effectively asserting employers' ownership of workers' time, was not the first clock to indicate and regulate owner-labor relations. Among the first shifts in the measurement of time in mercantile capitalism, the division of hours into 24 identical and equal-hour units was an essential innovation for the standardization of time on an arithmetic basis, a shift from feudal property relationship based on land − nature-based wealth − to one based on capital.

The medieval system of time as

---

[23] Whyte, Nicholas. *Hours Equal*, September 2002. www.nicholaswhyte.info/hours.htm#02n.

a property relation is a reflection of its time machines. Aristocratic and "princely" church ownership of time was arranged around "calls to prayer" in a system of time based on the seasons of the year. In order to maintain 12 daylight hours, depending how far north the clock was located, each hour needed to be shorter. By today's measurement, there would be fewer minutes in daylight hours—though minutes themselves were not introduced as units of time measurement until the late Middle Ages, when geared clocks were introduced and *discrete* tick-tock representation of time replaced the *continuous* flow of water, sand, and sundial clocks.

Medieval ownership of time was oriented around calls to prayer rung by church bells every three hours.[24] As is the case in modern time clocks installed to track employees' "punch in" and "punch out" times and, thereby, precisely determine the value of labor time, the peeling of church bells was not only a call to prayer but also a call to work. In the late nineteenth century, church bells were replaced by factory sirens that indicated the beginning and end of a work shift. Mechanized automatons, made to imitate humans, that came out of church-tower clocks on a temporal schedule of hours, were replaced by

workers imitating robots[25] whose "punch in" allowed them to enter precisely into mercantile time with employee pass cards.[26]

The shift in the ownership of time from land to capital in the marketplace in the fourteenth century is paralleled by a shift from natural time to arithmetic time. Hours unequal, as Whyte points out, is not so much consciously replaced as it is made irrelevant by the early stages of automatization (digitalization). Irrelevance and disruption are common aspects of and occurrences in technological evolution.

The quantification of time is a final divorce of mediated time and nature. Hours no longer reflect seasonal night and day, though medieval Books of Hours, the most common of medieval illustrated books, had already textualized and contextualized time.

Books of Hours are not only an example of the aesthetic textualization and intertextualization of time. These popular illuminated manuscripts served as handbooks to accompany the measured time of church bells and clocks that had appropriated and measured time to serve the church's ideological goals. The fifteenth-century illuminated miniatures of Simon Marmion, the "prince of illuminators" and "master of colors," undoubtedly stand as masterpieces the equal of any art before or after his time. They also mark off eight prayer

---

[24] Rung every three hours, church bells called clergy and laity to prayer and to begin their work day: Prime (6AM), Terce (9AM), Sext (noon), None (3PM), Vespers or Evening Prayer (6PM), Compline (9PM), Matins (midnight). This traditional continues today among Moslems.

[25] *Robota* (Czech)—forced labor.
[26] Seen as a stock character in late nineteenth- and early twentieth-century literature and film, Chaplin's *Modern Times* perhaps the best-known example.

times of the 24-hour day that the Church set in place. The textualization of time in a temporal guidebook for worship for the first two literate, medieval Estates (aristocracy and clergy) codified the measurement of time by clocks and provided a hermeneutics of religious temporality. Interestingly, the measurement of human time by discreet units served as a passageway into eternity through prayer. The time of past, present, and future as a property relationship was disguised as prayer intended as an opening to God's eternal "time" that had no past, present, or future.

The measurement of time in the Books of Hours was not yet divorced from nature, as it was when feudal property relationships gave way to early mercantile manufacturing. The "first hour" of the Book of Hours, known as "Prime," began at sunrise – so, while the religious expropriation of time serves as a "way to heaven," it is also rooted in nature. The contradictory unity of opposites – supernatural eternity and natural daybreak – is elevated in religious thinking to an eschatological "end time" that is shrouded in the theological concept of "mystery," that is, a supernatural, theological truth that, even if known, is ineffable.

The invention of the printing press and widespread availability of books demystified the measurement of time as it contributed to the mercantile take-over of time from the Church. The availability of mass-produced books gave accelerated impetus to the intertextualization of temporal hermeneutics, as it did for every field of inquiry, allowing limitless reference, connection, and allusion to non-religious as well as religious texts.

The textualization and inter-textualization of time should not be understood to mean that the explanation of time and the measurement of time was solely theoretical. Placing time in one text (for example, Simon Marmion's *Book of Hours*) also placed it within the *context* of texts. Intertextuality enforced theocratic ideology and its self-justification of the property relationship that benefitted land owners.

As throughout history, clocks of any technology and how they measure time are repressive state apparatuses used to enforce the property relationships of an economic hierarchy. Textualized time, as part of a general, historical shift in the expression of knowledge, is distanced from oral knowledge. Knowledge becomes *bookish* and *readerly*. Ideological power shifts from an authoritative writer to the newly literate. Literacy becomes an attribute of the bourgeoisie and petty-bourgeoisie as well as the aristocracy and clergy, and the process of detaching language from transcendent reality purred forward.

THE OWNERSHIP OF TIME
AND THE CLASS STRUGGLE

Early in the history of the technology of clocks, a class distinction between metal and wood clocks arose. More durable and accurate than wood mechanisms, metal clockwork mechanisms, for those who could afford them, facilitated the expropriation of time by the ruling class. Unlike late-medieval and early-renaissance sumptuary dress-code laws that were imposed by the aristocracy on the Third Estate, purchase of commodities such as clocks was regulated by the market. When the ownership of time passed from the hands of aristocracy and Church to those of merchants, the historical stage was set for accelerated exploitation of the working class.

In the early days of the industrial revolution, the legend of a revolutionary worker, Ned Ludd, took shape in folklore among the new working class. Whether Ludd existed or was the creation of discontented workers is debatable. What is not debatable is the folkloric efficacy of Ludditism that exposed the conditions of labor in the new mode of production.

At the beginning of the modern era, it was neither eternity nor death that underpinned time and served as its pivot. Measured time found a new underpinning in *productivity*. For the capitalist, sloth (unproductivity) replaced greed as the root of all evil (*Radix malorum est cupiditas*). The emerging industrialist complained that "lazy workers" were possessed of the greatest capitalist sin, sloth, because "time is money." Workers complained that it was capitalist greed that was the greatest sin. Both claims were measured in units of time, but the instrument of time measurement was owned by the employer, not the employee. The shift of the means and mode of production from feudal to capitalist was accompanied by an ideological shift. The theological ideology of the medieval seven deadly sins was upended and in the modern era sloth and greed contended to dethrone the "queen" of the seven sins, pride. The measurement of time became the battlefield of class warfare. Pride became a virtue – succinctly stated by Gordon Gekko in Oliver Stone's film, *Wall Street:* "Greed is good."

In the late eighteenth century, Ludd, a weaver from Leicester, England was said to have been unjustly whipped for idleness by the textile-mill owners who employed him. In response, he smashed two knitting frames and hammered the machine needles. After, whenever workers sabotaged weaving machines, they claimed that "Ludd did it." The point is that Luddites were not against technology. Luddites were workers who opposed exploitation through technology, as are today's neo-Luddites.[27]

Today, automation is the call word of manufacturing. Artificial-intelligence robots take the place of

---

[27] When the House of Lords considered a bill imposing capital punishment for workers who destroyed the means of production at which they worked, Lord George Gordon Byron observed that "... the real cause of these distresses, and consequent disturbances, lies deeper. When we are told that these men are leagued together, not only for the destruction of their own comfort, but of their very means of subsistence, can we forget that it is the bitter policy, the destructive warfare, of the last eighteen years, which has destroyed their comfort...?"

workers not only because they do not tire or complain, but because they are less expensive and more efficient and productive than their human counterparts. We are told that "timeless" robots will prevail and that certain manufacturing jobs will never return. Workers, blue and white collar alike, are told they are redundant and should become accustomed to "capitalist" techno-logical progress.

It is not automation or technology that oppresses workers. The delusion that automatization inevitably leads to unemployment because it is more *efficient* in traditional manufacturing is self-justification of the ruling class. Automation need not be uncritically tied to profit and the marketplace. It can just as readily lead to greater safety, greater productivity, and more leisure time for the working class *for the same or more pay*. If time were not appropriated by the bourgeoisie, a reduced work week at the same pay, for example, could just as easily be the result of greater machine efficiency. Except among libertarian fundamentalists, auto-mation is not of necessity an ingredient of profit for owners. Libertarian philosophers and economists elevate greed to a virtue, mistaking profit for efficiency, just as they misidentify working-class anger as class envy or resentment.[28]

The growth of factories in the industrial revolution saw the bourgeoisie expropriate time and create a new relationship between workers and time. Temporal efficiency and punctuality became inherent in the management of time. Assembly-line work, unlike farm labor, demands precise punctuality. The change in the mode of production meant that the working class was required to live by the clock rather than the sun, education became the preparation of efficient factory workers, and workers' leisure time became slothful. Punctuality and productivity became virtues. Franklin's proverb, "Time is money," became the mantra of the business world, and the publication of Frederick Taylor's *The Principles of Scientific Management* (1911) textualized a management theory based on the quantification of work flows to improve productivity.

TIME AS AN IDEALIST BANK ACCOUNT:
PHENOMENOLOGY AND LIBERTARIANISM

Two rails of an idealist political-economic ideology, laissez-faire libertarianism and phenomenology, run parallel towards the same destination: fascism.

Husserlian eidetic and transcen-dental phenomenology, blithefully unaware of political and economic reality and marked by purposeful naïveté in dealing with transcendent social problems, is irrelevant in our discussion of the measurement of

---

[28] The delusional ideology of the bourgeoisie mandates that time manage-ment is a term in business discourse, not labor discourse. Just as there is no "Labor Section" comparably to the "Business Section" of a newspaper and labor events are covered within the business discourse, so too was the measurement of time expropriated by capitalism.

time as money and, while the undercurrent of Nazi thought in Heidegger (a self-defined "inner truth" Nazi) is now accepted by all except his most devoted acolytes, much less attention has been given to phenomenological "realists." Yet, the relationship of phenomenological "realists" such as Alfred Schütz to the Austrian School of Economics and its collaboration with Austrofascism remains a neglected study. But the theoretical underpinning that "realist" (subjectivist) phenomenology provided Austrian libertarian economics and the justification of the expropriation of time by the owning class are ignored at the price of intellectual honesty. This line of investigation in relationship to time and the measurement of time demands a lengthy discussion. For the moment, a few brief and disconnected comments will suffice.

Before the *Anschluss* of 1938, when Hitler annexed Austria into Greater Germany, Austria was already a fascist state. The dictator, Engelbert Dollfuss, claiming to "over-Hitler" (*überhitlern*) Hitler,[29]

had constructed Austria as a Catholic "corporate state" modeled on Mussolini's fascism. The economic practice that Dollfuss set in place relied on libertarian-fascist theories of ultra-right economists – Ludwig von Mises, Friedrich Hayek, Eric Voegelin, and others – who came to be known as the Austrian School of Economics and, still later, the Chicago School of Economics, when its founders fled Austria after Hitler over-Hitlered Dollfuss and Austrian fascism. While in Austria, they served as economic advisors to Dollfuss.

When Mises immigrated to the United States, he became close to the extremist Ayn Rand and an early member of the reactionary John Birch Society. His brand of libertarian Austrofascism continues today in the Ludwig von Mises Institute in Alabama. Libertarians such as Tennessee's U.S. Senator Rand Paul have, for example, announced that, in the name of "individual liberty," they would have opposed the Civil Rights Act of 1964 that outlawed discrimination based on race, color, religion, sex, or national origin, while Heideggerians such as Hannah Arendt openly opposed

---

[29] Not unlike Heidegger's contention in a lecture given in 1935 that he was a better Nazi than others, his own Nazi ideology being the "inner truth and greatness of this movement": "*What today is systematically touted as the philosophy of National Socialism, but which has nothing in the least to do with the inner truth and greatness of this movement (namely the encounter of a globally determined technology with the man of the new age), darts about with fish-like movements in the murky waters of these 'values' and 'totalities'.*" Later, by way of self-justification, he explained that "*The whole lecture shows that I was at that time an adversary of the regime. The understanding ears knew therefore how to interpret the sentence. Only the spies of the party who – I knew it – sat in my*

courses, understood the sentence otherwise, as it must be. One had to throw them a crumb here and there in order to keep freedom of teaching and speaking." We note that "the freedom of teaching and speaking" of which he speaks was the "freedom" of the Nazi regime and applied only to those defined as Aryans – not Jews, Slaves, Gypsies, homosexuals, those handicapped, socialists, Communists, and others. For some, this explanation not only illustrates Heidegger's profound ignorance of the meaning of "freedom," but is wildly offensive.

legal integration. In the same way, Eric Voegelin, after coming to the United States, participated in the Philadelphia Society, a reactionary libertarian group also opposed to legislation assuring civil rights.

Libertarianism, the ideology of *laissez-faire* capitalism, is the polite word for what others call law-of-the-jungle capitalism. The cluster of Austrian intellectuals who revolved around von Mises accepted the basis of his subjectivist economic thought: the working class is driven by *envy of the rich*. This envy is not much different than Nietzsche's petit-bourgeois sense of *ressentiment*. It is envy – another deadly sin – that drives class conflict, according to von Mises, projecting bourgeoisie fear and demonizing working-class anger as envy.

Alfred Schütz may serve as an example of phenomenological libertarianism. His career as chief financial officer of an Austrian bank is indelibly reflected in his major work, *The Phenomenology of the Social World*. As Allen Oakley notes in *Alfred Schütz and Economics as a Social Science*:

> A number of interpreters with an interest in economics have given some attention to the work of Alfred Schütz. As intimated in this literature, the orientation of his delimited thought on economics stemmed from contacts with the Austrian school during his Vienna years.[30]

With a philosophical sleight-of-hand that is the idealist's stock trick, the subjectivized class values of the bourgeoisie are objectivized. The subjectivizing of economic experience through crude epistemological surgery that amputates transcendent reality and replaces it with a subjectivized "lived body" results in the objectivizing of values – in this case, the reintroduction of the medieval deadly sin, *envy*.

In "Time and Meaning," Luigi Muzzetto examines "the main limitations of Schütz's theory":

> Temporal structure determines the uniqueness of meaning: the latter is a function of lived-through time, of each individual's life-story. The structure of temporality seems to condemn the lived present to being excluded from the possibility of possessing meaning. In fact, the present is the privileged time frame for the construction of fundamental reality, of action, and of identity....[31]

In "On Rationality, Ideal Types

---

[30] Allen Oakley notes in *Alfred Schutz and Economics as a Social Science*. (rd.springer.com /article/10.1023/A%3A1005684608896?no -access=true).

[31] Luigi Muzzetto, "Time and Meaning in Alfred Schütz." *Sage Publications*, Volume: 15, issue: 1, page(s): 5-31 March 1, 2006. journals.sagepub.com/doi/abs/10.1177/09 61463x06061334dx.doi.org/10.1177/0961463 X06061334.

[32] Alfred Schütz, "Letter to Adolph Loewe," 7 December 1955 (Beinecke Library, Yale University). Cf. also: "Authors who consider all acting 'preferential acting' do not realize that with this thesis they provide a definition of acting as such and that thereby <unwittingly> have set themselves the task of separating this acting from other manners of human existence." (Schutz [1936] 1996:102, note).

and Economics: Alfred Schütz and the Austrian School," Peter Kurrild-Klitgaard notes that Schütz "raised the question of what he saw as Mises broadening of economics to all areas of human action." The passage Kurrild-Klitgaard refers to is from a letter that Schütz wrote to Adolph Loewe.

> But are not human activities called "services" also economic activities? And what is the criterion for these specific activities? [This definition does not answer] these questions unless you take, as my friend Mises does, the shortness of our life and the impossibility of performing everything we would like during a life span as a problem of scarcity; then time, like what you call matter, would be a scarce means for alternative ends.[32]

Schütz deftly dodges the consideration of time as a qualitative measure by false analogy with space, as though its measurement were a matter of quantification, which implies scarcity. What he shares with Mises is the notion that time is a subjective experience.

When I walk with a friend in a park and turn onto the left instead of the right path, can I meaningfully say that I preferred the left path? And are not what we call choosing and preferring complex processes occurring in elapsing time?[33]

I prefer to ask what sort of philosopher, astonished by the truism that he finds himself in time, says he prefers the certitude of the right path.

WORKS CITED

Franklin, Benjamin. *Advice to a Young Tradesman, Written by an Old One.* file:///C:/Users/Paul/AppDat a/Local/Microsoft/Windows/ Temporarypercent20Internetper cent20Files/Content.IE5/MJH V180J/1748percent20Franklinp ercent20Advice.pdf

Los Angeles Times Cf. articles. latimes.com/1998/aug/01/hom e/hm-9005

Lukács, Georg, *Existentialism,* 1949. https://www.marxists.org/archi ve/lukacs/works/1949/existent ialism.htm.

Majkut, Paul. *Smallest Mimes: Defaced Representation and Media Epis-temology.* Zeta, 2014.

---. "Untext," *Glimpse.* San Diego: Society for Pheno-menology and Media, 2009.

[32]Alfred Schütz, "Letter to Adolph Loewe," 7 December 1955 (Beinecke Library, Yale University). Cf. also: "Authors who consider all acting 'preferential acting' do not realize that with this thesis they provide a definition of acting as such and that thereby <unwittingly> have set themselves the task of separating this acting from other manners of human existence." (Schutz [1936] 1996:102, note).

[33]Alfred Schütz, "Letter to Adolph Loewe," 7 December 1955 (Beinecke Library, Yale University).

Marx, Karl. *Capital.* www.marxists
.org/archive/marx/works/1867
-c1/ch07.htm.

Muzzetto, Luigi. "Time and
Meaning in Alfred Schütz." *Sage
Publications,* Volume: 15, issue: 1,
page(s): 5-31 March 1, 2006:
journals.sagepub.com/doi/abs/
10.1177/0961463x0606133
dx.doi.org/10.1177/0961463X0
6061334.

Oakley, Allen notes in *Alfred Schütz
and Economics as a Social Science:*
https://rd.springer.com/article
/10.1023/Apercent3A1005684
608896?no-access=true

Piketty, Thomas. *Capital in the
Twenty-First Century* (trans.
Arthur Goldhammer). The
Belnap Press of Harvard
University Press: Cambridge,
Mass., 2014, 113.

Plato in Twelve Volumes, Vol. 9,
Timaeus: Sections 37c-38c,
translated by W.R.M. Lamb.
Cambridge, MA, Harvard
University Press; London,
William Heinemann Ltd. 1925:
www.perseus.tufts.edu/hopper/t
ext?doc=Perseuspercent3Atextp
ercent3A1999.01.0180percent3A
textpercent3DTim.percent3Asec
tionpercent3D37c.

Reid, Thomas. *Essays on the
Intellectual Powers of Man,*
"Chapter 5: Perception," 50,
www.earlymoderntexts.com/ass
ets/pdfs/reid1785essay2.pdf.

Schütz, Alfred. "Letter to Adolph
Loewe," 7 December 1955
(Beinecke Library, Yale
University). Cf. (Schutz [1936]
1996:102, note).

Trần Đức Thảo. *Investigations into the
Origin of Language and Consciousness.* Trans. Daniel J. Herman

and Robert L. Armstrong.
Dordrecht, The Netherlands: D.
Reidel Publishing Company,
1984.

Wells, H. G. *The Time Machine.* New
York: New York, 1995.

Eddington, Arthur Stanley. The
Nature of the Physical World,
35.file:///C:/Users/Paul/App
Data/Local/Microsoft/Windo
ws/Temporarypercent20Interne
tpercent20Files/Content.IE5/1
SNWDUSO/Eddington.2008.
pdf Whyte, Nicholas. *Hours
Equal,* September 2002,
www.nicholaswhyte.info/hours.
htm#02n.

GLIMPSE

GLIMPSE